Carried

Debra McDonald

PAGE PUBLISHING, INC.
New York, NY

First originally published by Page Publishing, Inc. 2017

ISBN 978-1-64082-545-1 (Paperback)
ISBN 978-1-64082-546-8 (Digital)

Printed in the United States of America

Preface

The mother of the defendant took the stand and swore "to tell the truth, the whole truth, and nothing but the truth." She testified that her son, Paul, was home in bed sleeping at the time of the crime. In fact, she swore that on the night of April 18, Paul went upstairs at 9:30 p.m. and took a shower. She put ointment on the cuts on her fifteen-year-old son's face, knees, and arms before he went to bed.

Mrs. Ferguson's favorite TV show began that night at ten, just twenty minutes before the attacker entered her neighbor's home. She testified that while she watched TV, she left her favorite show three times in the first fifteen minutes. She went upstairs to take care of her sick two-year-old, to correct her thirteen-year-old daughter for staying up too late watching television, and to stop her daughter from taking a shirt she wanted to wear the next day to school from Paul's closet without his permission.

Mrs. Ferguson swore that each trip upstairs allowed her to see Paul sleeping and hear him snoring.

Her attorney was careful to ask, "When you went upstairs to tell Natasha to turn off the television, were you aware of where Paul was at that time?"

"Paul snores. You can't help but hear Paul snoring," she clarified for the benefit of the twelve-member jury she was trying to convince.

Her attorney did not need to be convinced of Paul's whereabouts between 10:30 p.m. and 10:36 p.m. on April 18. It was his job to see to it that Mrs. Ferguson was able to convince the jury. "And during the time that you were up there taking care of your sick two-year-old and changing the linens on the bed, you're saying you did see Paul?"

"Oh, yeah. His room is right next to the linen closet. Like I say, you can't help but hear him snoring. I just would look over. You know, normal things I normally do," she testified.

When Mrs. Ferguson continued her account of the evening, she swore that she returned to her favorite show at 10:30 p.m., the exact time when her neighbor heard the floorboards in her hallway creak and got out of her bed to investigate the unexplained noises. Mrs. Ferguson would be up and down the stairs checking on her daughter two more times during her favorite TV program—once when Natasha went to the bathroom and finally when Natasha called her upstairs to look out the window at the police officers surrounding their home. Those trips upstairs would again provide testimony that she saw Paul sleeping and heard him snoring at the exact time that her neighbor was being attacked by an intruder in her home just two and a half blocks away.

Chapter I

The Attack

The red digital numbers on the clock displayed 10:30 p.m. The light was on. The red dot for the alarm was lit, and the alarm was not blasting. What a relief! It was not time to get up and go to work. In fact, Debbie wondered if she had even been asleep. The last time she had looked at the clock was 10:20 p.m. when she hung up the phone and fell asleep. That was just ten minutes ago. When the floorboards in the hallway creaked, she wondered if that was the sound that woke her and what was causing those boards to creak. None of her three children made trips to the bathroom during the night. Jaredd, her fifteen-year-old son, had been exhausted from baseball practice. He ate his normal large dinner, took a shower, did some homework, and then went to bed at 8:30 p.m. Her thirteen-year-old daughter, Alisha, and her ten-year-old daughter, Ashley, had been quiet since about 9:30 p.m.

There was another creak of the floorboards in the girls' room directly across the hallway; but in the dark, she could see only the outline of their open bedroom door. The moonlight coming through their bedroom windows cast just enough light to see the shape of their doorway, and it was the only light in the pitch-black upstairs. A momentary light flickered in the dark bedroom across the hall. Could Ashley or Alisha be playing with her Easter present? Those adorable trolls with removable bunny ears and eyes that lit up when you pushed their belly buttons were hard to resist even though all three of her children were too old to actually play with them. How odd it was for Alisha or Ashley to be awake and playing with a troll doll!

Convinced that one or the other was awake for some reason, Debbie called their names, but neither answered. As she stared across the dark hallway, she could no longer see that square, slightly lighter shape of their open bedroom door. She had just seen that doorframe, but now she could no longer see it. Her daughters' silence frightened her. The darkness and the silence of her house frightened her. Why were they not answering? Why was one of them just walking and playing with her troll? Afraid and confused, it occurred to her that this was not funny. Alisha or Ashley must be fooling around, and it was time to answer, settle down, and get to sleep.

This time the tone of her voice was stern as she called out, "Alisha! Ashley!" A tone that would surely send the message that an answer was imperative.

Still no answer.

With no little girls' voices responding to her call, she remained fixated upon the dark hallway. Where was that doorframe? Why weren't they answering? Squinting and moving her head did not help her see what she was sure she had seen just seconds ago. Why couldn't she see the doorframe? Why was the hallway as black as the rest of the upstairs?

Something huge and dark must be standing in the hallway—something big enough to block the moonlight shining through the doorframe. Debbie slowly sat up without making a sound. She needed to know what was standing there. She didn't want to see the outline of a huge man in her hallway. What she wanted to see was the outline of her daughters' bedroom doorway. How big and what shape was blocking the moonlight from their bedroom?

Be absolutely quiet, she told herself. *Make no noise. Listen to any sounds in the hallway*, her mind directed.

Whatever was in the hallway was huge—so huge that no light and no part of that doorway were visible.

Her phone was right there—on the nightstand next to her bed. She could pick up that phone and call for help by merely extending her left arm to the phone.

No, you can't do that. The light from the phone and the sound of the dial tone will signal your plan, her mind commanded.

Whatever was in that hallway would see her if she picked up that phone, she was sure of it. She had read too many Stephen King books to fall for that one. To be attacked in the dark was her worst nightmare. No, to be attacked in the dark in her bed, trapped beneath the covers was her worst nightmare. She needed to get her legs out from under the covers. She needed to get her arms and legs free to fight whatever was standing in that hallway. And she needed to do it quickly and quietly. She was terrified.

Debbie pulled her legs from her covers without taking her eyes off that dark doorway. Without making a sound and without looking away, she quietly put her feet on the floor. Now free from the restraints of her covers, she desperately needed light. She needed to see what was lurking in the darkness. She could not be attacked in the dark.

Please God, don't let this be a huge monster or man in that dark hallway right outside my door, her mind pleaded.

Could it see her? Was it watching her get out of bed? Was he waiting to attack? Would he charge into her dark bedroom any second? All those questions stampeded through her mind as she planned her move to her dresser, to the light.

She had to get to her dresser. She had to get a light on. She didn't want to see the huge monster in her hallway waiting to attack her, but she couldn't stand the fear of being attacked in the dark. Just three quick, cautious steps toward the dresser were all it took. Three silent, blind steps and she was there. Never taking her eyes off the black doorway, she was there. And her Braille method of finding the button on her antique hurricane lamp worked, unlike in so many horror movies. She relived where the woman got to the door, or the latch, but could not get it open in time to escape her oncoming attacker. Debbie had been watching and listening as she made her silent move across her bedroom to her lamp, and she was sure that the monster in her hallway had not started moving toward her. She had made it, and in an instant, her light was on.

No one was standing in the hallway. A tremendous sense of relief passed through her body. The feeling one has after a loved one jumps out unexpectedly from behind a door and yells, "Boo!" That physical feeling of the fight-or-flight adrenaline rush that was physically there but not needed that you could actually feel washing away. She could feel that incredible fear flow from her body.

What her eyes were sure they would see, what she knew had been blocking the moonlight through her daughters' open door was not there. How could nothing be there? Thank God nothing was there. Her mind was sure something huge had to have been blocking that light, but the monster was not there. It was all her imagination. Thank God! Thank God!

The fear that was flowing from her began to creep back as she realized the girls' door was closed. Not totally closed, but closed enough to block the moonlight. But Alisha and Ashley never closed their door. She never closed her door. They didn't use nightlights anymore, but they never closed their doors. That was understood—it was an unwritten but thoroughly understood rule. Jaredd, the only male in the house, always slept with his door closed, but Alisha and Ashley never allowed their door to be closed when they went to bed. How did their door get closed? Their pet cat, Ashes, could have pushed their door open if it had been slightly ajar, but she couldn't have pushed the door closed. Why was the door closed, and how did it get closed?

All those questions raced through Debbie's mind as she walked across her bedroom floor toward the hallway and their closed door. None of those past horror movie scenes flashed through her mind to warn her not to go there. Jaredd hated scary movies and would always tell the character on the screen not to go there. He would always end up asking his mom, "Why do they always do that? Who would go out in the dark alone like that? No one in real life would do that!"

If he had been watching his mother in one of those scary movies at that moment, he would have been screaming, "Don't push that door open! Get someone to help! Don't go in there!" But Jaredd wasn't watching his mother right then. He was sound asleep in the room next to his sisters' room, totally unaware of her actions. And Debbie was not recalling any of those past scary movies or hearing any warnings not to go to the doorway of her daughters' room. Still very frightened and confused, yet reassured by the absence of the monster in the hallway, Debbie approached her daughters' door. The monster was not there and the light was, dispelling the panic of being attacked in the dark.

Still frightened and perplexed, Debbie cautiously and slowly began pushing the door open, trying to remain as far away from it as possible while still pushing it open. Suddenly the door finished opening by itself. From the darkness of the girls' room a person emerged. It was not a little girl or the cat, but a much larger, taller person. As the light from her bedroom hit his face, she instantly recognized Paul Ferguson.

What was Paul Ferguson doing coming out of her girls' room? He was an ex-friend of Jaredd's and had not been in her home for years. Why was he here, what was he doing here? she wondered as she backed away from him and the doorway.

Unable to speak and too confused to think, Debbie backed across the hallway and into her bedroom, leaving the hallway clear for Paul to exit. Staring right into his face and being sure he would turn and flee down the hallway, she was stunned when he didn't. He came directly at her and began to punch her head.

Paul was several inches taller than Debbie, and over a hundred pounds heavier. Despite his weight and size advantage, his blows to her head did not hurt. Her arms reflexively rose above her head in a defensive fashion to shield her head from his fist. Surprisingly, her hands found a knife rather than his fist and instinctively began to grasp the blade.

A plastic knife, she convinced herself. It had to be a plastic knife! This was Paul Ferguson, the neighborhood kid who used to play with Jaredd. Perhaps if she got this plastic knife out of his hand, he would leave, her mind convinced her. He was aggressive because he had a plastic knife in his hand, and the sooner she got that knife from him, the sooner he would leave. She just wanted him to leave. She didn't want to know why he was there; she just wanted him to leave.

Each time Paul returned the knife to her head, Debbie grasped it tighter. She could see the gray plastic blade above her head as his right hand continued to pound it to her scalp. Although he managed to pull the blade from her grip time after time, he was struggling more with each attempt. She could sense he was weakening, and her confidence rose each time her grip on the plastic blade lasted longer. Determined she would get that knife from him and he would leave, she focused all her energy on that plan.

As Paul struggled more each time he tried to pull his knife back, he too must have realized that she was getting stronger and his efforts were failing. Perhaps he was getting too tired to risk losing this battle, and he needed a new plan.

At that moment, Paul grabbed Debbie around the back of the neck with his left arm, pulled her head to his chest, and took the knife across the back of her head. Debbie did not feel the cut Paul inflicted on the back of her head, nor did she expect to feel pain from a plastic blade. But she did feel her face against his chest, and that feeling was appalling! She had been in this position before—a position she would later recall as a trapped position set up in her college water lifesaving classes to teach her the lifeguard technique of how to release herself from a drowning, panicking victim. She did not need to think about her lifesaving training—it was automatic. She ducked her head, put her hands against his chest, and shoved him away.

Now free from his grasp and several feet away from him, Debbie stood in her bedroom facing Paul Ferguson. Still more confused about his presence in her house than frightened by his physical aggressiveness, Debbie felt pain for the first time. She had shoved Paul away from her with her hands, and her hands hurt. She looked away from Paul to the palms of her outstretched hands to discover, in horror and disbelief, that her hands were covered in blood. The knife was not plastic. The knife was real. She had been grasping the blade of a real knife with all her might, and it had been pulled through her hands repeatedly. Her hands were all cut up. She frantically began to count fingers. Were they all there? In all that blood, were all her fingers still attached? Surely her fingers must be dangling from strands of skin after all those slices.

Traumatized by the horror of her injuries and the realization that Paul had been stabbing her head with a real knife and she had been clutching its blade, she called for the only person in the house who could help her now. "Jaredd!" she called. Jaredd would get him to leave. Jaredd could kick the shit out of Paul Ferguson. He always could. He never had to because Paul knew better than to mess with Jaredd. Jaredd had always been bigger than Paul, taller and more athletic. Paul wouldn't take Jaredd on two years ago, and he wouldn't take him on now, either. She was sure of that.

Paul was sure of that too. He had no intentions of taking on Jaredd. That was evident in the tone of his voice and in the quickness of his response to her call when he shouted, "Shut up!"

And Debbie's rage was just as immediate, for she hated the words "Shut up." She had learned that from her mother. She and her brother and her sister were never allowed to tell anyone to shut up. It was rude and disrespectful, and therefore not tolerated. Furthermore, how dare this punk tell her to shut up in her own home? She felt the rage swell up inside her as she looked him straight in the eyes and told him, "Get out!" Still consumed by the shock and concern for her hands, and still unafraid of Paul, she looked back at her hands and yelled for Jaredd once again. She would continue to yell for Jaredd. It was her house; Paul didn't belong there, and he would not tell her what to do in her own home.

Without warning, Paul tackled her to the floor of her bedroom. His two hundred pounds of girth landed on her, causing her left shoulder to dislocate. The pain in her shoulder far exceeded the pain in her hands, and she rolled off her left shoulder to relieve the pressure. Paul was on his knees, straddling her as she screamed out for Jaredd. Repeating his name, she was determined that help from Jaredd was all she needed. Determined until Paul stabbed the knife into her right temple and then took the blade of his knife across her throat.

Her mind never stopped talking to her, directing her. From the first creak of the floorboards to the partially closed door, her mind desperately tried to sort things out—tried to make sense out of the craziness. Now it was telling her, *You're going to die here on your bedroom floor if you don't fight for your life.*

With over two hundred pounds sitting on her thighs, a slit throat, a dislocated left shoulder, and cut-up, bleeding hands, she had only two defenses left—her mouth, which never stopped yelling for Jaredd, and her right arm. With her fingernails pointed, she jabbed the nails of her right hand into Paul's face. He pulled back from her claws enough for her to pull her legs through his straddled knees. Her legs were free now to fight, and she began kicking him with all her might. She was as far away from him as she could get, and she wanted to keep it that way. But she was still lying on her back on her bedroom floor.

At that precise moment, while Debbie was kicking for her life, she heard Alisha's voice call her. "Mom" had never sounded so good, but the tone in Alisha's voice was one of fear and confusion. Paul heard Alisha call her mother's name and immediately turned his head toward the voice. He instantly stood up and ran out of the bedroom. Finally, he was gone. Debbie struggled to get up. Her left arm was no help due to the dislocated shoulder. Blood was running down her face, and she could not see out of her right eye. Convinced that the knife wound to her right temple had blinded her, she walked to her bedroom doorway to check on the children. She was sure Paul had left. With another person awake in the house, he would surely have fled.

Still calling Jaredd's name in a frantic voice, Debbie arrived at her door in time to see Paul coming back across Alisha's bedroom floor toward her. *He didn't leave! He's coming back! Shut the door! Keep him out!* Her mind once again was in charge, but like in those old horror movies, he was there before she could close the door. He was there, pushing on the door. Six inches of open space, and he was there, pushing to get in.

She was pushing the door closed with her bleeding right hand. It was awkward because she had to reach across her body to push on the door. Her left arm was useless. She put her left foot against the door as a stopper and tried to put her weight upon her foot. She needed to hold him out, but putting weight on her foot caused her to have to be close to the opening of the door—close to Paul. He was there, pressing against the door, and he was winning. How could she expect her one hundred and fifteen pounds to hold back the two hundred pounds pressing against her door? And her mind was not sure it wanted her to keep him out. If she succeeded in getting her door shut, the monster would be out of her room, but free to hurt her children. If she failed, he would be in her bedroom again with his knife. She was already too injured to handle that. She was already bleeding to death.

As all those thoughts fought with one another in her mind, she heard Alisha call again to her, frantically. Instantly, Debbie had another plan. Her screams for Jaredd changed to directions to Alisha. "Alisha, get Jaredd! Alisha, get Jaredd!" came repeatedly from her as she pressed against her door.

Suddenly Debbie fell into her door, and the door was shut. She had succeeded. The door was closed. But she did not want the door closed if Paul was on the other side with a knife and her three children. She grasped the doorknob with her bloody right hand and began to open it. It seemed like forever before she had the door open. Was he waiting outside the door? Was he waiting to stab her to death? Was she already dying, bleeding to death?

Overcoming the fear of encountering Paul yet another time was automatic. Her children were outside her bedroom door, and she needed to get to them. As she opened her door, she heard running and banging down the staircase, and she knew Paul was leaving. Finally he was leaving. She was as sure of that as she was sure that she was bleeding to death. Her throat had been cut open for what seemed like an endless amount of time, and she was sure that she would collapse any minute and die on her bedroom floor. She had survived all that horror and could still die. She needed to survive. She was still fighting for her life.

Debbie returned to her bed, propped her pillow up with her bleeding right hand, and carefully and quickly picked up the phone. She lay down on her bed using her pillow to force her chin to her chest. She had seen in some horror movie that she would later recall as *In Cold Blood* that a woman survived having her throat slit by lying

Chapter II

Trauma Bay

The sirens of the ambulances blared all the way to the Polyclinic Hospital. The six or seven blocks seemed longer with the only view being the ceiling of an ambulance. The hospital doors opened, and emergency technicians hurried through door after door, with the emergency room as their final destination. With the horrors of the attack behind her, Debbie was grateful to be finally in the hands of doctors. The fear of dying was slowly fading away into the bright white lights inside the large emergency room. She would later learn that she ended up in the trauma bay, an area of the emergency room that was reserved for patients who had extensive trauma or injuries, where multiple doctors could assess and treat the injuries.

Several doctors immediately began working on her wounds. They seemed mesmerized by her description of the last twenty minutes of her life. Dr. Albracht, the orthopedic surgeon, was particularly concerned and interested in every detail of the attack that caused her injuries. He was also very gentle, caring, and patient, not to mention extremely handsome. Debbie knew he was too young for her, but she could not help being attracted to his intense compassion for her as he cleaned her hands and assessed her injuries.

Debbie was forty-three years old and had been divorced for nearly six years. Despite her six years as a single parent, the fifteen years of marriage prior to her divorce still left her feeling less than single and available. When her ex-husband left for a business trip to Russia in December of 1989, *divorce* was not a part of her vocabulary. A month later, she was alone, doing divorce by phone to John in Russia, and wondering how she would ever manage to raise a ten-, eight-, and four-year old by herself.

Six years later, she had accomplished just that. She had three wonderful children whom she had managed to shelter from the major evils of divorce. When John left them, Debbie had a good ten-month job as a middle school assistant principal, so the financial impact of divorce was not devastating. She had a modest home in an excellent school district, with a swimming pool in her backyard to keep her children and their friends entertained at home in the summer months when she was not working. Her home was nearly paid for, and she could handle the monthly mortgage payments on her salary. Her family did not need to move.

In addition to handling the financial changes in her life, she had had a wonderful therapist, Elizabeth Hoffman, who helped her survive divorce, and she had attended a seminar on helping children deal with separation and divorce. She knew what she needed to do to help her children cope with divorce, and she did everything she could to minimize the changes in their lives and the harmful effects of divorce. She wanted to be a strong parent for her children, and she fought all the urges caused by her emotional neediness to find some new man to depend upon. She learned in counseling that she must first be able to manage her life and her children before she could be a good partner to anyone. She also knew that she would not attract or be attracted to a healthy person until she was healthy herself. The last thing her children needed was an adjustment and attachment to another man who might leave.

Perhaps the most important gift she gave her children as a single parent was that she truly loved them and was devoted to them. She had always wanted three children, and to have a son and two daughters was her absolute dream. The time and energy that went into providing for their needs and keeping them actively involved in all their sports, dance, and social activities never felt like a sacrifice or work. The demands were simply the commitment necessary to be a come into their home that night with a knife? Why had he come upstairs?

As she wrestled with questions, her shoulder was still giving her a great deal of pain. Earlier she had asked Dr. Albracht to put her shoulder back into the joint, but he assured her that proper medical protocol required that he address the most life-threatening injuries first. Her dislocated shoulder was secondary to her open wounds. Debbie remained patient and calm, enduring the pain of her shoulder, as she watched Dr. Albracht attend to her hands. She could not believe she was looking at such grotesque hands, and that they were actually her own. She never liked the sight of blood, and now she was actually studying open wounds. She hated shots too, but she was paying little attention to being repeatedly jabbed with needles. Somehow the horror of the entire event seemed to minimize the gore of the treatment process. She desperately wanted to be fixed, to be back to normal; and she knew she would endure whatever it took to accomplish that.

Dr. Albracht had completed the cleansing of her hands and was prepared to discuss with her his assessment of her injuries—the good news and the bad news, the latter of which she was not expecting. The tendons of the fingers on both her hands had been severed. As a result, she would be unable to flex the middle and ring fingers of her right hand or the little finger and the thumb of the left hand. Dr. Albracht could not repair her tendons because the injuries required surgery in an operating room. Surgery would be scheduled for the next day. He would not be closing the lacerations to those fingers since the surgeons would need access to the severed tendons and could possibly use those openings to repair the tendons.

After a full discussion of the six weeks of traction and hand therapy necessary to restore full use of the fingers affected by the severed tendons and the chance that full recovery may not be achieved, Dr. Albracht focused upon his more immediate concern. A large flap of skin on Debbie's left palm was barely attached. He explained that the blood flow to the filleted skin was seriously impaired by the extent of the cut. If the blood was unable to flow to that portion of skin, it would die. Loss of that amount of skin would require skin grafting from another part of her body.

Debbie had managed up to that point to remain attentive and focused on her open wounds, but a nauseous feeling began to overcome her. The roller coaster of positive and negative feelings she was riding was plummeting from the height of the joy of survival to the low of possible complications and permanent disabilities. She had always been physically active, and the thought of disabled hands was more than she could handle. She rested her head back against the bed and away from her damaged hands.

The room seemed to be swaying, and she was afraid she was going to throw up or pass out. Dr. Albracht's voice faded into the background of her physically sick feelings and her tremendous fear of the long-term consequences of Paul's attack on her. She did not want to be in the trauma bay. She wanted to wake up from this dreadful nightmare and be back in her home, asleep with her children. But she knew she had experienced all too vividly every detail of the past four hours for this not to be real. How could this bizarre chain of events be happening to her?

The reality of the situation seemed more manageable after Dr. Albracht had wrapped her hands with gauze and reduced her dislocated shoulder, the source of her greatest physical pain. With her scalp, temple, neck, and hand wounds sutured and her shoulder back in place, she was ready to be transferred to a hospital room. After four hours of intensive treatment by several doctors at a time, she was wheeled into her room.

She had a lot to be thankful for, and she related those emotions to her nurse. Mary was a blonde, angel-like young nurse who, like Dr. Albracht, seemed intent on knowing every detail of the attack. Her interest and compassion was soothing to Debbie. Mary promised to be by her side throughout the rest of the night, which was morning by then. With her hands totally bandaged, Debbie would be unable to buzz for assistance, so Mary would remain in her room.

It was three o'clock in the morning, and Debbie needed some rest. As Mary secured Debbie's blankets and encouraged her to relax and trust that she would be there for her, she said, "I think you saved your daughters' lives."

Debbie wept for the first time since the whole ordeal began. She sobbed at the acknowledgment that her children could have died at the hands of Paul Ferguson just hours ago. It was a chilling reality that had it not been for the phone call at 10:20 p.m, the floorboards creaking, and her actions, her children could be dead. Tears of grief and gratitude streamed down the sides of her face, marking the end of the worst night of her life.

Chapter III

That's What Friends Are For

Friday, April 19, was a typical workday for most people, but not for Debbie and her friends in the East Pennsboro and Susquehanna Township School Districts. Just two hours after her nurse dimmed the lights in her hospital room and began the vigil of watching over her, she was surprised by visitors. At five o'clock in the morning, Debbie's superintendent, Dr. Glenn Zehner, and his assistant superintendent, Keith Voelker, were standing in her hospital room, both with looks of grave concern. Still unaware of the impact the news of the attack would have on her family and friends, Debbie was surprised by their visit.

Where can you work that the top two people in your business are the first people at your bedside? she wondered. They had received a call from John McGreevy and had initiated a phone chain in the district. They needed to know she was all right, and she reassured them that she was.

The rest of the day was filled with visitors. Her best friend, Rainie, was there by 7:30 a.m. Rainie hugged Debbie, and they cried. They had been through a lot together. Rainie's ex-husband left her soon after Debbie's divorce; and, although Rainie was ten years younger, they shared a special bond and a deep friendship. Rainie was visibly shaken up, and she had had a fellow teacher drive her to the hospital. She had not received the phone chain call due to a phone problem, but she was convinced it happened for a reason. She lived forty-five minutes from school and the hospital. If she had gotten a call at her home, she would have been too upset to drive herself to the hospital.

As fate would have it, she had teacher friends standing in the parking lot waiting for her when she arrived at school. She could tell something was wrong, but she had no idea the news would be so upsetting. Fortunately, and true to form, the East Pennsboro staff had already planned to take her directly to the hospital, and she had someone to talk with on the way.

She was there by Debbie's side, and she was there to stay. She took over for Mary, and she needed to know the whole gory story, even though it hurt and upset her. She cried through the parts where Paul hurt her friend and gritted her teeth with anger at his violence. She was happy that the police had arrested him, but was incensed by Paul's and his mother's denial.

Debbie was validated and touched by how much Rainie's emotions mirrored her feelings and thoughts, a warm feeling that she had experienced so many times throughout their relationship. She recalled the day Rainie came to her office to share with her the start of her divorce. "If we are going to do aerobics after school today, we will need to borrow someone's stereo. Gary took the one we had been using when he moved out," was all she needed to say to hurl them into an emotional journey of recovery from divorce—not a quick fix but a commitment to do it perfectly. A pair of strong and proud women determined to follow the book; and as it turned out, every book on divorce that they could get their hands on, to ensure that they understood what happened in their first marriages so they would not repeat them in their next.

Elizabeth Hoffman was their hero. Although Rainie had never met Elizabeth, she felt she owed her a weekly consultation fee for her support and advice, a la Debbie. Debbie had already begun her journey, outlined by Elizabeth, when Rainie joined her. She had done everything Elizabeth recommended, including Chit Chat's Family of Origin Program, group counseling, individual counseling, books, and seminars. She had done them alone and scared, but with a firm belief that she needed professional help to get her through the toughest part of her life—the toughest, at least to that point. Debbie welcomed and appreciated having the love and support of a true friend through divorce, and now her best friend was there for her again.

Rainie's first marriage had lasted only eleven months. She adored children and dedicated her professional career to caring for learning-disabled children, but she longed for her own. Jaredd, Alisha, and Ashley had become the closest thing for her to nurture as her own, and Rainie soon grew to love each one of them. While children could tie down single women, Rainie never saw Debbie's children as anything but a blessing, and she could not get enough of them. While Debbie and Rainie needed to get out and meet new people, they planned as many Saturday nights in as out, just getting pizza and videos and hanging out with the kids. They spent summer days riding their bikes in the neighborhood and swimming and picnicking in the backyard by the pool, always surrounded by Debbie's children and their neighborhood friends.

Rainie was enough a part of Debbie's family to know Paul Ferguson. Paul was often a part of the bike rides and swimming. He wasn't Jaredd's best friend, but he was one of the regular neighborhood kids who would hang around with Jaredd and his best friend, Dorsey. Dorsey, on the other hand, was like a part of the family. He was a bright, honest, wonderful, true friend whom Debbie loved as a son and welcomed to and included in all the family activities. He was a quiet, respectful, and polite young man who was the only son of a neighborhood couple who had children from their prior marriages but only one child in their marriage together. Dorsey had older half sisters, but being much younger than them, he felt and seemed like an only child. Being included in Jaredd's family made him feel that he had a brother and two little sisters. He always seemed to cherish his relationship with Jaredd's whole family and the love they felt for him.

Rainie loved Dorsey too, but she never was too fond of Paul. Unlike Dorsey, Paul was loud, ill-mannered, and hyper. His presence with Jaredd and Dorsey often resulted in arguments, household items or toys being broken or missing, or pranks of a negative or destructive nature. Paul frequently showed up uninvited, never had rides to the movies or activities that the boys wanted to attend, needed to borrow a bike for bike rides, and was even, occasionally, locked out of his house and needed a place to stay. There was always an air of deceit or manipulation surrounding Paul, giving him an Eddie Haskell sort of personality.

Jaredd and Dorsey were by nature very honest and respectful boys. They were frequently amazed by Paul's risk-taking mischief and enjoyed describing his behaviors as funny or just plain stupid. Debbie at times felt sorry for Paul. When Bradon, the fourth neighborhood buddy, joined Jaredd, Dorsey, and Paul, Paul always seemed to be the underdog. Bradon picked on him and teased him more frequently than the others. Paul was the slowest and least athletic of the four, making the competitive games like basketball or ball-tag a bit one-sided. Despite their differences, they remained neighborhood friends until February of 1994, when Paul's mischievous pranks escalated to criminal acts, which separated him from the others.

What clues from the past could explain Paul's attack on Debbie's family? Reflecting on all those memories, Debbie and Rainie, together, could not come up with the motive, despite their combined professional expertise and experience with children. They had lots of time to discuss and analyze human nature, as they had done for years in an effort to understand and make sense of their failed marriages. Their wounds from their respective divorces had healed, but they had new wounds to care for. This, too, they could and would handle together.

Rainie needed to see Jaredd, Alisha, and Ashley. She was sure they were safe, but she needed to see them and hold them as much as Debbie needed to see them and hold them. Rainie left for only a short time that day. She went to Debbie's home to check in on the kids, then drove to her home to pack her bag for the weekend. Before she was even missed, Rainie had returned to the hospital with a heart-warming story of her reunion with Debbie's children. She always saw the best in each one of them, and she was very emotional and proud as she described the strength and beauty of each one of the children.

Debbie was surprised when Rainie put her suitcase by the extra hospital bed in her room and declared it her bed for the weekend. Debbie had not asked nor expected Rainie to stay overnight with her. Rainie had recently remarried, and she had a husband and a life of her own. But Rainie had arranged with her husband, Douglas, that she would stay at the hospital with Debbie for the weekend. She was settling in and making herself at home like it was a girls' weekend retreat. The company and support of a strong and compassionate best friend was just what Debbie needed.

When Debbie realized she could not shower, brush her teeth, or go to the bathroom without help, she understood and experienced the true meaning of friendship. Debbie hated being dependent on anyone; she was so used to taking care of herself and others; but with both hands wrapped in gauze, she was helpless.

Surprised at Rainie's plan to stay, Debbie was not sure the hospital would allow her to stay there; but Rainie was sure. Whether they allowed it or not, she was staying. If they needed the extra bed for another patient, Rainie would be sleeping on the chair in the room. She was staying, and Debbie was grateful. It was not until that evening, when the hospital was quiet and it was time for Debbie to sleep for the first night since the attack, that Rainie's presence was of utmost importance to her. Trying to sleep meant she would have to allow herself to shut down the mind that had been so helpful in saving her life and the lives of her children. Having no use of her hands to defend against another attack was frightening too, but she had her strong friend by her side. After all, that's what friends are for.

Chapter IV

The DA's Office

April 19 was not a typical day in the office of the district attorney. The fourth floor of the Dauphin County Courthouse was buzzing with the shocking news of a multiple stabbing in quiet Susquehanna Township. District Attorney John Cherry had arrived at work early as usual, and his secretary had the Patriot Newspaper opened to the article entitled, "Mother, Son Stabbed." It was a short article that read,

> A mother and her 15-year-old son were stabbed last night after what police believe was an attempt by another teen to burglarize their Susquehanna Township home. The mother, identified as Debra Bird, and her son, Jaredd, of the 3300 block of North Third Street, were taken to Polyclinic Medical Center. Their conditions were undisclosed last night. Lieutenant Don Fleisher said officers were questioning a neighborhood teen. Fleisher said he believes both boys attend the same school. No charges have been filed. Police were called to the Bird home shortly before 11:00 p.m. for a burglary in progress. When police arrived, Debra Bird and her son had been stabbed by the

intruder, Fleisher said. Police determined there
was forced entry at the front door of the home.

George Matangos was skimming the paper at the same time
that he was listening to the morning news on television and eating breakfast. As a resident of Susquehanna Township, the television report caught his attention immediately. As he glanced up from
his paper, he caught sight of the television news coverage of a Third
Street home and watched ambulance crews carrying victims from the
home. Did they say a teen stabbed the residents of this home? The
newspaper could tell him what he missed on the TV. He needed to
find the article in the paper fast. As deputy district attorney in charge
of juvenile crime and violent offences, he needed to know more.

George's breakfast was no longer of interest to him. Besides, he
had lost his appetite, and he knew enough from the television and
newspaper to be in a big hurry to get to work. When his wife, Elaine,
entered the kitchen to join him for a cup of coffee, George was ready
to leave with briefcase in hand and the morning paper tucked under
his arm. "I've got to run, hon. A big case is breaking today. Some teen
stabbed a family in the township. I'll call you later this morning."
With a kiss good-bye and a passing "Love ya," he was out the door,
leaving Elaine with lots of questions. She would get the story from
him later, but the coffee was calling her. With three little ones sleeping peacefully, she savored the quiet morning moments.

George's office was crowded when he got to the courthouse. His
assistants, Shawn and Bev, couldn't wait to tell him that the attacker
was Paul Ferguson. They knew George had prosecuted a case against
Paul in juvenile court several years ago and he had overseen a second
case involving Paul just two days ago.

"Do you mean the same Paul Ferguson who was just found guilty
of vandalizing three homes did the stabbing last night?" George was
floored. He was excited too, and he knew he shouldn't show it; but
Paul was only fifteen years old. If Paul was truly the perpetrator of the
crime he had read about over breakfast, George would have a good
chance of prosecuting the case, or at least assisting the prosecution.

George had only been deputy district attorney a little over a year and a half. This would be his biggest case ever. His fellow prosecutors would be begging for this case. If he got the case, he could finally focus his talents on an important case that would receive a lot of attention and media coverage. Was he too new to get this assignment? He deserved it. After all, he was the expert on juvenile crime.

John Cherry and the first assistant district attorney, Ed Marsico, were discussing the case in the small boardroom when George arrived. Ed appeared stunned and a bit rattled. George knew Ed was an intense prosecutor, but informal discussions of cases usually were handled in an impersonal, detached fashion. Ed's concern immediately became clear. "I know the victim," Ed repeated for George's sake. "Mrs. Bird was my high school physical education teacher. I think she's an administrator now, but when I attended East Pennsboro, she taught PE and coached the girls' field hockey team. She was a great teacher and coach. I can't believe anyone would want to hurt or … I have to make some calls and find out how she is doing," he concluded as he pushed his chair from the large table and left the room.

"George, I'd like you to prosecute this case," Mr. Cherry said in a voice that communicated that he too was shaken by Ed's description of the victim. "You and Ed are my best, and Ed obviously is too personally involved to handle this case. I need my best to prosecute this case. It will be the first case in the state to bring a juvenile charged with a violent crime directly into adult court instead of bringing him through the juvenile justice system."

George was well aware of the new law that Governor Tom Ridge had just signed in December of 1995. In fact, he was the only staff member who knew enough about the new law to conduct seminars to explain what the changes actually meant. And what they meant was that George Matangos would be prosecuting the first juvenile as an adult under the new law in the state of Pennsylvania. The case would go directly to adult court, and Paul Ferguson would be tried as an adult.

His excitement was overwhelming. As his thoughts shifted from the prominence of the case to its substance, an incredible sense of dread came over him. What if the victims that were being carried out of the home had died? What if children lost their mother or they sustained serious, permanent injuries? He wanted fulfilling work. He wanted to make a difference in the lives of the people he defended, but he wasn't looking forward to dealing with the tragic and painful consequences of the violent crime he had read about in the news that morning.

Chapter V

A Daughter, a Sister, a Mother

Debbie was not ready to deal with the painful reactions of her parents when they arrived at her hospital room that morning after the attack. It always upset her to see her mother crying or her dad worried, and that's exactly what she saw as they approached her bed. She wondered who had called them and what they must have heard and thought and felt as they drove from their home an hour away from Harrisburg. Parents should not have to see their child hurt in such a way, and she felt sorry for them. She remembered how hurt and worried they were about her when she told them she was getting a divorce. She never wanted to hurt or disappoint them. They should not have to go through another emotionally painful trauma, but they were there and grateful to see her alive.

Marti, Debbie's sister, was there for her too. They had always been close. Growing up, they had shared a bedroom, but the closeness they shared as adults was marked by a genuine love and respect for each other. Even though there was five years difference in their ages and fifty miles between their homes, they were as close as any two sisters could be. Marti was always so sweet that Debbie could not get into an argument with her, let alone a fight. Marti did not have a harsh or unkind word for anyone, except when she called John a "creep" for leaving Debbie. Paul was a "creep" now, too, so Debbie knew Marti was really upset.

Debbie's brother, Dave, came to see her too; and he did have harsh words to say. Debbie could see the hurt in her brother's eyes as she explained what Paul had done to her and the children. She could not remember seeing her brother cry, but as his eyes filled up with tears, he focused on his anger rather than on his pain as he described what he'd like to do to this kid if he got his hands on him. "No one does this to my little sister," he vowed as the protective big-brother instinct kicked in. Debbie and Dave had had their share of fights growing up, but as sibling rivalry changed with maturity, they too shared a special love and respect for each other.

Debbie was blessed with a very close and caring family, a normal family that was not used to violence and aggression. She had a mother, a father, a sister, and a brother who did not deserve to see her hurt any more than she deserved to be hurt. The reason and the details of the attack continued to plague her as her family gathered around in support of her.

Rainie was back again, and this time she had the children. It was so good to see Alisha and Ashley. The last vision she had of them in her mind was when she was looking across her room into their room and seeing Alisha comforting Ashley in the top bunk of her bed. What a nightmare it was for them to awake to such horror! And how good it was for them to see their mother alive and without the blood. They were eager to share stories.

They even found opportunities to find humor in some of the events of the previous night. Alisha remarked on how slow John McGreevy was when she had summoned him to follow her to her house. He had to turn off the television, find his flashlight, put on his shoes, lock his door; she thought they'd never get back to the house. They laughed out loud as Jaredd described his memory of John taking over the 911 call. He had answered a few of the operator's questions and then promptly told the operator, "Debbie's just covered with blood. We need an ambulance here."

Debbie's whole family knew John as Debbie's wonderful neighbor and friend, and they could all appreciate the humor. It was the first time they were able to laugh, and the laughter felt good.

Chapter VI

Intent to Kill

When the Susquehanna Township police visited her room, Debbie was alone. It was one o'clock in the afternoon. Rainie and Debbie's family had gone to get some lunch. Debbie had been watching television and was both amazed and troubled by the news coverage of the attack. It was an eerie feeling to watch herself and her son being carried out of her house on stretchers. Her house was surrounded by yellow crime tape, and a news commentator was describing a crime. It gave her the chills to view the aftermath of her nightmare, but what bothered her most was the newscaster's description of the event as a burglary.

Paul did not come into her house the previous night at 10:30 p.m. to steal. If he wanted to take things, he could have helped himself to anything downstairs. Paul was upstairs by ten thirty. He wasn't there to steal, so why were they calling it burglary? She felt threatened, and at the same time angry that Paul's attack on her family was being portrayed to the public as an attempt to steal items from her home.

The two officers, Nelson and Heilig, were all ears as Debbie presented her theories and questions about the newscast to them. She told them her account of the attack from start to finish, as she had told it so many times before. They learned the details that Debbie could provide, but they had information to add to her story.

The police brought a tracking dog to the house, and the dog led his trainer to Paul's house. What a relief! That would surely prove what she had said from the start about Paul being the perpetrator of the assault. She wondered, a bit smugly, how Paul's mother would cover that up.

The officers remained serious and intent on gathering as much evidence from her as possible. They wanted to know what Paul was wearing at the time of the attack. That was a question no one had asked of her. From Dr. Albracht to her family, she had not included a description of what he had worn. As she described the plaid shirt Paul was wearing, she could see it as clearly as if it was right in front of her again; a navy or black and white large plaid shirt with a dark collar. They had not found the shirt that she described.

"Was Paul wearing pants during the attack?" one of them asked.

Debbie could not recall if he wore pants or not since his shirt was big and covered most of his upper body. It occurred to her at that moment that she had no memory of looking down at Paul at any time during the attack; but at the same time, she knew he must have had something on, otherwise he would have appeared half naked. If that were the case, she was sure she would have noticed. Her total attention had been on his face or upper body, so she could not come up with an image of pants.

The officers seemed to have an explanation for Debbie's inability to recall Paul's pants. They found pants and sneakers on her kitchen floor that, according to Jaredd and Alisha, did not belong to them. "When Alisha chased Paul from the house, he must have left his pants and shoes where he took them off," Officer Nelson theorized. They had interviewed Alisha at eight o'clock that morning at John McGreevy's house, and Jaredd at 10:15 a.m. at Mandy's house. Both children were very helpful and cooperative. "You have great kids," they complimented Debbie.

The questions and suppositions continued between the three of them, but two questions haunted Debbie. One was when Officer Nelson asked her if she put up a fight. Debbie had not fought, and she could not understand why. In fact, she was disappointed in herself to the point of being ashamed that she did not kick him or hit him. Why did she just back away and tolerate his blows? But the officers did not seem to be satisfied with her answer. "Are you sure you did not mark or scratch him in any way?"

She wished she had scratched him, but she would remember if she had dragged her claws down his face. Why were they so sure she must have scratched him? "Because he had scratches on his face and arms when he was taken to the police station," and they were wondering how he got them. She remembered jabbing the nails of her right fingers into his face, but not dragging her nails down his face. That was the only defensive action she had taken against Paul, and it occurred when she feared she would die on her bedroom floor if she didn't fight for her life.

The officers seemed to be content with their interview with Debbie and reassured her that they were impressed and appreciated all the help that she and her children had provided. Debbie had one final question of the officers before they left. She had already told them that she rejected the burglary theory and that she was sure Paul did not come into her house the previous night to steal. As difficult as it was for her to say it, she had to ask them the burning question that had occurred to her since they had mentioned that Paul's pants had been found on her kitchen floor. "Do you think Paul Ferguson came into my house last night to rape Alisha?"

Officer Heilig responded with only two words, which ran through her like a bolt of lightning. His two-word response to her question was "Or murder."

Despite the number of times she had thought or spoken about dying as a result of the assault by Paul, she had never realized that he was trying to kill her, and it all made sense to her now. A chill ran up her spine, and the events of the previous night took on a whole new horror. That's why he didn't leave when he had the chance. When she called out her daughters' names in the dark, he could have walked right down the hallway, down the staircase, and out the door. He would have gone undetected. Instead, he waited with a plan to kill.

"He may have intended to kill your whole family last night," Officer Nelson concluded.

His words would haunt her thoughts for years to come.

Chapter VII

Thank You

When her ex-husband appeared at the foot of her bed, Debbie was truly surprised to see him. Rainie greeted John with an expressionless "Hello John," making it clear that she had not forgiven him for leaving her best friend six years ago. She told Debbie later that her protective instinct to stay by her side and support her fought with her need to provide privacy at such a difficult time. John's humble, concerned demeanor and Debbie's strength despite the ordeal were the deciding factors. Rainie had some items she needed to attend to at the nurses' station.

John began by explaining that he had stopped by the house and checked on the children. They were all doing just fine. His next words were the most sincere, heartfelt ones he had ever spoken to Debbie. He said, "Thank you for saving our children." He grasped her hand, bowed his head, and wept. They wept together.

John's words reminded Debbie again of her role in saving her children's lives, alone; and she instantly responded with, "You should have been there."

She couldn't help feeling lonely, vulnerable, and sorry for herself. She shouldn't have been alone raising three children, and she shouldn't have been alone at night fighting off an intruder in her home. For the first time since their divorce, she sounded as though she wanted him back. She knew she didn't want him back, but she didn't like being alone, and she didn't like the fact that her children had only one parent to depend on, only one parent to be there when they needed them. She didn't blame John for the attack or for not being there, and she could tell that he understood when he said, "I know." That was really all that needed to be said.

She reflected later on the brief exchange between her and the father of her children. She had often wondered, in her years of single parenting, if the fathers who left their children ever really allowed themselves to feel guilty about their choices. She was sure, in the moments he had spent with his children that morning, that John must have sincerely wished he had been there to protect them, to prevent such a horrible event from happening to them. Perhaps that's why he acknowledged she was right, that he should have been there.

But she didn't want him there, not anymore. She just never quite forgave him for the way he left her and the children, so unaware and unprepared. And for the first time since their divorce, he didn't have an excuse, an explanation, or a reason to defend his choices— just an acknowledgment that he should have been there. And for the first time since their divorce, Debbie heard the closest thing to an apology that she would ever need to hear from him. And finally, a genuine expression of his appreciation for her being there for his children—the much-needed expression of contrition and gratitude that got lost in the legal battles over visitation and child support. Although she was sure he didn't know it, his words went a long way toward healing her emotional wounds from the divorce. He spoke the kindest and most important words she had ever heard from him when he said, "Thank you for saving our children."

Chapter VIII

The Doctor Is In

Friday continued to be a long, emotionally packed day. By early evening, Rainie had become a full-time nurse and secretary. The news of the attack was widespread, as evidenced by the flowers, cards, and phone calls that poured into Debbie's room. Rainie was busy greeting friends, finding a place for another planter, or holding the phone for Debbie's phone conversations. Debbie's tears were frequent, but generated by more positive feelings about caring friends and the celebration of survival.

Rainie didn't recognize Elizabeth Hoffman's voice when she answered Debbie's phone because she had never met Elizabeth. But Debbie recognized Elizabeth's voice instantly. Elizabeth's gentle words comforted her and caused a flood of tears. "What do I do now, Elizabeth?" Debbie asked through her sobs.

And as always, Elizabeth had the answers. She would see Debbie as soon as she was out of the hospital.

"But what about my children? What should I do for them?"

Elizabeth had a plan for them as well. She knew a therapist who was great with children. She would make an appointment for Debbie and the children with Deb Salem. They could get help together, and they would all be just fine.

Elizabeth always had the answers. Debbie had told her one time in a counseling session that she just wanted an Elizabeth Hoffman in her pocket so she could look into it for all her needs and questions and get instant answers. It was at that point in the session that Elizabeth reminded Debbie that the answers were always with her, inside her. She just needed to learn to take better care of the little girl inside her, learn to trust her, and she herself would provide all the guidance, help, and answers Debbie needed.

When she began seeing Elizabeth, Debbie just wanted Elizabeth to tell her how to fix her husband. But Elizabeth wasn't interested in John; she was interested in Debbie. Much of what Elizabeth expected of Debbie didn't make a lot of sense to her, but she did what she was told. Elizabeth's lessons became clearer as Debbie learned how to pay attention to her own needs rather than the needs of others. She found herself looking less and less into her pocket for Elizabeth and more and more to herself as she made decisions and choices in her life. But now she was facing the second greatest hurdle in her life, and it was good to know that Elizabeth would be guiding her recovery again. She was touched that she was important enough for Elizabeth to call her in her hospital room the day after the attack. She hadn't seen Elizabeth in years, yet she was there the day she needed her the most—not in her pocket, but in person over the phone. What a relief to know she and her children would get the professional help they needed!

Chapter IX

Girls' Club

Debbie had just finished updating Rainie on Elizabeth's call when Edee arrived. Edee and her husband, Bill, had been friends since Debbie's oldest, Jaredd, and their oldest, Nick, began playing township soccer at the age of six. Alisha was only four and Ashley was just a baby when Debbie and Edee found themselves sitting on lawn chairs next to strollers on the sidelines of the soccer field. With six-year-old boys and babies, Ashley and Andrew, who were one month apart in age, Edee and Debbie had a lot in common and instantly became friends.

Nine years later, Edee was still happily married to Bill, but busy with two more boys who were clones of Nick and Andrew. Not too busy, however, to get to the hospital as quickly as she could upon hearing the news. Edee always had a hundred and one questions to ask even on a boring day, so her visit was a tidal wave of requests for details that needed to be explored.

When Judy and Karen entered the room, the gang was all there. Debbie's most intimate girlfriends surrounded her. She couldn't have planned a girls' night out better if she had sent out invitations. In fact, the gathering reminded her of the fortieth birthday party that Rainie had planned for her. They spent an evening eating, drinking, and relaxing in Debbie's living room, all reminiscing and reliving funny experiences. Edee always had the best stories, like the time she paraded across the Top of the Sixes Restaurant in New York City with a dinner roll stuck to her crotch. It never took long for the group of women to be having a good time discussing women issues, parenting, embarrassing moments, and men.

What perfect timing for Dr. Albracht to stop in to check up on and prepare Debbie for her hand surgery, which was scheduled for the next day. Debbie had told Rainie all about her handsome orthopedic surgeon, but Edee, Judy, and Karen were in for an unexpected treat. As Dr. Albracht explained in his professional, thorough fashion every detail of Debbie's injuries, he used his own hands as a visual aid. He had all her incisions drawn on his own hands and made a presentation that could have been a medical school lecture to the group of women in the room.

Debbie would, at a crucial time later in her recovery, remember every word of his analysis of her injuries and the concerns he stressed about possible complications. She would remember because he was so passionate about her injuries and the upcoming surgery. What kind of surgeon would take the time to draw a patient's injuries in ink on his own hands and visit the patient to explain in such precise and complete terms the surgical procedure and aftercare physical therapy required for complete recovery? She was impressed and grateful to have had such personal and special treatment.

You could have heard a pin drop in the hospital room throughout Dr. Albracht's entire explanation. Even Edee was speechless. When he asked if they had any questions, Rainie, in her protective style, wanted to know why the surgery was not scheduled sooner. Dr. Albracht assured her, and Debbie, that tendons do not atrophy and that surgery could be scheduled weeks later without comprising her chances of full recovery.

Debbie was not anxious for Dr. Albracht to leave, but she could hardly wait to see her friends' reactions, which started the second he was out of the room. The swooning and panting over Dr. Albracht was as predictable as if John Kennedy Jr. had still been alive, had decided to become an orthopedic surgeon, and had just left her hospital room. They were like silly teenage girls, with Rainie and Edee arguing over whose hand he could use for his next presentation.

In the moment, Debbie's fears of the next day's surgery were drowned in laughter and sheer delight over a room full of thirty- and forty-year-old women acting like giggling schoolgirls.

Chapter X

Q-Tips

Debbie's girlfriends assumed age-appropriate conduct when the teenage boys began entering Debbie's hospital room. Debbie was surprised to see Jaredd's friends collecting in her room, and she soon saw the common theme of her visitors. Jaredd had lots of friends, but this group of guys was his baseball team. Their Friday practice must have been focused upon Jaredd and the attack, and they were in the hospital to check on Jaredd's mother soon after their practice ended.

When a son plays baseball from township T-ball to high school junior varsity baseball, his mother gets to know a lot of players and parents through season after season of wins and losses. How sweet it was to be surrounded by teenage boys who took time from their Friday evening activities to get rides to the hospital to see her, Debbie thought. They had so many questions and concerns, most of which Debbie could answer, but the reason for the attack remained purely speculation.

The teens had their own ways of handling the gruesome or horrifying aspects of the incident, but PJ Connor used humor to handle his struggle with Debbie's hand injuries. "Nice Q-tips!" he said, referring to her bandaged fists. And he was right; her hands looked like giant Q-tips. His spontaneous observation gave some comic relief to the otherwise-difficult visit for teenage boys who don't always have the words to express their feelings.

Later that evening, when Debbie returned from having her shoulder x-rayed, her family, Rainie, and the Susquehanna Township boys' basketball team were waiting. Jaredd's basketball season had ended in March, but Jaredd's basketball friends were as familiar to Debbie as his baseball buddies. Debbie's mother was so impressed with how committed the boys were to seeing Debbie. When they learned Debbie was getting her shoulder x-rayed, they stayed and waited for her return. Her mother was particularly touched by Reggie Guy's concern. The six-foot three-inch varsity basketball star wanted to know each part of the attack. But as Debbie's mother related each part of the incident, Reggie would moan, turn away, collect himself and his emotions, and then turn back with "Then what?" or "What happened next?" The details were more than he could handle, but he seemed compelled to know everything.

Debbie was very touched by the efforts her children's friends made to see her in the hospital, especially when Dorsey arrived. Dorsey's mother brought him to the hospital, and as she waited and talked with Debbie's mother, she explained that she had to bring Debbie's "second son" to see her. And Dorsey's reactions were those very similar to Jaredd's reactions. He was hurt, angry, and confused by Paul's attack on her. Why would he do such a thing? Jaredd and Dorsey could never understand why Paul did a lot of the things that he did, but this act was unimaginable.

As Dorsey struggled with how badly his childhood ex-friend had hurt his "second mom," Debbie was reminded of Jaredd and Dorsey's commitment to seeing the best in all people. Two years ago, Dorsey could not believe that Paul had sneaked into Jaredd's home and taken items and money until, one month later, he and Bradon had to testify against Paul in juvenile court as witnesses to Paul's breaking into and stealing from cars parked at the neighborhood Jewish Community Center.

Dorsey and Jaredd must have been the last two supporters of O. J. Simpson as the yearlong trial presented overwhelming evidence that O. J. killed his wife. They had tried their best to keep believing in their football hero. Too bright to argue with the facts of the case, they eventually gave up their wide-eyed, fairy-tale hopes that O. J.

was innocent, but not without a great deal of disappointment and disillusionment.

Debbie could see that struggle in Dorsey again. Just as he had wondered how O. J. could have done such a violent, evil act, he wondered how Paul could have become so evil. She was sure Dorsey would wrestle with the reality of Paul's attack on her as they were all trying to make sense out of the unexplainable.

Chapter XI

Under the Knife Again

Debbie awoke Saturday morning in a panic. Her heart was racing, and her startle reflex had her prepared for battle again. But it was just a bad dream. She was safe in her hospital room, with Rainie sleeping in the bed next to hers. She had slept well—very soundly from the exhaustion of the previous day, which began with the 5:00 a.m. visit from her school administrators and ended with her family leaving her hospital room and Rainie helping her prepare for bed.

As she reflected upon the previous day and how blessed she was to have such loving, caring relatives and friends, the pain in her shoulder and hands reminded her of less positive concerns. What if the surgery does not go well? What if her hands were permanently disabled? She didn't want to think of such morbid thoughts, but she couldn't help but worry.

As the nurses were going in and out of her room doing their morning rounds, she was visited by a nurse who happened to be the parent of one of her students at East Pennsboro Middle School. Kathy introduced herself and expressed her sincere regrets and shock over the horrible attack. But she had an even more important mission. She had overheard Dr. Mauer expressing an interest in performing Debbie's hand surgery. While it was not appropriate for her to be discussing the matter, Kathy felt compelled to let Debbie know that Dr. Mauer was an expert on hands—truly the best orthopedic hand surgeon around. Dr. Mauer was not assigned to do the surgery, but if he asked Debbie for her permission to be involved in the surgery, Kathy urged Debbie to allow him to do so.

Then quickly, Kathy was gone. And sure enough, not long after Kathy's visit, Dr. Mauer entered Debbie's room. He introduced himself and explained that Dr. Brown was scheduled to do her surgery, but that he had a great interest and specialty in hands. He had studied her case and was wondering if Debbie would have any objections to having him assist Dr. Brown in the operating room.

That was a no-brainer. Having two doctors working on the repairs to her hands was very reassuring. Not to mention, and she didn't, that Dr. Mauer came so highly recommended by the hospital staff that a friendly nurse would go out of her way to encourage a patient to allow him to work on them.

After Dr. Mauer left her room and it was time for surgery, Debbie's confidence at having dual surgeons was shattered by an overwhelming fear of being put to sleep for surgery. She was so afraid to face the chance of death, again. How ironic to have lived through the attack only to die on the operating table having her tendons repaired. Having survived a near-death experience, she did not want to tempt fate again. She didn't want to be put to sleep and run the risk of not waking.

But, like so much of the last thirty-six hours of her life, the choices she had been presented with were not good; they were choosing the lesser of two evils. Stay in the dark and be attacked or turn on the light and see the monster? Push the door closed and keep Paul out of the bedroom with her children or let him in to stab her again? Risk dying of anesthesia or have crippled hands for the rest of her life?

Isn't there another door to pick from? she wondered, feeling sorry and afraid for herself again. And she worried about her children losing their mother after all the trauma they had just experienced. The tears ran down the sides of her face and onto her bed as she was wheeled on her way to the operating room.

And the tears of joy ran down the sides of her face and onto her bed as the staff wheeled her from the recovery room. She had survived the dreaded surgery. And what a welcome party she had as she moved through the hallways lined with six-foot- and some less-than-six-foot-tall basketball players. Her family was there, and they all celebrated her return from surgery. Debbie had survived yet another hurdle on her long road to recovery. She was so grateful and happy to be alive and loved.

Debbie's mother would later tell her about the one person who was happier than Debbie herself was when she returned from surgery. Alisha saw immediately what was under the giant Q-tips—her mother's fingers. It didn't matter that her mother's hands were bandaged from her elbows to her fingertips. Nor did it concern Alisha that several fingers were attached to wires and pulleys. What mattered to Alisha was that her mother had all her fingers. She was so excited that she talked about it to her grandmother all the way home that day. Grandma was tearful as she told Debbie about Alisha's fears. How sad to think that Alisha had been afraid since the attack that her mother had lost fingers and the gruesome remains were hidden under those gauze Q-tips.

How unfortunate it was that any of them should have to experience such pain and fears. The haunting questions returned. Why was Paul in her home that Thursday night? Why didn't he leave when she called her daughters' names and he knew she was awake? He could have walked down the stairs in the dark, collected his pants and sneakers, and left the way he came in, leaving Debbie with unexplained creaky floorboards. Did he think she would fall back to sleep so he could finish what he came there to do—rape or murder, or both? Her thoughts faded as she fell asleep on her third night in the hospital.

Chapter XII

Reliving the Trauma

Sunday was a pleasant day—full of visitors, phone calls, and flowers. Debbie's mother and Rainie were busy caring for her and making trips back and forth from the hospital to Debbie's home with the many flowers and planters that no longer fit in the hospital room. Rainie packed herself and prepared to return home.

The weekend was over, and Rainie would be back to work the next day. She had updated many of the middle school teachers by phone, but tomorrow would be a busy day of personally sharing the details of her friend's tragedy with their caring, worried staff and students.

While Rainie anticipated the return to work, she was relieved that Debbie had the use of her right thumb and index finger and could push her own hospital buzzer. Each day, Debbie showed marked improvement in both her physical and emotional strength. Rainie was grateful to have had the entire weekend to spend by her friend's side. She enjoyed Debbie's family and friends, especially Debbie's mother. She knew she had been greatly appreciated by Debbie and her mother.

Things had a way of working out; Debbie would be reminded over and over through her traumatic experience. She had lost track of the days of the week, and the day hadn't felt like a Sunday until it was time for Rainie to leave the hospital. Debbie would be leaving the hospital the next day as well. She had a scheduled visit to the physical therapy unit for the next morning, after which she would be discharged from the hospital and free to return home.

She had grown accustomed to the care and security of the hospital, and her first night without Rainie was more difficult than she expected. The quiet, dim atmosphere of the hospital after visiting hours created the perfect setting for a horror movie—the kind where the bad guy returns to the hospital, disguised as a hospital orderly or doctor, to finish what he intended to do in the first place. She knew Paul was locked up, but what about his father? She had never met him, so it was easy to imagine him as an angry, crazy man intent on killing the woman who was accusing his son of a crime he didn't commit.

She stared at her open hospital room door, wishing she had a guard sitting outside her room. Rainie had provided such a sense of safety. Now she was alone for the first time since the attack, and she was too frightened to close her eyes despite her exhaustion from another long day. Her thoughts began to fade with the effects of the sedation and pain medication.

Suddenly, without warning, a noise in her room startled her into a sitting position. A nurse had banged her metal water pitcher into the table as she made her nighttime rounds. That feeling of adrenaline and rapid heart racing was uncontrollably back as she tried to make sense of the danger around her. The nurse was not Mary. Mary had promised Debbie that she would stay by her side and protect her, that she would not let anyone hurt her again.

The new nurse apologized for frightening her, but she was sure she had no idea of the level of panic she had created by her unannounced visit. Debbie explained that she had been a victim of an attack, and that unexpected noises startled her.

"Perhaps if you could talk as you enter my room rather than just quietly walking in, it would help," Debbie pleaded. Her sense of safety was shattered, and her insecurity disturbed her. She eventually fell asleep, but the sleep was medically induced. She wondered if her life would ever feel natural or normal again.

Chapter XIII

It Was Then That I Carried You

Debbie's mother brought real clothes from home and helped Debbie get out of her hospital gown. Debbie's splints on her arms and her painful shoulder made it impossible for her to do anything for herself, creating a helpless, childlike feeling that was foreign to her. Even when she had gotten her foot caught in the lawn mower at the age of five, she didn't need any help. She recalled her grandmother checking in on her in the bathroom where her injured right foot was propped up on the side of the tub and commenting to her mother that she was so independent. Debbie considered that a compliment, and she was always proud of her ability to take care of herself. It was difficult now to be so needy, so dependent upon others for help; but she was grateful to her mother and to her best friend for being there for her most personal needs.

When she exited the hospital with her mother, John McGreevy was waiting with a vehicle to take them home. As she sat in the back of the car, she reflected upon the seven-block trip from her home to the hospital in an ambulance. She was in such a better place now with her injuries healing and her family out of danger.

As the car pulled up in front of her house, she saw the crime tape was still there surrounding the house. She was overcome by intense fear of returning to her home. She wasn't sure she could go back in there, yet this was her home. How could Paul have destroyed the comfort and safety of her own home, for herself and for all three of her children?

She fought back the tears as she walked slowly up the sidewalk. She had no tissues, and she wouldn't be able to wipe her own tears anyway. She would need help for even that. As she entered her home, she noticed the broken banister and the charcoal-covered walls: damage from the attack and the fingerprinting for evidence. When Debbie turned and entered her living room, she was surrounded by her family, neighbors, and friends. She was so touched by the room full of love and flowers—flowers on every shelf, on the mantel, and on the table from her living room into the sunroom and dining room. There were flowers everywhere! She was so overwhelmed that she spontaneously asked, "Who died?"

Expecting to hear laughter at her humor and getting none, she was reminded of her doctors' silence when her hair was so covered with blood and she jokingly asked them how she looked as a redhead. She was able to joke about the morbid, but those around her were not there yet.

When Debbie looked up the staircase to the second floor, her sense of humor was gone, and she was sure she did not want to go there. Alisha and Ashley must have sensed her apprehensions and immediately asked her to come upstairs with them. They were anxious to show her that the upstairs was all cleaned up—the blood was gone. They took her splinted arms, being careful not to touch or hurt her hands, and led her up the stairs. As they walked together down the hallway toward their bedrooms, the floorboards creaked, and Debbie's tears returned—tears of joy and gratitude. Her floorboards never sounded so good, and she thanked them, out loud, for saving her life.

Alisha and Ashley were so proud, so happy to display their bedroom and their mother's room without all the blood. Debbie's room was different. The phone was gone, the doorknob was off the door, wall items by her door were missing, and her wicker wastebasket was crushed on one side. The dresser by the door was pushed farther from the door, and she began to replay the attack in her mind. When Paul tackled her, she must have hit the dresser, pushing it out of place. She must have fallen onto part of her wastebasket as she fell to the floor beneath Paul's weight. She didn't remember knocking items from her wall, or hitting anything on her way to the floor, just the incredible pain in her left shoulder and Paul's knife attack on her temple and neck.

She remembered not being able to see out of her right eye when she struggled to get off the floor and thinking the stab wound to her right temple must have blinded her. Remembering John McGreevy's and her children's descriptions of her face as "covered with blood," she realized, in that moment, that the blood from the stab wounds to her scalp must have run down her face and into her right eye. It was sickening to imagine not being able to see because so much blood had poured into her eye. Thankfully, the blood had not run into her left eye too, or she would have been unable to see Paul returning to her door or find the phone to dial 911. She was amazed at how clearly she could always see the positive in the very worst of events, a quality that had always been a part of her personality. Her cup was always half full. She would later, and frequently, marvel at how the positive always seemed to outweigh the negative, as good always triumphed over evil.

She stayed upstairs a long time that first day home, reclaiming her house, focusing upon the positive and counting her blessings— the creaking floorboards that alerted her, her grandmother's hurricane lamp that illuminated her room, the clock that displayed 10:20 and 10:30, the frame of her daughters' bedroom door. It was when she reread her favorite poem, which was hanging on her bedroom wall, however, that she got in touch with her ultimate blessing. Her mother had given her the framed poem entitled "Footprints" on her first birthday as a single parent.

Debbie knew at that time of her life that she had questioned God's plan for her. She was at the lowest and saddest time of her life, and God reminded her, through the poem, that he had not abandoned her but, rather, carried her.

She had not questioned God for a minute through the second trial and suffering of her life. She felt him carry her as she reflected upon the phone call that woke her, Alisha's waking to help, the timely medical assistance, her friends, her loved ones, and Elizabeth Hoffman. She understood fully that when she needed him most, it was then that he carried her.

Chapter XIV

Forever Changed

Nighttime was difficult again for Debbie. Home in her own bed, she could not sleep on the side of her king-sized bed, which was closest to the door. Despite the awkward feeling of sleeping on the opposite side, she felt safer and more secure farther away from the door. Her mother would sleep on her old side of the bed for the time being.

Something else would change at bedtime in the Birds' house. The hall light would remain on. Alisha had often argued with Ashley over nightlights: Ashley wanted a nightlight in their room, but Alisha could not get to sleep with a nightlight. Alisha had won the argument until April 18 of 1996. After that night, there were no more arguments. The hallway light would remain on all night—even Alisha agreed that she slept better with the hall light on.

Debbie's new position in her bed and the hall light on gave her a different look from her bedroom. She could see Jaredd's bedroom door and farther down the hallway. His door was closed as always when he slept. No wonder he couldn't hear her screams for help.

She couldn't get to sleep her first night at home. She found herself reliving the attack, followed by imagining Paul's dad coming down her hallway with a gun. Jaredd couldn't sleep either. He called out several times to his mother that he couldn't sleep. Debbie was tucked in between pillows supporting her shoulder and arms in the least painful positions. She didn't know what to do for her son until she offered him room at the foot of her bed. He accepted her offer and was there in a flash. With his favorite blanket and his pillow, he was comfortable and secure at the base of her bed. Her six-foot-tall, strong, athletic son was sleeping at the foot of his mother's bed. What a traumatic experience the attack must have been for Jaredd to make him need her closeness and reassurance!

Debbie cried herself to sleep that night worrying about the long-term impact of Paul's attack on her family. She had an appointment with Elizabeth Hoffman the next day and an appointment with Deb Salem for her children in a week, and those appointments couldn't come soon enough. It was time to put her life in the hands of professionals, again.

Chapter XV

A Return to Elizabeth

Debbie's return to Elizabeth Hoffman's office was quite a contrast to her first visit. Seven years ago, she felt like Angie Dickenson in *Dressed to Kill* as she walked up the steps to her office. She had no idea what she was going to say, and she felt embarrassed to even be entering a therapist's office. She knew her marriage was falling apart, and she wanted help to fix her husband; but she didn't want anyone to know that she was struggling or anyone to see her going for help.

Seven years later, she knew just what she needed from Elizabeth Hoffman. As she waited to see Elizabeth again, she reflected on how she felt so many years ago and was sorry for that little girl who was so alone, frightened, and confused about her emotions. Back then, she was like the princess in *The Princess Who Believed in Fairy Tales*, and she was *drowning*. She wanted the porpoise to carry her to the shore, but the fish insisted that she learn to swim. And she'd have to let go of the *leaky boat* that she was hanging on to in order to do so. Her visits to Elizabeth were never easy, but she did learn to trust and let go of the leaky boat and swim.

She was no longer embarrassed about needing help, and she wasn't ashamed or afraid to be returning to Elizabeth. The reunion was warm and comforting. In the sessions to follow, Elizabeth would guide Debbie through the personal challenges of grieving the losses, understanding the changes, celebrating the blessings, and getting on with her life just as she had done before.

The first session was focused upon helping Debbie learn how to accept her helplessness and allow others to do things for her. Elizabeth had in the past challenged Debbie to do what was necessary to help her children if she was unable to do it for herself, because Elizabeth knew that was one sure way to ensure that Debbie would accomplish the task before her. Elizabeth again reminded Debbie that her children needed to be able to help her. In fact, all her loved ones would try to find ways to help, and Debbie needed to allow them to help in order to promote their own healing process.

That evening, after her mother had helped her bathe and get dressed for bed, Debbie was alone in the bathroom, struggling with the toothpaste. She could barely hold the toothbrush between her right index finger and her thumb, but her left hand had no available fingers or functional shoulder to negotiate the toothpaste tube. In her frustration with her helplessness, she remembered Elizabeth's words: "Let your loved ones help."

She called out from the bathroom for anyone to help her brush her teeth, and three children ran from their bedrooms in a race to be first. She was amazed at the pleading and arguing between Alisha, Ashley, and Jaredd. Huddled in the bathroom, her children took turns brushing her teeth. Jaredd expressed a need to do more, and Debbie, in jest, told him he could be her "official nose picker." Even that job he would have done if she had been serious.

As a person who once saw asking for help as a sign of weakness, Debbie had to come to terms with being dependent on others. She was amazed and touched by Elizabeth's insight one more time into her life. And so the healing process would continue for all of them.

Chapter XVI

The Crazy Family

On the way to the first family counseling session with Deb Salem, Debbie recalled feeling a little like the porpoise in *The Princess Who Believed in Fairy Tales*. Because she had led Rainie through divorce with the insights Elizabeth had given her, she was confident that her experience and strength would prove valuable in guiding her children through the recovery process. Deb Salem had agreed to schedule counseling sessions starting at six thirty in the morning so that her children wouldn't have to miss school.

As Debbie's mother drove them to Deb Salem's office, Debbie recognized her own initial counseling reactions in her children. Their questions about what they would do or talk about in counseling turned into nervous jokes about being crazy. By the time they got to Deb's office, they were all laughing hysterically as Jaredd announced the crazy family's arrival.

The laughter ended as the session began. After introductions, Deb Salem led with, "How do you think you have changed through this horrible event?"

Debbie burst into tears with an angry protest: "I don't want to change, I don't want to be different, and I don't want my children to be different." With that, they were all in tears, and the journey of recovery began.

Jaredd felt angry with himself for not waking up. He hated hearing what happened to his mother while he slept. He was sure he left the window to the garage unlocked from the last time he had forgotten his key to the house and had to crawl through the garage window.

Alisha figured out from the police questions that Paul must have come in for her. She was sure that she left the garage door unlocked. Ashley cried that she wished she had woken up to help. She was sorry she slept through the whole attack, and she was sure she left the garage door unlocked when she put her bike away.

Each of the children cried through their feelings of guilt, and Debbie realized that guilt over feeling responsible was the first stage of recovery. Her children somehow were blaming themselves for this horrible event, and she had had no idea they felt such guilt. They were not responsible for her injuries; they did nothing to create such evil, and Deb Salem wasted no time in helping them understand that leaving a door unlocked or not waking up to help did not cause the evil actions of Paul Ferguson. And whether he came there for Alisha or Debbie or the whole family, he had no right to enter their home and hurt them.

Alisha, still focused upon Deb's first question about how they had changed, confessed her fears about the changes the injuries to her brother and her mother might have caused. She worried that her brother might no longer be handsome, and that her girlfriends had always commented on how handsome he was. And her mother always had such beautiful hands, with long, thin fingers. Alisha worried that her mother might no longer have pretty hands.

Debbie had always been amazed by the counseling process, but she was even more so as she learned the fears and unspoken thoughts of her children. Jaredd confessed in a later session that he always hated hearing his mother tell the details of the attack. He would have to leave the room because he couldn't stand it. He was so angry with Paul, and angry that he couldn't do anything to him. In the same session, Jaredd asked his mother the very question that she struggled with since the attack: "Why didn't you fight him? Why didn't you kick him? Why did you just let him stab you?"

As she blamed herself for not being more aggressive, Debbie admitted that she instinctively avoided saying or doing anything that would make him angry. She gave him room to leave, and she said nothing to him, nothing until she called for Jaredd and Paul told her to shut up and she told him to get out.

Deb Salem reminded her that she did exactly what she needed to do to survive and to save her children. Had she done anything differently to change the course of events that night, she and her children could have died. From that moment on, every time she would replay the attack and imagine her kicking Paul in the crotch, grabbing the knife and stabbing him with it, she would remember Deb Salem's words and remind herself that she did exactly what she needed to do to survive.

And there wasn't a day that she didn't replay the attack, or reflect upon the blessing of the footprints in the sand. She was sitting with Alisha when the theme song from the movie *Up Close and Personal* came on the radio: "You were my eyes when I couldn't see / you were my voice when I couldn't speak."

Debbie and Alisha held each other and wept as the words expressed Debbie's gratitude to her daughter for being there for her and saving her life. What a hero she was! What a brave thirteen-year-old girl who confronted Paul, went to her brother's room for help, and ultimately chased Paul from their home. Her bravery did not end when she saw her mother covered with blood. Alisha ran into the dark night to the neighbor's house to get help.

There were many stages of recovery ahead for the Bird family. They were through the denial stage immediately because there was no denying the events of the attack. Their first counseling session was clearly focused on feelings of guilt and grief. They all felt better as they hugged Deb Salem on their way out of her office. But no one was more relieved than Debbie was as Deb Salem embraced her and whispered, "You have three great kids, and you saved their lives. You will all be fine. See you next week."

By the time Debbie and her mother caught up with the kids at the car, they were deep into an argument over who called front seat first, and whether they could go to McDonald's for breakfast before going to school. The kid debates that used to be draining for Debbie were music to her ears now. In many ways, they hadn't changed a bit, and she was incredibly grateful for that. There was nothing crazy about this family—just a crazy act of violence that they would sort out with the help of Deb Salem, Elizabeth Hoffman, and the Footprints in the Sand.

Chapter XVII

The DA

George Matangos did not know Elizabeth Hoffman; nor did he know the Bird family. The preliminary hearing for the *Commonwealth of Pennsylvania vs. Paul A. Ferguson* was set for May 1 before District Justice Raymond Shugars, and he had his work cut out for him. He and Detective Jim Nelson talked the day after the attack. They would be working together on the case; and between the two of them, it was hard to tell who was more excited.

Jim updated George on the progress of the case: Paul requested a lawyer when he was picked up at his home the night of the attack. "A typical response from an innocent fifteen-year-old," they sarcastically agreed.

Detective Kevin Fox was in charge of the evidence, and he hoped to get fingerprints from various items from the Birds' home. "The clothing items and weapon that were left at the crime scene were sent away to be analyzed," Jim related rapidly to George.

All the evidence would be addressed in due time, George thought as he listened and took notes on Jim's report. "How are Mrs. Bird and her children?" George interrupted with genuine concern.

"They are doing fine." Jim switched gears with increased enthusiasm. "Mrs. Bird is pretty cut up, and Jaredd has a huge cut on his face, but he is already out of the hospital. Mrs. Bird provided an excellent account of the crime from her hospital bed, which was sup-

ported by Jaredd and the middle
views. The youngest daughter, A
could not provide any eyewitne
an amazing woman," Jim reass
any trouble getting a full stor

That's what George re
Nelson would have many
much more interested in r
to arrange the meeting, D
in just a minute, he was talking .
dering when she would hear from the Distr
sounded concerned and insecure.

Two days later, when George arrived at the Birds' home, he wa
surprised by Debbie's normal appearance. Debbie's mother answered
the door, but Debbie was standing next to her to greet him. She was
wearing blue jeans, a white shirt, and a baseball cap, and apologized
for not shaking his hand. Aside from the splints on both her arms,
there was no evidence of the serious injuries she had sustained. Even
as she described the injuries in detail throughout the course of their
first interview, she had to point out the cuts to her temple and her
neck while the majority of her injuries remained hidden by the cap
on her head and the bandages on her hands.

Debbie did not look or act like a woman who had just gotten
out of the hospital after a serious physical attack. She was clear and
assertive about the details of the crime. Her amazing ability to recall
the details of her nightmare was almost like she was experiencing it
again as she spoke. He could have continued for hours with her, but
he had three children to meet and talk with, and it was a school night
for them. Debbie called each one of her children to the living room,
introduced them to Mr. Matangos, and then disappeared, allowing
them privacy for their individual interviews.

Two and a half hours later, after completing his interviews,
George had a tremendous understanding of his prime witnesses and
the nightmare they shared. After his tour of the entire crime scene
from the kitchen floor, where Paul left his pants to the bedroom
floors where he left his knife and his evil, George had enough knowl-

e was investigating for one night. Professionally,
y. Personally, however, he had had more than he
ces and personalities of three sweet children and a sin-
ho were victimized in their own home haunted him on
me. How could such a normal American family have expe-
such a horrible attack? And if such a normal family experi-
it, any family could. Jaredd's face faded to the face of his oldest
d, Alyssa, who was just five years old. And Debbie's middle child,
lisha, could be his middle child, Stefan. He had three children too, and it was not hard for him to picture sweet, timid little Ashley as looking a lot like his baby, Christina, when she was only a year old. His family was all alone as he drove home to his quiet Susquehanna home. Elaine was not a single parent, but she was alone with his children every night he worked late. His safe, secure world was shattering as he reflected upon the innocence of the Bird family.

Elaine noticed immediately that George's hug was different that night as he greeted her—a little longer and tighter. Perhaps Alyssa and Stefan didn't notice in their sleep that their dad's kiss good night was different, but George was sure that Christina noticed as he held her and rocked her to sleep that he and his reality had changed. He felt better having his family close to him. He needed them close to him. Elaine had no idea the impact this new case would have on their lives, but she would in time. She would live this one with him because he would need her support.

Chapter XVIII

Let Them Help

Debbie felt much better after her meeting with Mr. Matangos. He was warm and patient and had taken the time to come to her home to meet with her and her children. Perhaps he knew how helpful he was in reassuring her, in answering her questions, and in preparing her and her children for the legal road ahead of them; but she was sure he wasn't aware of how helpful his home visit was for her. It was one less outing to schedule with all three children and her mother to chauffeur. She would not fully appreciate the convenience until weeks later when she would be juggling counseling appointments with Elizabeth and Deb Salem; hand therapy appointments; doctor's appointments; and legal meetings, hearings, and phone conferences.

What she was juggling at the time was her inability to do anything with her hands and the enormous amount of time it took to do the simplest tasks of eating, dressing, and bathing. The phone was ringing constantly during the day with calls from caring friends. Between phone calls and the doorbell ringing with more flower deliveries and visitors, Debbie's mother could barely attend to Debbie's needs and the needs of her children. Rainie visited daily after school, as did friends from school and neighbors. They helped with grocery runs, phone calls, kid pickups, and school project demands.

Cyd Cohen, a teacher at East Pennsboro, organized a district meal delivery plan providing Debbie's family with dinner each weeknight. Although Debbie's children resumed their afterschool activities of baseball and dance, they were even more excited to come home each day to a delicious home-cooked meal. Debbie's schedule prior to the attack allowed for some home cooking, but not the extensive meals that her district friends were providing.

Debbie's neighbors soon realized that her family so appreciated the meals provided during the week by the teachers at East Pennsboro that they planned meals for the weekends. Debbie's mother expressed her appreciation for the meals to every visitor that came to the house. While she was a great cook, she had no idea how she could manage cooking with all the demands of her full-time job as personal nurse and nanny.

Debbie's mother was never good with hair, and in the shape Debbie's head was in, she could barely manage to gather it and cover it with a baseball cap. According to hospital directions, Debbie was not permitted to get her stitches wet for five days. Although she was incredibly anxious for clean hair, she would not have remembered those directions with all the other medical instructions she was given at the hospital. But her hairdresser, Sue, did.

When Sue had heard about the attack, she called and talked with Debbie in her hospital room. Along with the horrid details of the attack, Debbie filled Sue in on the condition of her head and her hair. Sue visited her the next day in the hospital and, to Debbie's surprise, brought all her supplies to wash her hair. They were both disappointed when a nurse told Sue that the stitches could not get wet for five days.

Sue must have made a mental note of the date because she called Debbie at home the day before and offered to pick her up at her home the next day, drive her to the salon, and wash her hair. With such an offer to help, Debbie had to remember Elizabeth's words: "Let others help you. They need ways to help. They need ways to heal their pain too." Sue's plan was way too much, but she insisted, and Debbie really needed her help.

And her help Debbie got. It took four hours of standing over her head at the sink removing blood clots. Sue persisted like a surgeon to gently and carefully clean Debbie's hair without disturbing the stitches that closed the nine or ten stab wounds. She was amazed by the extent of the injuries and occasionally found a small cut or two that the surgeons had missed suturing. With a handheld mirror, Sue showed Debbie the wounds to her scalp that she had never seen.

Debbie did not know at the time how helpful Sue's hours of work would be for the removal of stitches. She had an appointment four days later at the hospital to have her scalp stitches removed, and that appointment took several hours, with two nurses working on her head at the same time. They weren't sure when they were finished that they had gotten all the stitches, but they would have had a much more difficult time if Sue hadn't washed her hair and removed all the dried blood.

When Sue had finished, Debbie had clean hair styled in a French twist to hide the need for a perm and the uneven edges and hair loss from the knife attack. Debbie was due for a perm at the time of the attack, and her hair needed one desperately; but Sue knew it would be weeks before she could put harsh perm chemicals on Debbie's damaged, tender scalp. When Debbie asked Sue what could be done to prepare herself to attend the preliminary hearing without the baseball cap that she had been wearing daily to cover her permanent "bad hair" days, she was amazed at Sue's solution. Sue made an appointment to French-braid Debbie's hair at 6:00 a.m. on the day of the preliminary hearing.

When Sue dropped Debbie off at her home that day, all her hair concerns had been taken care of. She also had a hairdresser and friend who had been there for her and her children for the most important events over the last ten years. Debbie could almost feel each step as she reflected upon her blessings and visualized the Footprints in the Sand behind her.

Chapter XIX

The Preliminary Hearing

When Debbie and her family arrived at Justice Raymond Shugars office on May 1, Debbie had clean hair prepared in a French braid that made her feel a little older, but very professional; and she was ready for the preliminary hearing of her life. They had never been to District Justice Shugars's office, but Debbie had made many visits to District Justice Robert Manlove's office in Cumberland County. As East Pennsboro's attendance officer, Debbie was quite familiar with school-related hearings. But this hearing was different, very different. It was much more serious, and Debbie was nervous as her mother delivered her and the children to Justice Shugars's small Canby Street office.

Mr. Matangos was waiting outside as promised, and Debbie was just slightly more relaxed at the sight of him. He greeted them and escorted them to the waiting area. He could sense their nervousness and reminded them that they had nothing to worry about. "I'll lead you through your testimony. We need only to establish the facts of the crime and that you each can identify Paul Ferguson as your attacker. We don't want to give the defense attorney any more information than necessary."

It occurred to Debbie as she scanned the empty courtroom that Paul would be in attendance and would actually be in the same room again with her and her children. She was angry, and she wasn't sure how she wanted to respond to him. She didn't even want to look at him. Jaredd, on the other hand, knew just how he intended to deal with Paul. He was going to stare directly into his face for his entire testimony.

When Justice Shugars entered his courtroom, two police officers led Paul from the back of the room to the table in front of him. Paul was dressed in an orange, prison jumpsuit and had shackles on his wrists and ankles. He was seated in front of the judge, next to his attorney, Jeff Foreman; and the proceedings began.

Just as George had described, he called Debbie to the stand first. She was sworn in with her left splinted hand on the Bible and her right, splinted hand raised in front of her. With George's leads, she quickly and clearly described the details of the attack on her and her children that had occurred just thirteen days earlier. As it turned out, she didn't need much prompting from her attorney. The story seemed to be taking on a life of its own. George did stop her when she described Paul coming out of her daughters' room and asked her if Paul was in the courtroom, forcing her to focus her attention for the first time on Paul.

"Yes, Paul is sitting at that table with Mr. Foreman," she said with disgust as she pointed in his direction.

Paul was sitting soberly next to his attorney, *in the attire and chains that he deserved*, Debbie thought, but refrained from saying it out loud.

Her testimony was easy. She trusted Mr. Matangos and she was half finished. She needed only to be cross-examined by Attorney Foreman. Mr. Foreman acknowledged the events she included in her testimony. He had recorded them in the order she had described them, beginning with the phone call she received that disturbed her sleep on April 18 and ending with her 911 call for help. He then proceeded to ask her to tell him the time each event took place. He started by asking her how long she talked on the phone when she received the call that woke her at 10:20 p.m. Less than a minute was the time her friend had taken to confirm arriving home twenty minutes from her house that night.

"You testified that at 10:30 p.m. on your bedroom clock, you heard the floorboards creak. You looked into the dark hallway and saw a small light flicker in your daughters' room. How much time elapsed from the time you heard the floorboards creak until you saw the light flicker?"

He must be kidding, she thought as she tried to estimate the time and offer him a guess as to the number of seconds involved. He wasn't kidding, because he wrote down her answer and then asked, "And from the time you saw the light flicker, you said you stared into the darkness, trying to imagine what caused the flicker of light. Just how much time did that take?"

With the dissection of each event of her testimony, Debbie found herself trying to replay each incident and count in her head the seconds in order to give Mr. Foreman the answer he sought. She confessed that she could not be sure, she could only guess, but Mr. Foreman insisted that she continue to answer and pointedly recorded her times with each event she recounted.

Debbie didn't like the nature of Foreman's questions because her answers were clearly guesses, and she didn't understand the point he was trying to establish. She did recall in her meeting with Mr. Matangos that she thought the attack took fifteen minutes and was shocked to learn that it actually took less than five minutes. George had received verification on the time of the 911 call. It was received at 10:35 p.m., just five minutes after Debbie first heard the floorboards creak. George assured her that it was common for victims of traumatic events to describe the events as taking place over a much longer period of time.

Debbie knew what Mr. Foreman was planning to do with her answers. He was going to add up all her times to show that her testimony was inaccurate because it went beyond the established time frame of the attack. At that moment, she interrupted Mr. Foreman's questions with the declaration: "If you are trying to establish the time of this attack, it began at 10:30 p.m. when the floorboards creaked and ended at 10:35 p.m. when my 911 call was received."

Debbie never did confirm the point of Mr. Foreman's line of questioning, but her statement brought an abrupt end to his time questions. In fact, it brought an end to Mr. Foreman's questions for her completely.

Debbie was relieved to be finished testifying, but Jaredd and Alisha were next. After Jaredd was sworn in, he did exactly what he said he was going to do. He looked directly at Paul and proceeded to answer all of Mr. Matangos's questions.

Paul's head went down almost instantly when Jaredd faced him and their eyes met, and Paul never again looked back up at Jaredd. It was painful to watch and listen to Jaredd describe a childhood friendship with Paul that had been so brutally and callously violated. Debbie wept through most of Jaredd's testimony, particularly when he said, "Paul had been a friend of mine."

In between her tears, Debbie was amazed and proud of her son, especially during Mr. Foreman's cross-examination.

"Jaredd," Mr. Foreman challenged, "didn't you testify that you were sleeping and did not actually see the person who cut your face?"

"That is correct. I did not see Paul Ferguson in my room that night," Jaredd agreed. "I heard him."

"You testified that all you heard spoken by your assailant were the two words, *good* and *night*. Isn't that correct?" Mr. Foreman continued.

"Yes, that is correct," Jaredd confirmed in a tone that begged the question, *So what's your point?*

"How is it that you could be so sure that you heard Paul Ferguson's voice that night in the dark when only two words were spoken?"

Jaredd's response came as quickly as the question when he explained, "You know how when you answer the phone and your friend says, 'Yo,' and you know instantly it's your friend's voice? He doesn't have to tell you who he is, you just know."

Jaredd's answer made perfect sense. Debbie recalled asking George how Jaredd could be an eyewitness when he never saw Paul that night. George had explained that individuals who hear voices or sounds, or even smell or feel aspects of a crime, provide what is referred to as eyewitness accounts. In fact, those witnesses have been considered by the courts to be just as reliable and substantial as witnesses who provide visual testimony. Jaredd's example was an even better explanation of how he knew it was Paul who said good night to him that night. And whatever Paul meant by his cocky, smart-ass remark to Jaredd after he cut his face, it cost him. It provided a third eyewitness against him in court.

Foreman seemed as stunned as Debbie was enlightened by Jaredd's answer to his question, but he was not finished. "Jaredd, you testified that Paul was no longer a friend of yours and, in fact, hadn't been a friend of yours for years. If you hadn't talked to Paul for years, how can you be sure it was his voice you heard in your room on the night of April 18?"

Jaredd's response to Mr. Foreman was instant and now possessed a tone of anger as he replied disgustedly, "Because I hear that voice every day on the bus."

How could Mr. Foreman have known that Paul shot off his big mouth daily on the bus? He set Jaredd up for another perfect addition to his already impressive testimony. Mr. Foreman was done with this witness and ready to get this hearing over with.

Alisha was called to the stand next and provided a riveting account of the attack from a whole different perspective than Debbie's. She described a thirteen-year-old daughter waking up to hearing her mother's screams and seeing Paul Ferguson kneeling over her. As Alisha relived the horror of the attack, Debbie realized that her nightmare was a nightmare for Alisha as well. Alisha ran from Paul as he chased her into her room. She kicked at him as she held her pillow in front of her for protection. When she saw him leave her room, she bravely crawled out of her bunk to see Paul still there and pushing on her mother's door. She followed her mother's direction to get Jaredd without hesitation. As she desperately tried to wake her brother, she kicked at Paul again to keep him away from them.

Debbie wept quietly as she listened to her daughter's nightmare. Alisha described Paul slashing her brother's face, saying "Good night" and running from Jaredd's room. She chased Paul down the stairs, through the hallway and the kitchen, and out the back door. She said she stopped at the open back door, looked outside into the dark backyard, and knew she wasn't going out there. She was not chasing Paul into the dark backyard. It was when she hesitated and said, "And I wondered why I chased him in the first place," that Debbie sobbed out loud, in pain, over the extent of the horror her sweet, innocent thirteen-year-old daughter had experienced. And all the while, she lay bleeding on her bed that night waiting for the 911 operator to answer. Alisha said she locked the door, bolted it, and ran back upstairs to help her mom.

Debbie remembered Alisha's return to her and her reassuring words that she had chased Paul out of the house and he was gone. But Debbie didn't realize that when she directed Alisha to go get John McGreevy, she was sending her daughter out into that very darkness that she feared. But Alisha did exactly what she had been told to do. She ran to the front door, looked out into the darkness, wondered if Paul was out there, and went there anyway. She ran as fast as she could to Mr. McGreevy's house and knocked frantically on his door. All the while she waited for him to open the door, she looked over her shoulder, guarding her back in fear that Paul was following her.

Debbie was so proud of her daughter's courage and so sad and angry that she had had to experience such a frightening event. Alisha knew her attacker, and she had no trouble pointing him out in the courtroom. She had also named him to John McGreevy when she had summoned him for help that night. "Paul Ferguson stabbed my mom," were her words to John, and they were the words he would later recall as well.

As Debbie reflected upon Alisha's testimony, she realized that she had never mentioned Paul's name to Alisha the night of the attack. She had told Alisha to get Jaredd, and later to get John McGreevy; but she had never said the name Paul Ferguson until she spoke to the 911 operator. By then, Alisha was gone in pursuit of help from John. Alisha had known who her attacker was without any help from her mother or her brother.

Mr. Foreman had completed his cross-examinations of three eyewitnesses who did not depend upon each other for their convictions that his client was the perpetrator of the crimes. And Justice Shugars did not need any more evidence to change the charges against Paul Ferguson from two counts of aggravated assault to two counts of attempted homicide and to set his bail at $100,000.

Mr. Matangos was proud of his three eyewitnesses, and he told them so. And they were proud of him as well. It had gone just as he promised. Paul would be returned immediately and directly back to prison. The trial would be set at a later time, and it would be a long way off. In the meantime, they were becoming quite a team, and they had their first victory to celebrate. They also had a lot for which to be grateful. George was now officially a part of their Footprints in the Sand.

Chapter XX

Special Delivery

The results of the preliminary hearing were front-page local news. In addition to the daily calls and visits from friends, the news media was calling. Debbie refused the first several requests of area television reporters to interview her, but their interest and persistence were compelling. Debbie called George Matangos and asked him if there was any value to her talking to the press about the attack. She was surprised by George's lack of concern for the media's involvement in the case. She actually sensed his encouragement of her if she felt up to it, but he did caution her to refrain from discussing details of the attack that might jeopardize the prosecution's case.

Debbie did not have to contact the news. Shortly after her discussion with George, WHTM Channel 27 called her. Kim Garris professed to be very interested in the positive outcome of the preliminary hearing and encouraged by Debbie's recovery. She had heard of the wonderful outpouring of community support for Debbie and her family, and that was all Debbie needed to hear to be launched into a lengthy dialogue with Kim.

Kim asked again for an opportunity to meet with Debbie in her home to discuss the incredible story. Debbie found herself agreeing to a time for the interview, but was emphatic about her conviction to not discuss details of the attack.

Kim arrived precisely at the time they had agreed on for the interview. Debbie was a little intimidated by the presence of two cameramen and loads of camera equipment. While Kim introduced herself and engaged Debbie in conversation, the cameramen made themselves at home and began setting up cameras, lights, and cords all around Debbie and Kim. Kim was easy to talk with, and Debbie was soon absorbed in showing her the magnitude of cards, balloons, and flowers that led them on a tour of the downstairs. The gestures of love and caring were overwhelming, even to Kim, who had not met Debbie prior to the interview, but felt she knew her through the messages from her students and friends at East Pennsboro and her neighbors and friends in Susquehanna Township.

Throughout their two-hour-long meeting, the phone continued to ring with calls from friends, and the doorbell continued to ring with flower deliveries and visitors.

Debbie's friend Judy realized immediately when she arrived for a visit that Debbie was busy talking with Kim and offered to take Debbie's mother to the grocery store. Debbie's mother was grateful for the help and knew Debbie would not be alone if they left during the interview. Each phone call Debbie took during the interview was further evidence of the tremendous positive support she and her family were receiving as a result of the incident Kim was there to investigate. Just as Debbie had completed her tour of the many flower arrangements they had received and her account of the need for her mother to make trips back and forth from the hospital with flowers too numerous to fit in the hospital room, the doorbell rang. With her mother at the grocery store, Debbie answered the door to another delivery of flowers. She could not have been more convincing about the extent of support if she had staged this arrival herself.

With lights and cameras on, the deliveryman said, "I remember you. I made so many trips to the hospital to deliver flowers to you that I knew just which room to go to without asking at the nurses' station."

Touched and almost embarrassed by the coincidence of his visit and his statements, Debbie thanked the gentleman and showed him to the door. If Kim wanted a story on the positive response of caring people for a family in need, she had it.

Kim had wanted to report on the positive things that happen in response to an evil act, but she also wanted to know as much as she could about the evil act itself. Debbie was careful to avoid details, but was able to describe in general what had already been in the newspapers. Kim respected Debbie's limitations and appreciated the personal account she was able to provide. Kim promised Debbie she would get her a copy of their interview, and then she and her cameraman were on their way. Debbie was relieved that she had the opportunity to share her story, especially the positive parts, and was particularly amused by the flower deliveryman's added touch.

Chapter XXI

Second Opinion

Debbie's days remained very busy, and she and her mother could hardly believe where the hours of each day went. The day of the doctor's appointment that Debbie had been anxiously awaiting had finally arrived, and she and her mother found Dr. Brown's office with no trouble. The first three-week follow-up appointment after surgery would include the removal of the stitches, and Debbie was looking forward to seeing her hands without the bandages. She had been doing her hand exercises faithfully, extending her injured fingers the full distance the rubber bands would allow and making sure the bands returned her fingers to their flexed position. She also knew that when the stitches were out, she could begin to soak her hands and arms in the bathtub—a simple pleasure that she had been unable to enjoy for three weeks.

Dr. Brown was professional and thorough with his examination. He removed all the bandages and stitches from the many cuts on Debbie's hands. Debbie was amazed at how thin and light her hands and arms appeared and felt without the thick bandages and splints. Her cuts had healed well, and the stitches were no longer needed. Her concern, however, was with the appearance of the three fingers that Dr. Brown had repaired through surgery. Even though she had been intent upon following Dr. Albracht's recovery directions to make sure her fingers were fully extended during the exercises after surgery, her fingers were not straight. She had stretched them to the full extent of the rubber bands, but with the bandages off, she could see that her fingers were not straight.

As she listened to Dr. Brown provide routine information, Debbie pulled on her fingers in an effort to straighten them, with no success. She could recall Dr. Albracht's concerns as clearly as if she was still in her hospital room surrounded by her girlfriends. "Fingers with tendon damage must be manually moved through the straight and flexed positions to ensure full recovery. If this is not done, the fingers will fuse permanently in a locked position, unable to flex or extend."

When she asked Dr. Brown about the position of her fingers and their inability to straighten, he assured her that that mobility would return. He reattached the splints and rubber band pulleys to her hands and fingers and directed her to the nurses' station to schedule her next appointment in three weeks.

Debbie did not feel good about Dr. Brown's examination. As her mother drove her home, she should have felt relieved that the surgery had been successful and that she was halfway to full recovery. She had known that she would have to suffer the ordeal of not being able to use her hands for six weeks. Dr. Albracht had prepared her for the recovery time. She had known that her damaged tendons would take six weeks to heal, and that any use of those tendons prematurely would cause the surgical repairs to the tendons to rip. She remembered him sympathizing with her by telling her that even those who schedule carpal tunnel surgery have one wrist repaired at a time so they have at least one hand to use during the recovery process. Unfortunately, she would have both hands recovering at the same time, resulting in a tremendous inconvenience for six full weeks. She had known all of that and accepted it, but she also knew that any range of motion that was not maintained during the six-week period would be permanently lost. She trusted Dr. Albracht more than she did Dr. Brown, and felt she needed a second opinion.

By the time Debbie and her mother had arrived home, Debbie had a plan. She was unable to find Dr. Albracht's phone number in the phone book, but she was able to find Dr. Mauer's office number.

He had a local office, and he was available to take her call. Debbie introduced herself by reminding Dr. Mauer of her tendon damage and his request to assist in her hand surgery. He immediately acknowledged a memory of her and her tendon damage. She confessed that she had some concern with her follow-up appointment with Dr. Brown and asked if he would examine her fingers for a second opinion. He cautioned her that she was Dr. Brown's patient and so he would not be able to treat her, but he said he would take a look at the progress of her hands.

"Could you see me today?" she pleaded, knowing full well that there wasn't a doctor anywhere who would see a patient the same day without an appointment.

Dr. Mauer's response was, "Sure, I'll see you whenever you are able to get here."

"Great! I'll be there as soon as I can get there, and thank you," Debbie responded.

She and her mother were back in the car and on their way to Dr. Mauer's office, which they had never visited before. By skipping lunch, they had the time to squeeze in another appointment. The waiting room was filled with people with obvious injuries to their limbs, as one might expect at an orthopedic office. The number of patients waiting for their appointments did not discourage Debbie; she was just grateful to be able to get a second opinion on her hands as quickly as possible, and she did not care how long she needed to wait in an office waiting room. While they waited, she worked on her hand exercises with an increased determination, but also a much graver outlook.

When Dr. Mauer greeted Debbie in the waiting room, he invited Debbie's mother to join Debbie in the examination room. Dr. Mauer was patient and relaxed as he gently removed the splints and rubber bands from Debbie's hands. As he studied and manipulated Debbie's fingers, he confessed that Dr. Brown had denied his request to assist in the surgery, and he had only been able to observe. He was interested in assessing the results of the surgery since hands were his specialty and he was familiar with the injuries.

Debbie was disappointed that Dr. Brown did not take advantage of Dr. Mauer's expertise, but she felt privileged to have a second doctor to consult. When Dr. Mauer invited his hand therapist, Donine, to join them, Debbie's disappointment in Dr. Brown turned to anger and disgust. As Donine manipulated Debbie's fingers, she asked Debbie when her surgery had been done and what kind of hand therapy she was undergoing. It was clear to Debbie that Donine not only did not like the answers she was getting, but they alarmed her. When Donine asked, "Do you mean you have gone three weeks without any physical therapy on these hands?" Debbie could feel the blood draining from her face. Again she could hear Dr. Albracht's warnings and was sure that her fingers were frozen in clawlike positions forever. That feeling she had in the trauma bay, when Dr. Albracht was telling her more bad news than she could handle, was back. Only this time, she was sitting up on an examination table wondering if she was going to faint or throw up, and unable to rest her head back to compose herself.

Trying desperately not to faint, Debbie barely heard Donine suggest that she return to whoever created the splints and pulleys and have them redone. They were not done properly. Donine told Debbie that her doctor should write a prescription for physical therapy to begin immediately. As Donine continued her appalled assessment of Debbie's hands, Debbie reflected on her visit to the physical therapy department of the Polyclinic and the time she had spent getting fitted for the splints and the intricate pulley system that was supposed to ensure that her fingers were in the proper positions. The woman who created the splints and pulleys had not said anything about physical therapy, and Debbie was discharged from the hospital with instructions to do her own exercises.

Debbie did not want to go back to the woman in the physical therapy department, and she did not want to go back to Dr. Brown. They obviously did not know enough about tendon damage to recommend the right treatment. "Can you fix my splints and do the hand therapy that I need?" Debbie begged Donine.

Donine looked at Dr. Mauer and then back at her patient, who was obviously more distressed than she could ever imagine. "Not without a prescription from your doctor," Donine said emphatically.

Dr. Mauer reinforced Donine's ruling with a reminder that Debbie was still Dr. Brown's patient, and he would have to prescribe the hand therapy.

Dr. Mauer maintained his professional commitment to not treat Debbie, and Debbie proposed, "What if I don't want Dr. Brown as my doctor? What If I decide to drop him as my doctor? Will you see me then?"

Sensitive to the obvious panic in Debbie's voice and the desperation in her request, Dr. Mauer agreed to see her routinely to monitor the progress of the physical therapy without billing her as a patient, provided she continued as Dr. Brown's patient. That was good enough for Debbie. She would have Dr. Mauer's help. She agreed, but she still needed Donine.

"If I get a prescription from Dr. Brown, can you be my physical therapist?" Debbie asked with persistence.

Donine agreed. "And if I get that today, can you start today?"

Debbie was not giving up. Donine assured her that if she got the prescription, she could return that afternoon, and she would fit her in.

It was already one o'clock in the afternoon so Debbie did not have any time to spare. She and her mother returned home. After making a quick call to Dr. Brown's office, Debbie and her mother picked up the prescription and were back in Donine's office. Once again, Debbie was sitting in a waiting room filled with people with obvious orthopedic injuries, patiently and gratefully waiting her turn. Her mother dropped her off this time, since the children would be returning home from school soon and she would need to be there for them.

Debbie had no idea of the painful ordeal ahead of her as she watched Donine put patients "through the vise." Nor did she have any idea that her first physical therapy appointment would last three hours. Donine totally redesigned new splints and pulleys, explaining in detail the purpose of each angle created by each pulley. It was clear why the previous design was ineffective. When the actual physical therapy began, it was clear how ineffective it was. Debbie's fingers not only did not straighten to the normal position, they also did not flex enough. After three weeks of fusion, it was going to be an extremely painful and long process to restore Debbie's hand functions, and there was no guarantee that it would be successful.

Donine was encouraging, but realistic. Even aggressive hand therapy performed immediately after surgery does not always achieve the desired results. "Depending upon the severity of the injuries and the effectiveness of the surgery, full and complete recovery may not be realistic," Donine cautioned.

Debbie knew Donine was speaking professionally and impersonally on the facts about her injuries, but Debbie was personally committed to full recovery despite the pain and obstacles.

If Donine did not learn that from Debbie during their first session, she would through all of the sessions to come. Debbie came to every appointment for the next four weeks, dropped off and picked up by her mother for each session since she was restricted from driving for six weeks following the surgery. They met two to three times a week for two to three hours a session. Debbie endured the pain; experienced every new and different treatment technique, from electric stimulation to squeezing clay; and trusted Donine through it all. At times she feared that Donine would manipulate too aggressively and rip the surgical repairs Debbie had been cautioned to protect. But each session, Debbie put her hands, literally, in Donine's hands and trusted that she was the person that could restore her hands to their normal strength and mobility.

Debbie met some unique and interesting people in Donine's care. By the nature of the injuries, it appeared most patients were hurt in violent ways by gunshot or knife injuries or accidents on the job. One woman ran through a glass door, and her whole right hand was clawlike. She didn't make her appointments and seemed content to allow her hand to be permanently disabled so she didn't have to return to work. Debbie was amazed at her willingness to sacrifice the use of her hand for the opportunity to collect disability.

Debbie would meet people one time, spend hours with them as Donine took turns with their individualized therapy, and then never see them again. When she would ask about them, the follow-up stories were not always pleasant. One teen with a gunshot injury was using his therapy time to get out of his house arrest monitoring to pursue his drug habits. Donine had to call his probation officer each time he didn't attend his therapy session, and he finally had to be dropped from therapy.

There were always different clients in Donine's therapy sessions, and they all shared one room with Donine. They took turns being treated by Donine and exercising on their own with her equipment and under her instructions. Sooner or later, they would be discussing each other's injuries. Debbie could always anticipate the question she was asked by the patients in Donine's office and strangers outside the office.

"Did you have that carpal tunnel surgery?"

"No," Debbie would respond, anticipating their reaction when she would continue to explain that a kid attacked her with a knife. The discussion never ended with her answer, because even remote strangers were intrigued and craved every detail of the attack. Regardless of the number of times Debbie told the story of the attack on her and her family, Donine was as captivated by the details as she was the first time she heard them; and she would add the points of interest that Debbie might have missed.

Just when Debbie would meet a "normal" patient, like the father who cut his tendons trying to fix a fan in his attic, Debbie would tell her story, and realize that she must sound like some woman who lived in some violent part of the city. She would always find herself defending her neighborhood and reassuring her new acquaintances that the attack was not a normal occurrence. And each session, she would leave Donine's office wishing her new acquaintances could know just how normal she, her children, and her neighborhood really were.

At least Donine knew that Debbie was normal, and that she had done nothing to deserve such an ordeal. Appointments with Donine were often as much psychological therapy as physical therapy, as Debbie and Donine discussed and analyzed the whole attack.

What continued to plague both of them was Paul's motive for the attack. Debbie had come to suspect that Paul attacked her family because he was angry that she had stopped allowing him to come to her house two years ago. After he cut school and hung out in her house in February of 1994 while she and her children were at work and in school, he was no longer welcome. He had never admitted or apologized for being there, taking money, food, and jewelry and killing their fish, so allowing him to play basketball, swim, or visit their home was out of the question.

And with all the times Debbie had included Paul in their family activities of bike riding, swimming, sleepovers, and trips to the movies, she did not deserve to have her privacy and trust violated by his intrusion in February. She had come to the conclusion that Paul had lost his second home when he was no longer permitted at her home, and that her home had provided him with more than he had in his own home. His mother had not been home in the summers, and Debbie could not remember her ever taking the boys anywhere. When Jaredd, Dorsey, and Paul had a plan that required transportation, Debbie and Dorsey's parents always provided the rides. The sleepovers were always at Jaredd's or Dorsey's house.

During one of the extremely painful hand therapy exercises, Debbie felt sorry for herself and expressed her anger by suggesting that Paul's mother should be sitting in Donine's office instead of her. "Mrs. Ferguson should have these injuries and be feeling this pain. Her son should have taken his anger out on her instead of me."

Donine picked right up on Debbie's feelings by sharing a story about another client she was treating who had similar injuries. The woman's daughter tried to stab her in the back as she was at the kitchen sink doing dishes. "Kids watch too many horror flicks and believe them," Donine went on to explain, "and this teenager thought her mother would just drop dead when she stuck the knife in her back. But that only happens that way in the movies. In real life, you don't drop dead."

When the mother turned around, she had to defend herself from her daughter's continued knife attack. She had ended up with tendon lacerations and the need for hand therapy just like Debbie.

The images Donine created for Debbie caused an instant real-ization that Paul, too, must have thought that stabbing Debbie in the head would cause her to drop dead instantly. "That's why Paul stabbed my head," Debbie exclaimed. "He thought I'd just drop dead and he could continue what he came into the house to do. No won-der he stood stunned in my bedroom when I shoved him away after his repeated stabs to my head did not kill me. And that certainly explains why he stabbed my temple and slit my throat. He needed to try another way to kill me."

Debbie was stunned by the whole revelation. Confirming once again that Paul truly intended to kill her sent shivers down her spine. Donine did not need further convincing. She was sure the first day they had met that Debbie had escaped death, and she was sure that Debbie was a normal woman who did not deserve the violent attack Paul Ferguson had committed against her and her family. While many of her clients needed her help as a result of their own careless or risky lifestyles, Donine knew that Debbie was there because of evil acts she could not have prevented.

Chapter XXII

He's Back

After three weeks of being out of the hospital, Debbie still wasn't feeling very normal. Although the daily throbbing pain in her shoulder and fingers was gone, she still could not totally dress herself or do many routine activities that most people did without thinking or help. Despite not feeling normal, she looked normal. In fact, other than the splints on her arms, Debbie looked great. Rainie could see improvements in her condition every day she visited, and she was anxious to get her back to work. The middle school needed her leadership, and the staff and students needed to see that she was well and back to normal.

When Rainie asked Debbie when she could return to work, Debbie's answer was, "At the end of the six weeks when I get these splints off." Rainie no longer saw the helpless friend with both hands wrapped in balls of gauze. When she visited after school, Rainie saw a healthy, strong woman with splints on both arms, and she didn't see the daily struggles Debbie endured. Just to eat, Debbie needed someone to cut her food, and then she needed to balance her fork or spoon with her thumb and index finger and slowly and carefully feed herself. Rainie wasn't there when Debbie's mother had to write her thank-you notes as Debbie dictated. When Rainie persisted, Debbie assured her that when she could "write, put on my own pantyhose and drive myself to work," she would be ready to return. "We'll drive you to work and help you with all your needs," Rainie promptly promised, with no success at changing Debbie's mind.

Debbie struggled with her helplessness and really tried to allow others to help her as Elizabeth Hoffman had counseled her to do, but she was not about to go into her work world and be treated like an invalid. Her staff and students would just have to wait and manage without her. She owed that to herself and to her mother, who was working so hard each day to help her. Besides, Debbie was still overwhelmed with the time she needed for being helped with routine tasks, hand therapy appointments, counseling sessions, and resting enough to keep up her strength. Even though she could finally sleep without propping the arm of her injured shoulder on a pillow, she still didn't sleep well at night.

In addition to missing Debbie at work, Rainie wasn't sleeping well either. After playing over and over the trauma Debbie experienced, she was afraid to be in her home alone in the city of York, and she hated nights even when Douglas was there with her. She had convinced Doug that they needed a security system because she could not stand the fear. Rainie filled Debbie in on all the details of the security system she was planning to have installed, but Debbie was too overwhelmed with household repair bills, therapy session fees, and medical bills to handle the thought of a fifteen-hundred-dollar security system. But the idea of pushing a button at night and knowing that if any door or window on the ground floor was opened an alarm would warn all of them sure sounded great.

They were all afraid to be in the house, especially at night. Without telling anyone, Jaredd had been sleeping with a large kitchen knife under his pillow. When Debbie's mother discovered it while making his bed, she told Debbie out of her concern that Jaredd was afraid to be in the house at night. The upstairs hall light remained on every night, but the fear of falling asleep still haunted Jaredd and Ashley, oddly enough, more than it did Alisha.

When Debbie brought the concern up in counseling with Deb Salem, it made perfect sense to her. She explained to all of them that Jaredd and Ashley felt much more vulnerable when they lay down to sleep because they didn't wake up to defend themselves the night of the attack. Since Alisha, on the other hand, did wake up to defend herself, she felt less vulnerable.

Debbie clarified, "So even though Alisha saw the attack and the blood and experienced the whole trauma with me while Jaredd and Ashley slept, she feels more powerful and more able to defend herself?"

"Exactly," Deb confirmed. She also reassured them that time would help reduce their fears and insecurities as they regained the trust in their lives. "It may never be as it was before the attack, but time has a way of healing the fears and pains," she promised.

Debbie had her children in counseling to prevent those long-term scars. She desperately wanted to do everything she could to see to it that Paul did not haunt their lives forever.

But a week later, the haunting returned. While Debbie was unable to do a lot of daily tasks, she had learned to answer the phone with the thumb and index finger of her right hand. When she answered the phone that morning, the operator's voice said, "You have a collect call from a correctional institution, will you accept the charges?"

Debbie was stunned and speechless. While the automated operator repeated the message, Debbie was frozen with fear. She couldn't speak, and she couldn't hang up. After the third recording, the line went dead.

There was only one person that she knew in a correctional institution, and she had never received such a call prior to Paul going into prison. How could he call her home? This couldn't be happening. She would tell no one. Perhaps it was a wrong number. It had to be a mistake. She was relieved that she had said and done nothing so that if it had been Paul, he did not get through.

It was several days later when Alisha answered the same call. She too did nothing because she didn't understand the message and was sure it was a wrong number. But something about the call disturbed her enough to tell her mother, and now Debbie was more disturbed. She wanted to know exactly what the message said and exactly what Alisha had said or done. The message was the same, and Alisha had done just about the same as Debbie, except that Alisha had hung up after the first recording, and she was not frozen with fear like her mother had been.

Debbie commended Alisha for hanging up and telling her about the call. She also encouraged her to do the same thing should she ever receive any more calls. Debbie told Jaredd, Ashley, and her mother to do the same. What was Paul trying to do? Whom did he want to talk to, and what would he say if one of them took his call? This was no longer a coincidence. She was sure it was Paul, and she was sure she did not want to know what he had to say to any of them. She needed this violation of her home and her family to stop.

When Debbie told Elizabeth Hoffman about the calls, Elizabeth was outraged. "Paul is as much as in your house traumatizing you and your children again. You must change your phone number and get this terrorizing to stop," Elizabeth directed with a certainty that Debbie had heard many times before regarding certain issues in her counseling sessions.

"I have had this phone number since I moved in to my home in 1976. All my friends have this number to reach me, not to mention every document I ever signed that required a phone number," Debbie protested. "Paul has changed my life enough, and he is not going to make me change my life anymore."

Debbie was as sure that she was not letting Paul win the battle as Elizabeth was sure that she must do something to stop the re-traumatizing of her and her family.

"Every time he calls, he is in your house again, and this isn't healthy for you or your children," Elizabeth reminded Debbie. Elizabeth knew that if Debbie was reluctant to do the healthy thing for herself, all she had to do was remind Debbie that she needed to do it for her kids and it was as good as done. Debbie knew she had to stop the calls, but she was not ready to change her phone number. There were ways to block calls. There were other things she could do before changing her number. After all, Paul hadn't gotten through to them yet. She was angry, and she was scared. She would have to do something—she just wasn't sure what to do just yet.

When Debbie called Mr. Matangos to report the calls that they had received, George was angry. He was sure it wasn't a coincidence.

He just couldn't believe that a fifteen-year-old kid in the trouble Paul was in would "have the balls," as George put it, to be calling the family he nearly killed. He knew Paul from his years of working in the juvenile system, so he knew Paul wasn't stupid; but for some reason, Paul just wasn't getting it. He would talk with Paul's attorney, but, he cautioned Debbie, they really had no proof that Paul had made the calls, and he was sure that would be the response of his attorney as well. Debbie had hoped that George could fix this for her, but he left her with very little assurance that the calls would stop.

And George had very little leverage to persuade Jeff Foreman to get Paul to stop calling the Bird home until Debbie called him with what she had decided to do on her own. If they needed proof, she had an idea on how to get proof. The next time Debbie received the automated call from a correctional institution, she took the call. She pressed the number 1 button on her phone and waited for whatever would happen next.

A male voice said, "Hello."

And Debbie responded with a stern "Hello." She was trembling, but she wasn't sure if it was from her fear or her anger.

The male voice asked, "Who is this?"

And Debbie demanded in return, "Who are you?"

Silence fell between the two voices, and Debbie grew concerned that the caller might hang up. "You called me. Who are you, and what do you want?" she challenged. Any fear Debbie had at the beginning of the call was replaced by anger, and she was on the attack.

"Is Raymond there?" the caller asked tentatively.

"Raymond doesn't live here, and you didn't call here to talk to Raymond. Who gave you this number to call?" Debbie demanded, knowing that the voice was not Paul's. Perhaps Paul didn't have the balls, as George put it, to harass her family himself; but Debbie was sure he had put someone up to the call. He apparently didn't prepare his caller well enough, because he hung up from what seemed to Debbie as a lack of knowing how to respond to her questions.

After the phone call, Debbie called the operator and requested the origin of the call. The operator could not tell her, but assured her that the call would be charged to her account. When she received her phone bill, she could get the information she needed. George was amazed with her plan, and when the bill arrived, she saw that the call was not only made from Paul's prison, it was made from cell block C, the section of the prison where Paul was housed.

George had all he needed now to approach Mr. Foreman regarding his client's behaviors. Given the job he had to do to prepare for Paul's defense, Mr. Foreman did not need further problems. Although Debbie had received several more calls from the correctional institution that she hung up on, the calls ended just about the time it took for Mr. Foreman to confront Paul with a copy of Debbie's phone bill. Debbie had won that small battle, but the war was still being fought every day as Mr. Matangos and the Susquehanna Township Police continued their investigations and trial preparations.

Chapter XXIII

Police Work

Detective Nelson and his partners at the Susquehanna Township Police Department had their work cut out for them. This was a near-double homicide, and there was a lot of ground to cover. By the time Detective Nelson made his first follow-up visit with Debbie, he had gained a lot of insight into Paul. He explained to Debbie that he went to Susquehanna High School to talk with students and had never interviewed so many angry students. The students at Susquehanna were so angry with Paul that Detective Nelson commented that it was a good thing that Paul was in jail. He was convinced they'd kill Paul if they could get their hands on him. It was clear that Jaredd had a lot of friends at the high school, but even guys they talked with who didn't know Jaredd well and had actually been in trouble themselves were angry and couldn't understand why Paul did such a thing.

As Detective Nelson went on about the level of concern for Jaredd and the anger at Paul, Debbie reflected upon the similarity in the responses by the men in her life when they were told about the attack. They all wanted to get Paul. Jaredd frequently expressed his anger that he didn't wake up to fight Paul. Debbie's brother clearly conveyed the desire to go after Paul if he could. It was such a common response from the men who were close to Debbie that she even heard it from her Uncle Harold.

Uncle Harold, a seventy-nine-year-old man who needed to drive his golf cart right up to the green to physically be able to complete a round of golf, told Debbie, "I'd just like to have a few minutes in the cell with that kid."

Debbie found the whole image rather amusing, but her answer to him was, "You'll have to get in line. Every man in my life has already made similar requests."

Now the guys at Susquehanna High School were feeling the same way, and it was very touching to hear that the school was so supportive of her and her family.

It did not surprise Debbie that the Susquehanna Township School District was so affected by the news of the attack, since Jaredd and Paul were students in the high school; Alisha and Paul's sister, Natasha, attended the middle school, and Ashley was in Susquehanna's Herbert Hoover Elementary. The morning of Friday, April 19, must have been as difficult a day for the staff and students at Susquehanna as it was for those at Debbie's middle school.

Detective Nelson could not say enough about the overwhelming support he witnessed for Jaredd and Debbie, but he had other items of importance to share with her. He reviewed Debbie's description of the shirt Paul had worn the night of the attack. They had been unsuccessful at finding that shirt. Debbie could not believe they didn't have the shirt. It would have two perfect handprints of her blood on the front of it from when she shoved Paul away from her.

"How could you not have the shirt?" Debbie questioned, and Detective Nelson could only conclude that somehow Paul or his mother did something with the shirt. When they picked Paul up the night of the attack, he was in bed wearing sweatpants and a long-sleeved white shirt—not exactly nighttime attire for a mild April night. He and his mother maintained that he had been sleeping, but he had beads of sweat on his forehead consistent with having just run several blocks.

Fortunately, the tracking dog they brought to Debbie's house followed a trail right out of her back door, down the alley, and down several blocks to Paul's house. "If Paul ran down the alley, perhaps he threw his bloody shirt into a trash can in the alley," Debbie suggested. Her alley was lined with her neighbors' trashcans, but it was too late to check them now. "Were the trash cans checked the night of the attack?" Debbie asked.

Detective Nelson assured her that the officers on duty would have checked the trash cans, but Debbie didn't believe him. The police didn't even know about the plaid shirt until the morning after the attack when she had provided the description to Detective Nelson and Detective Heilig in her hospital room. She was sure Paul threw the shirt with her bloody handprints into a trash can and it was long gone by now. She was distressed by that news. She was really counting on her description of Paul's shirt matching a bloody shirt found in Paul's home and having the DNA testing prove it was her blood. That shirt would be a piece of evidence that would convict Paul for sure.

"Just what physical evidence do we have to support us in court?" Debbie asked Detective Nelson, and he assured her that Detective Fox, the expert on physical evidence, had everything under control. They sent the knife Paul dropped in Jaredd's room to be analyzed for fingerprints as well as the glass doorknobs and a picture of Alisha that had been knocked off the wall of the staircase. Debbie finally knew why the police had removed all the doorknobs and taken only Alisha's picture from the staircase wall.

"Your daughter, Ashley, had also found a small flashlight in her laundry basket that we believe to have been dropped by Paul when he left your daughters' bedroom," Detective Nelson went on to explain. "Your children confirmed that it was not a flashlight from your home. We sent it for fingerprinting as well."

"So that's what created the small flicker of light that I saw in the girls' bedroom." Things were all making sense to Debbie now. If Paul had flicked a small light in the direction of the girls' beds, he could have seen them, and that was the light she thought must have been one of her girls playing with her Easter troll. She was excited to be putting together the missing pieces to her memory of the attack, but she couldn't stop being concerned about the missing shirt. Had the police failed to check the trash cans? Did they lose a key piece of evidence? Her fears made her keenly aware of how much she needed the police to do a great job with her case. The O. J. Simpson case still haunted her, and she didn't want to be victimized by the legal system as well as by Paul.

The thought of being victimized by Paul reminded her of her fears about Paul's father, so she asked Detective Nelson about him. She admitted that all the years Paul had hung around her house with Jaredd and Dorsey, she had never met or seen Mr. Ferguson. She did recall one Halloween when Paul's sister, Natasha, wanted to go trick-or-treating with Alisha and Ashley. Paul's parents were either separated or divorced at the time, so Mrs. Ferguson and her boyfriend followed along the trick-or-treat route with Debbie and the other neighborhood parents and kids. That was the only time Debbie could recall meeting or seeing Mrs. Ferguson, and the man with her that night was not Mr. Ferguson.

Detective Nelson related to Debbie that the night of the attack, Mr. Ferguson was not home when they picked up Paul. Mrs. Ferguson followed slightly behind the police as they took Paul to the police station, and Mr. Ferguson came to the station much later. Detective Nelson personally explained the facts of the attack to Mr. Ferguson, and he was very cooperative. "Frankly," Detective Nelson went on to conclude, "I think he knew his son had done the crime as it was described to him by me, and he wanted no part in Mrs. Ferguson's cover-up."

Detective Nelson assured Debbie that he seemed to be a "level-headed, reasonable guy" and that he didn't believe she should be at all worried about him. That was a relief. Perhaps the bad dreams about the gun-wielding, crazy, outraged father of Paul would stop.

Paul's mother, on the other hand, was not levelheaded or reasonable. She clearly was trying to cover for her son and was creating alibis throughout her interview at the police station the night of the attack. Paul had scratches on his arms and face that she could not account for without making up lies as she went along. It was clear that she was uncomfortable about the detailed lies she was creating, because they would not match Paul's statement, so she finally refused to be interviewed any further until she had an opportunity to speak to her son.

When she finally got to see Paul, the police were taking him to be arraigned before District Justice Shugars. Mrs. Ferguson had just enough time to tell Paul to remember that he got the scratches on his arms playing football, consistent with her feeble attempt to excuse the scratches he sustained during the attack.

Debbie was furious with Mrs. Ferguson once again. "Why would a mother lie for a child when she knows full well he is guilty?" She just couldn't understand. But she did recall stories that Dorsey and Jaredd had told about Paul and his mother that were consistent with the pattern. One such story was that Paul had set off the high school fire alarm three times in one day, and nothing happened to him. Even though he bragged to other students that he had done it, he told the school authorities that he was only kidding. He admitted that he had told other kids that he had pulled the alarms, but he really hadn't. He later told Jaredd and Dorsey that when the principal called his mother, she accused him of picking on her son and blaming him for something he didn't do. Paul didn't worry about getting into trouble because he knew that his mother would lie for him and keep him from having to suffer any consequences for his wrongful acts.

Detective Nelson agreed with Debbie that her story sounded just like Paul and his mother. He had recently heard that Mrs. Ferguson was claiming to have a tape of Jaredd telling another kid over the phone that Paul really wasn't the person who attacked his family. She was really getting ridiculous in her attempt to get Paul off, but he was not concerned that she would be able to get him out of this one. Even though the mention of the tape was a whole new concern for Debbie, he reassured her that they had too strong a case against Paul for any of Mrs. Ferguson's defense tactics to work. He was counting on Detective Fox to come through with the fingerprints.

When Detective Fox made his appointment with Debbie to discuss the evidence, he apologized for having her doorknobs for so long, and he promised to bring them with him. When he arrived, he had a box full of items in individual brown bags. Each doorknob was in its own bag, as was Alisha's picture. He joined Debbie in the living room with Rainie and Edee, who were visiting at the time. Unfortunately, they found no fingerprints on any of the items. Despite the fact that the knife handle had been wrapped with electrical tape, there were no prints. They had hoped that Paul had used the wall to support himself as he ran down the steps and that his hand had hit Alisha's picture, causing it to fall. Since the picture was covered with glass, it might have Paul's handprint on it, but dusting the glass for prints revealed no useful results. The doorknobs were glass, but they too had no fingerprints on them. The broken piece of banister spindle that the police surmised Paul grabbed to make the turn from the staircase to the hallway was clear of prints as well. Detective Fox acknowledged that the movies and crime shows make fingerprinting look so easy when, in fact, it is difficult to get a full, clear print even from surfaces that lend themselves to leaving prints such as glass and tile.

Once again, Debbie was disappointed that the evidence she was counting on did not exist. She understood that Paul may not have touched the doorknobs or Alisha's picture, but he clearly had his whole hand wrapped around the knife. When she had learned that he had dropped the *attempted murder* weapon on the floor of Jaredd's room, she had been sure the crime lab would find prints on it.

Detective Fox acknowledged to Debbie that he was disappointed that no fingerprints were found, but not discouraged by it. He knew they had the right guy locked up and that the crimes in the neighborhood would seriously decrease. His statement caused Rainie, Edee, and Debbie to wonder what he meant, and Detective Fox quickly elaborated. He explained that the police suspected Paul of being involved in a lot of neighborhood crimes. They knew he wandered the neighborhood during the day and was in the area a number of times when women had reported that their purses were stolen. In one such case, the woman had briefly carried her groceries into her house from her car; and on her return trip to her car, her purse was gone. Paul had been walking down her sidewalk as she went into her house.

The police had also suspected that Paul was routinely stalking the neighborhood at night looking in windows and breaking into houses. The thought of Paul standing outside in the dark at night looking in her windows gave Debbie the creeps. He could have actually been doing that on the night of the attack, just waiting for her company to leave and the lights in her house to go out.

Detective Fox did not realize he was freaking Debbie out as he continued to describe a specific series of incidents that occurred to an elderly gentleman who lived on the 3400 block of Fourth Street, just one block northeast of Debbie's home. The gentleman woke up one night to find his bedroom light on and a boy fitting the description of Paul Ferguson standing at his dresser going through his wallet. When the old guy got out of his bed, he was afraid for his life and told the kid to take what he wanted. Paul, as Detective Fox referred to him for the rest of his story, patted the man on the back and said, "Now, you won't be telling anyone about this, will you?" in a threatening tone.

When the police questioned the gentleman during their investigation of the burglary, the man said that the same boy had knocked on his door earlier that day and offered to shovel his sidewalk. When the man said his son would be over to help him, the kid asked him if he lived alone. The man confirmed that he lived alone, that he had lost his wife a couple of years ago and that his son helps him a lot since his recent heart attack. Detective Fox was convinced that Paul was casing the house for an opportunity to rob the man and had found the perfect target—an old man who lived alone and had a heart problem. The image of Paul having the evil intent to prey upon people in the neighborhood was all becoming clear, and the images were alarming.

Detective Fox was not finished. The very next night after the man found Paul standing in his bedroom, his son spent the night to offer support to his frail father. The son woke up to the sound of breaking glass and went downstairs to witness a boy matching Paul's description running away from his father's house again.

The whole idea of Paul stalking the neighborhood at night reminded Debbie of her neighbor and friend Karen and her son's story about Paul. Several weeks after the attack, Karen shared with Debbie that her son, Nate, was struggling to believe that Paul actually broke into Jaredd's house and stabbed him and his mother. Nate was one year older than Jaredd and frequently played with Jaredd, Dorsey, Paul, and Bradon. Nate told Karen that he was sitting on their front porch late one night and saw Paul walking between the houses across the street. When Nate called out to Paul, he asked him what he was doing. Paul explained that he was playing the "ring the doorbell and run" game that they used to play to see if they could stir up some excitement or trouble.

As Nate struggled to make sense of the horrible attack on the Bird family and Paul being named as the attacker, he recalled the night that Paul claimed that he was playing the "ring the doorbell and run" game. He realized that that game was only fun if it was played with at least one other kid. Nate suddenly realized that Paul was not playing that game that night. He was stalking the neighborhood. But why would he break into the Birds' house and stab Jaredd and Debbie? He knew Paul had been getting into some trouble, but he had no idea that he had gotten that bad.

Debbie couldn't help wondering throughout Detective Fox's horror stories of Paul's neighborhood crimes why the police hadn't put this kid away a long time ago. If they had, Paul wouldn't have been around to attack her family. She recalled the morning she called the Susquehanna Township police to report Paul Ferguson for burglarizing her home. She told Detective Fox, Rainie, and Edee that she came home one day in February of '94 and noticed that the fish aquarium on the kitchen counter was out of place. When she went to adjust it, she noticed that it had been stirred up. Four of the six small fish were missing, and the other two fish were dead. She called Alisha and Ashley to the kitchen to question them, and neither had any idea what had happened to the fish tank.

Debbie was in a hurry as usual to get both girls to dance, make dinner, and pick up Jaredd at the middle school after his basketball practice, so she had dismissed her concerns about the fish aquarium and began her normal after-school routine. When Debbie picked up Jaredd and Dorsey from basketball, the boys did their normal chatting about the day, which, not uncommonly, included a story about Paul. According to them, Paul had not been at practice because he cut school. Debbie even recalled Dorsey wondering why a bus driver would drop a kid off the bus after he had gotten on the bus, but one more story about Paul getting into trouble was of little interest to Debbie.

The next morning, Debbie slid open the lower drawer of her antique sewing machine in her bedroom to expose the far back part of the drawer and discovered that the large roll of one-dollar bills she had hidden for daily lunch money was missing. Each morning, she would give three ones to Jaredd and two ones to Alisha and Ashley for their school lunches. Searching for seven one-dollar bills daily in her wallet became too unmanageable, so she collected and hid large amounts of ones for this purpose. The roll of ones was missing, and she knew her three children did not know the money existed, let alone that it was hidden in the back of her old sewing machine drawer.

Debbie stood in her bedroom trying to make sense of missing money and felt much like she did the day before as she studied the fish aquarium in disarray. If her children had not done these things, someone else had. She went to Jaredd's room and asked him about Paul cutting school the day before. Jaredd explained that Paul got on the bus at his bus stop so his mother would think he went to school. Two bus stops later, he got off the bus.

With that information, Debbie was sure that Paul had been in her house. He had pushed on her front door in October at Halloween and had broken the lock. Debbie hadn't gotten the lock fixed because the locksmith told her that the door was damaged as well and she needed a new door. She had gotten a chain lock for the inside of the door to assure her family was safe and secure at night and left the door latched but unlocked during the day. She lived in a good neighborhood and did not worry about leaving her door unlocked while they weren't home, at least until she could make a decision on a new door.

Paul knew the lock was broken on Jaredd's front door and that it was not locked during the day. He knew he could walk right into their house, but Debbie never worried that he or any of her children's friends would enter her house alone without permission, at least not until that moment. She knew that Paul had been there, but she couldn't imagine him cutting school and hanging out in her house alone.

So Debbie continued the questions of Jaredd. "Who got off the bus with Paul yesterday morning?"

Jaredd confirmed that Paul got off alone. "Was Nate on the bus?"

Debbie continued the questions. "Yes," Jaredd reported.

"Were Dorsey and Bradon on the bus?" Debbie asked, and Jaredd answered yes to all her questions.

Paul was the only friend in the neighborhood who cut school, and he did it alone, Jaredd was sure of that. But Jaredd did not know why his mother was asking so many questions until she announced, "Paul was in our house yesterday." Her jewelry box was stirred up, and her engagement diamond ring that she no longer wore was gone. While she was calling the police, her children systematically reported items missing from their rooms. Jaredd was missing his gummy worms, and Ashley was missing the five-dollar bill that she had gotten in the mail for her birthday on February 3. Alisha discovered that the chameleon cage was stirred up in much the same fashion as the fish aquarium. Both tanks looked as though someone had been trying to catch the fish and chameleons.

By the time the police arrived, the children were on their buses and Debbie had called work to report that she would be a little late. The police took a full report and promised to get back to her as soon as their investigation was concluded. Three weeks later, the officer responsible for getting back to Debbie called to report that he was sure Paul had committed the burglary, but the police could not prove it. Paul's mother was not cooperative, and Paul was denying it; so unfortunately, they couldn't go any farther with the case.

Debbie understood that it was a small crime and that she hadn't had her door locked. She didn't fault the police for not dusting the fish aquarium and the chameleon tank for Paul's fingerprints. She knew that from the police perspective, this crime probably amounted to a kid who hung out in his neighbor's house, ate their food, fed their fish to their cat, and took the money and jewelry that he found. But from her perspective, Paul had violated her privacy and her trust.

The police may not have been able to give him consequences for his behavior, but she was not allowing a kid like Paul to come back into her house. Jaredd understood that this time Paul had gone too far, and he agreed that he didn't want Paul in his house either.

A month after Paul was questioned about burglarizing Debbie's house, he was caught breaking into cars at the Jewish Community Center, which was just several blocks from his house. Debbie originally had heard about the incident through Dorsey when he mentioned to Jaredd that Paul was wearing one of Jaredd's ties in juvenile court.

Debbie got the full details of Paul's crimes at the JCC when Bradon's mother, Deb McLamb, visited her after the attack. Deb's visit started with her expression of sincere sympathy for Debbie and her family. She went on to describe a day in March of "94, when Paul and Dorsey left the Jewish Community Center after playing basketball. Paul began to break into a car parked at the JCC to steal a purse left in the front seat. Dorsey warned him not to do it and then left the scene and returned home.

Paul had burglarized so many cars at the JCC that the JCC hired a private detective to solve the crimes. The detective had set up video surveillance and planted a purse in a vehicle parked in the JCC parking lot. When Paul began his break-in to the car that day, an alarm went off, and Paul ran to Bradon's house. Bradon and his parents were not home, but Bradon's sister, Kayleigh, saw Paul go into their house. When he came out of the McLambs' home, Paul was wearing a different shirt. Paul lived across the street from the McLambs, and Kayleigh watched him return to his house.

When the police arrived at Paul's door in response to the JCC burglary report, Paul denied being involved and told them that Bradon McLamb had committed the crime. When the police went to Bradon's house, they found the stolen purse and the shirt worn by the thief in Bradon's room. When the case went to juvenile court, Bradon and Dorsey had to testify against Paul. Paul was ultimately found guilty; and Dorsey, Bradon, and their families were through with Paul. Paul had lost all his neighborhood friends by his own criminal acts and dishonesty, but his mother continued her lies and cover-ups. She maintained that Bradon was guilty of the theft and that, once again, her son was innocent and wrongly accused.

According to Mrs. McLamb, Mrs. Ferguson maintained such animosity toward Bradon and her family that Deb was uncomfortable living across the street from them. She didn't trust what Paul would do next, so when she heard about his attack on the Bird family, she had to express her condolences and share with Debbie her own ordeal with Paul and Paul's mother. She also wanted to attend the trial and offer any support she could to Debbie and her family in their fight against Paul and his lying mother.

Debbie went on to explain to Detective Fox that since the attack, she had met a lot of neighbors who had negative experiences or concerns about Paul. They consistently expressed a sense of relief that Paul was finally locked up, coupled with feelings of sadness that Debbie and her family had to suffer such a horrible experience for that to happen. While Debbie had heard many neighborhood concerns about Paul, she was surprised when Mr. Wilborn approached her at one of Jaredd's baseball games and expressed the same concerns, since he lived in a totally different neighborhood in Susquehanna Township. Mr. Wilborn's son, Earl, and Jaredd had played baseball together for several years, so Mr. Wilborn was a familiar, supportive father at baseball games. Despite Debbie's injuries, she did get to Jaredd's games, and the first game she attended after the attack, Mr. Wilborn approached her, expressed his sorrow for her and her family, and said, "This could have happened to our family."

As in the case of Mrs. McLamb, Debbie asked what he meant, and he went on to describe his frightening experience with Paul Ferguson. Paul had become friends with a couple of troubled guys in his neighborhood, and they had burglarized his home. In addition to stealing stereos, VCRs, TVs, and other valuables, they trashed everything in their family room. They took weights and smashed the coffee table and end tables and totally destroyed their place. His family went to court, and Paul was found guilty of that and several other similar burglaries in his neighborhood.

After Mr. Wilborn's story, Debbie was just amazed at how bad Paul had become in just two years. He went from committing neigh-

borhood thefts to burglarizing cars and homes, and finally, he burglarized the Bird house and attempted to commit murder. And after
being found guilty of burglarizing cars and later homes, why hadn't
the criminal justice system done something to stop his criminal activities? If they had, she wouldn't be sitting with Detective Fox with
splints up to her elbows and a horror story to tell that was suitable
for a Stephen King novel.

Detective Fox was aware of Paul's juvenile criminal record, but
he didn't know that Paul had burglarized Debbie's home once before.
He assured her that it took the strength of someone like her and her
children to put Paul away, and he and his police force would see to it
that he was prosecuted to the fullest extent of the law. He wasn't in
juvenile court this time. He had committed an adult crime and he
would do adult time. He reminded Debbie of how fortunate she was
that the law had changed and that Paul would be tried as an adult.

When Detective Fox was gone, Debbie tried to focus upon the
positive, but she found herself worrying about missing evidence and
all the evil acts Paul had committed that went unpunished. Although
she was surrounded by friends and reminded each day that she and
her family were loved and supported by so many good people, she
still worried that somehow the justice system would fail them and
Paul would get away with this crime too.

When George Matangos called Debbie, he was well aware of
the angry students at Susquehanna Township High School and of
the progress of Detective Nelson and Detective Fox. He was not concerned about the lack of fingerprints because he had a theory of his
own to explain it. But he had more important matters to discuss with
Debbie. Attorney Jeff Foreman had petitioned the court on behalf of
Mrs. Ferguson for a bail hearing, and George needed to meet with
Debbie and the kids to prepare for the hearing.

"What is a bail hearing?" Debbie asked George, and he explained
that the amount of bail set by Justice Shugars could be challenged by
the defense in an effort to get bail lowered. When Justice Shugars
set Paul's bail at $100,000, it essentially required Paul's family to
put up $100,000 in order to get Paul out of jail until the trial. Since
most people do not have that kind of money, a bail bondsman can

be hired to put up the bail money for a fee. The fee for a bail bonds-man is usually 10 percent of the total bail. Paul's mother would have to pay $10,000 to a bail bondsman who would, in turn, pay Paul's $100,000 bail. The bail bondsman assumes responsibility for getting his client to court, and if his client does not attend court for trial, the bail bondsman loses the $100,000.

Debbie didn't know what to worry about first—Paul getting out of jail or Paul's mother getting his bail lowered so that a bail bondsman would enable Paul to get out of jail. Debbie had not even considered the possibility that Paul could get out of jail by any way other than being found not guilty in court. How could this be? How would she manage having Paul out of jail and living less than three blocks away from her and her family? She had as many questions for George as she had fears, and she encouraged him to come to see her as soon as possible.

This was the first negative call Debbie had received from Mr. Matangos since she had met him. She had spoken with him fre-quently since their first meeting, and he always had good news. She recalled his call after the judge was assigned to their case. He couldn't wait to tell her that Judge Joseph Kleinfelter was their judge, and Debbie didn't know if that was good or bad, even though she could detect excitement in George's voice.

"Debbie, this is really good. We couldn't have asked for a better judge for this case," George exclaimed, and Debbie could almost pic-ture the smile on his face. "In fact, this is so good that I want you to call Detective Nelson and tell him."

Debbie didn't understand the ins and outs of the legal system enough to know that a judge assignment was important in criminal cases, but she didn't waste any time calling Detective Nelson and giv-ing him George's news. Detective Nelson was ecstatic. When Debbie asked him why Judge Kleinfelter was a good judge selection for their case, Detective Nelson said, "Because when Judge Kleinfelter gets a bad guy, he slam-dunks him!"

Debbie guessed that was Detective Nelson's way of saying that Judge Kleinfelter was a strict, tough judge who would be very hard on Paul, and that was just the kind of judge she wanted.

Things had been falling into place prior to George's call about the bail hearing. Debbie recalled calling George with as much excitement as George had about the judge assignment when she found Paul's picture in Jaredd's yearbook because he was wearing the same plaid shirt that he wore when he attacked her. Debbie had visitors at the time, and one of her guests asked her what Paul looked like. Jaredd's yearbook was on Debbie's living room coffee table, and it occurred to her that Paul's picture would be in the yearbook. At first she couldn't find Paul in Jaredd's class of students. Jaredd explained that Paul had failed so many courses that he was not considered a sophomore. When Debbie turned to the freshman section of the yearbook, she nearly dropped the book when she saw Paul in the same navy- or black-and-white large plaid shirt with the navy or black collar. She was on the phone to Mr. Matangos immediately.

George was in another trial at the time, but when he returned her call, he was as excited as she was about her discovery. They may not have the shirt, but at least they would have the proof that he had such a shirt. George did caution Debbie that the yearbook picture was black-and-white, so he would have to try to obtain the colored picture to prove the dark color was actually navy or black and not another dark color such as green or maroon.

Debbie and George had become quite a team as they worked to put their prosecution together. Debbie reflected upon the progression of their partnership from George's first interview with her and her children to his next calls to her as he discovered new aspects of the attack.

George had called Debbie the day he saw Lieutenant Fleisher's pictures of her in the emergency room. He was stunned by the condition she was in, and had no idea how badly she had been hurt. He had met her several days after the attack, and she had looked great. After looking at the gruesome pictures of her, he had to call her to express his even greater compassion for the horror she had experienced that only the pictures could convey. He also wanted to express his profound admiration for her strength to have survived such a brutal attack and her courage to be able to recall the details with such clarity.

George was even more amazed with her insight after she got to see the pictures herself. The picture she wanted to see most was the picture of Paul's face. Ever since that first day in the hospital when Detective Nelson told her that Paul had scratches on his face, she wanted to see them. When she saw the picture of Paul's face, he had an inch and a half scratch from the middle of his forehead to the bridge of his nose and a moon-shaped cut on the left side of his nose. She studied those marks on his face and tried to recall jabbing the nails of her right hand into his face. She knew her nails caused Paul to pull away, but she couldn't understand why there were only two scratches on his face.

She couldn't understand, until that evening when she was ready for bed. She lay propped between her pillows on the far side of her king-sized bed, with her bedroom door open and the hall light on. She could see Jaredd's closed bedroom door and her splinted right arm. Her middle and ring fingers were flexed tightly closed by the rubber band pulleys that Donine had just tightened that day in therapy. Debbie's index finger and little finger were free to move about, and it suddenly occurred to her that there were only two scratches on Paul's face because at the time she jabbed him, she only had two fingers that could flex—her index finger and her little finger. So when she jabbed her nails into Paul's face, her index finger hit the middle of his forehead and scraped to the bridge of his nose as he pulled his head back. Her little finger dug into the side of his nose, causing the moon-shaped cut. Her middle and ring fingers never touched Paul's face because they did not flex. The tendons that would have enabled them to flex had been severed. Debbie was so excited by her discovery that she wanted to call George right away. They were a team, but they were not on a "Call me anytime day or night" basis. It took her a long time to fall asleep that night, anticipating George's reaction when she called him in the morning. He didn't disappoint her. He was elated.

George's call to Debbie after he received a copy of her 911 call was very much like his call about the emergency room pictures. He was again amazed at Debbie's clarity and composure as he listened to the recording of her call for help. After seeing pictures of the knife wounds she had sustained, he knew what condition she was in when she made that call. He was amazed that she could be so calm and clearheaded. George knew at that time that Paul's mother was claiming that Debbie was confused about her attacker, and George told Debbie, with tremendous pride and conviction, that "this is not a tape of a confused woman."

George had a way of making Debbie feel proud of herself, and every time she and George talked, she was more assured and confident. This call, however, was bad news; but once again, George was telling her that she had nothing to worry about. He was confident that Judge Kleinfelter would not lower Paul's bail. Paul's crime was too serious, and he was too much of a threat to the community. The hearing was just another part of the legal process they would have to accept.

Chapter XXIV

Bail Hearing

Thursday, May 30, marked the end of Debbie's six weeks of recovery. Dr. Brown provided her clearance to return to work during her final follow-up examination, but Donine was the person who reassured her that it was okay to begin using her fingers in a normal fashion. Dr. Mauer had checked in on Debbie from time to time during her therapy sessions with Donine. Donine's office was adjacent to Dr. Mauer's office, which made the process very simple.

Debbie's therapy sessions had been reduced to once a week, and she had made tremendous progress. Donine was almost as proud of Debbie's hands as Debbie was. Most of the exercises that Debbie needed to do could be done at home with massage clays that increased in hardness. Debbie's determination to do everything she needed to do to restore the strength and functioning of her hands had paid off. Donine gave her the okay to begin doing normal activities with moderation.

Debbie drove home from her session for the first time in six weeks, and her mother was happy to be in the passenger's seat. Debbie could now write, drive a car, and if she could get her own pantyhose on the next morning, she would be back to work. She had only been back to visit school one day during her six weeks of recovery, and she was anxious to drive herself to work and walk into the building carrying her own purse. She was aware of how much she appreciated being able to do simple, routine tasks like eating without help, plucking her eyebrows, and writing her own checks.

She was amazed at how things had a way of working out, like the day Rainie brought the daily pile of cards and notes from students and teachers at school and a card from her staff with a check for $900. Debbie was overwhelmed by the compassion and generosity of her many friends. A week later, Judy, her friend who lived in Susquehanna Township, visited and had a card and check from the Susquehanna Township community for $600. Debbie did some quick addition and was sure that Rainie and Judy planned a collection for the $1,500 security system that they both knew Debbie and her children desperately needed. But neither claimed any awareness of the other's financial gift. If that was true, it was an amazing coincidence that put Debbie into tears and convinced her that the security system was meant to be.

And what a blessing it was. On June 6, Debbie's forty-fourth birthday, the system was installed and working. Debbie's mother had returned to her home the day Debbie returned to work, so Debbie and her children were alone again in their house. But they didn't feel alone. They memorized their individual codes to the system and together pushed the button that secured their home. The words "system armed" that appeared on the panel box were very comforting. For the first night in their home since the attack, they knew that it was truly safe to fall asleep because if anyone tried to enter any door or window on the first floor, the alarm would warn them, and they could be prepared to defend themselves. They also knew Paul was locked up—at least until his bail hearing scheduled for July 3, less than a month away.

The weeks prior to the bail hearing went quickly. George prepared Debbie and her children by promising them that they wouldn't need to testify. He was having Detective Nelson provide the facts of the attack because he didn't want Paul's attorney to be able to gather any information about the case through cross-examining Debbie or the children.

Having Detective Nelson do the testifying suited Debbie's children just fine because they weren't anxious to testify anyway, but

Debbie was not sure she wanted Judge Kleinfelter to have just a police report to make his decision. She wanted him to know what horror Paul had created and how much she was outraged at the very thought of allowing such a monster back into her life. George assured her that he knew what he was doing, so she placed her trust in him once more.

As Debbie's family and friends filled most of the seats in the left side of the courtroom, Paul's mother and several aunts sat in the first row of seats on the opposite side. Debbie had her mother and her father to her left and her sister and Ashley to her right. Alisha was right behind her mother between her two best friends, Jason and Elsa; and Jaredd sat behind Rainie between his two best friends, Mandy and Dorsey. Deb McLamb and John McGreevy sat behind Jaredd, and they were ready to fight the next battle.

As George and Detective Nelson prepared for the hearing to begin, George walked over to Debbie and handed her a document. He briefly explained, "A prison inmate had a hearing the day of our preliminary hearing, and he told Detective Nelson that Paul was bragging in prison that he did the crime. He agreed to a taped interview and this is the transcript. I think you'll find it interesting."

Debbie began reading the transcript:

STATEMENT BY INFORMANT

DATE: 5/7/96
TIME: 1415 Hours
INC. # 960003274

DETECTIVE NELSON: This is Detective James Nelson, from the Susquehanna Township Police Department. The time is now 1415 hours, on May 7, 1996. The location is the Susquehanna Township Police Department, at 1900 Linglestown Road, in Harrisburg, Pennsylvania.

BY DETECTIVE NELSON:

Q. Do you understand that this interview is being tape-recorded?

A. Yes, I do.

Q. And do you consent to it being tape-recorded?

A. Yes.

Q. Has any—have any offers of promises or deals been made to you in return for your statement?

A. No deals and no promises, no.

Q. Okay. You contacted me yesterday, which was May the 6th of 1996, and you indicated to me that you had some information concerning the Paul Ferguson case, is that correct?

A. Yes, I do.

Q. Okay, Where are you currently located?

A. Dauphin County Prison, 501 Mall Road, Harrisburg.

Q. Why are you in Dauphin County Prison?

A. Ah, I've been charged with felony forgery and theft by deception.

Q. Okay, how long have you been in?

A. Since the 16th of February of '96.

Q. The 16th of February '96?

A. Yes.

Q. Okay, what information can you—do you have to tell me that concerns Paul Ferguson?

A. Well, basically, Paul Ferguson and I have been talking about the crime that he committed, and the information that I have is that he has admitted to me that he was responsible for stabbing the family in the house in Susquehanna.

Q. Okay, Paul Ferguson was arrested on April 18 of 1996, when did you first meet him?

A. I would say maybe six days after that, maybe even two weeks after that, because I know he went to the quarantine block at first, and then he came over to C Block, but I met him, I would say, the last week of April on C Block. It was in the dayroom on C Block.

Q. Okay, did you know him before this?

A. No, I didn't.

Q. Okay, did you ever meet him before this?

A. I've never met him before.

Q. Okay, what has he told you about that? Continue on with that.

A. Well, basically, he's admitted that he was responsible for the stabbing of the family. He, ah, the conversations he and I had initially started with me having seen him at the preliminary hearing that he went to, and he came and started talking to me about what was said at the preliminary hearing, and he was stating that they weren't worried about the case, because you didn't have all the evidence. You couldn't prove how he got into the house, and that his fingerprints weren't on any of the weapons or anywhere in—on the weapon, the knife itself, or anywhere in the house.

Debbie was so excited to read that Paul had actually confessed to someone that she didn't care that the truth was told to a fellow inmate. In fact, she was instantly grateful to the informant for his willingness to come forward and tell Detective Nelson the truth. But she was concerned about Paul's confidence and the fact that he "wasn't worried about the case, because (they) didn't have all the evidence." He was right. They didn't have the shirt, they didn't know how he had gotten into the house and "his fingerprints weren't on the weapon, the knife itself, or anywhere in the house." She returned to the transcript:

Q. Okay, so you're saying he first came to you on
or about the date of his preliminary hearing?

A. Well, we had talked prior to his preliminary
hearing, like about a week before his preliminary hearing. I had known he had that case,
and he and I was talking, and he was admitting that he wasn't worried about it because
they really didn't have all the evidence. That
there was no way that they could prove that
he did it, plus they're not gonna—what he
said was they're not gonna fry me because I'm
a kid, so I'm not even worried about it. But
he admitted at that time that he had done it.
This was, like, about a week before his preliminary hearing. Then after seeing me at the
preliminary hearing, I was there for one of my
charges also. He was leaving, I was coming in,
and that evening he spoke to me about more
detail and more specifics, and he has up until
this date been talking about his case.

Q. What did he indicate to you concerning any
motive for this? Did he know the family? Was
he going in to do a burglary? Did he indicate
to you anything of why he was going in?

A. Well, he had admitted that he had known the
family, ah, a number of years prior to this happening. He had said that what he had done
was, he had stolen some stuff out of the mother's house. The son and him were friends. I
think they even went to the same school. And
he said that he had stolen some stuff out of
the house, but he said, "There's no way she
could even prove that I did it. She just said
that I stole it because I was black," and then he
said that she said, "Nigger, I don't want you in
my house anymore," or, you know, associating

with my son. I don't know if she called him
nigger or not, but that's what he said she did,
and he got really angry when he was talking
about it.

How dare he say I blamed him because he is black? Debbie thought
as she continued to read. His statement offended her, but when she
got to the claim that she used the N-word, she was angry. Not only
had she never used the N-word, she found it offensive and totally
unacceptable for anyone else to use it. And she didn't appreciate Paul
telling anyone lies about her.

Furthermore, she never talked to Paul after the burglary. Jaredd
and Dorsey never brought Paul to the house again, so she never had
to tell Paul anything. She assumed that Dorsey and Jaredd told Paul
that he could not come back to her house, but she was sure they
didn't use the N-word in any of their conversations. After all, Dorsey
and Bradon were also African American, and that was never an issue
for any of Jaredd's friends, or Alisha's or Ashley's friends, for that
matter.

Debbie was drawn back into the informant's interview:

A. He said, so I was always planning on getting even with her. When him and her son
were friends, prior to this happening, prior
to her telling him a couple years ago, I think
it was, that she didn't even want him to have
anything to do with her son, at that time he
already had a key to their house. The son had
some keys, and he had a key made. He said he
had a key made off the son's, without the son
even knowing about it. I don't know if the boy
stayed over at his house one night. It made it
seem like he snuck the key the way he said it.
So I don't know how he got it, but he said he
got a key made. 'Cause that's how he was able

to get in the house without them even knowing about it.

So that's how he got into the house the night of the attack. Debbie reflected upon the number of times Jaredd had misplaced or lost his house key, but she had never thought for a minute that one of his friends had stolen it. Jaredd was a bit disorganized as a little dude, and she had finally gotten to the point that she kept a magnetic box under her car with an extra car key and house key in it for emergencies. Jaredd used it frequently when her car was home and he was locked out of the house and had forgotten his key.

The police had expressed some concern for Debbie's lost-key solution, particularly when they questioned her as to whether Jaredd ever got the key from her magnetic box in front of his friends. Debbie was sure that was a possibility because Jaredd was very trusting of his friends and would not have seen a problem with them knowing about the key. If the police thought Paul had gotten the key from her magnetic box, they would soon learn, from the informant's statements, that Paul had stolen one of Jaredd's keys. Paul had slept over many times with Jaredd and Dorsey, but no one was ever concerned that he would steal Jaredd's key to his house. She now found herself wondering what else he had stolen from their house while he and Jaredd were friends.

Debbie was relieved to know how Paul had gotten into her home the night of the attack, and she was anxious for her children to know. During their first counseling session after the attack, they each had felt so guilty for leaving doors unlocked. They should feel relieved to know that they hadn't. Paul left himself in with his stolen key.

Debbie was getting angrier with Paul as she continued to read:

Q. Okay, so he told you then that he didn't like
    this family, or at least didn't like the mother.
A. He didn't like the mother.
Q. And wanted to get back at her, is that what
    you're saying?

A. That he wanted to get even with her, exactly. He said he was just waiting for some way to do it. He said he had done something to their—lawn in the backyard at one time or something, he said, "but I don't even think they knew about it." I don't know if he poured some chemical on their lawn or what, but it sounded like it was a little childish prank thing that he had done. But he said that they weren't even aware of it, he said, but he was planning on getting back at her.

Debbie remembered the "childish prank" the informant was describing. She recalled the morning she went to the pool shed to get the lawnmower to mow the grass and noticed white powder on the grass in front of her shed. She recognized the powder immediately as the diatomaceous earth used in her pool filter, but she was puzzled as to why it was spilled all over the grass.

When she opened the shed door, she discovered that the powder was all over her shed and lawnmower. A sense of dread came over her as she struggled to interpret the cause of the mess in her shed. The many pool toys and floatation devices were in their normal locations, so her kids did not accidentally make the mess while searching for something to play with. Someone intentionally poured diatomaceous earth on the lawnmower and, upon closer scrutiny, had even poured it into the gas canister. Her mower was ruined, and her shed was a shambles.

In a panic over unanswered questions and a need for help with her mower, she called Mr. McGreevy. He was always just four houses away, and if he wasn't out walking around the neighborhood, he would surely be willing to help her. When he answered the phone, he told her that he was finishing his breakfast and he would meet her in the backyard.

Debbie continued to clean up the trashed shed. As she picked up the empty plastic acid and alkaline test bottles that had also been poured on the lawnmower, she wondered who would have done such a nasty thing. Jaredd was getting along great with Nate and Bradon, so they'd have no reason to do such a thing. That left Paul Ferguson, but she hadn't seen him since February when she had reported him to the police. It had actually been a much more pleasant summer without him hanging around. Jaredd, Dorsey, Bradon, and Nate seemed to be enjoying the basketball, swimming, and Nintendo without him. None of them had anything to do with Paul since Dorsey and Bradon had to testify against him in juvenile court. So if the vandalized shed was Paul's evil doing, she could handle it.

John arrived at the back gate and joined her in the shed. He too was concerned about the damaged lawnmower. As they studied the gas container, Debbie noticed the small hose that allowed the gasoline to flow from the container to the motor. She realized that since she hadn't started the lawnmower and the powder was poured into the gas container, the powder was not in the motor of the mower. When John showed her how to remove the hose from the canister, she noticed that the canister could be lifted right off the mower. How excited she was to learn that her mower was fine, and that all she had to do was to dump the powder into the trash and rinse out the plastic gas container.

Debbie was mowing her lawn in no time, and John found a broom and swept the shed. The powder on the grass was easily absorbed into the lawn with a brief hosing, and Debbie was ready for an afternoon of fun in the pool with her children and their friends. She chose not to discuss the mess in the shed and the yard with her kids, so only she and John ever knew about it, except for the person who committed the vandalism.

With the informant's information, there was no doubt that Paul Ferguson had vandalized her shed. How else would an inmate know about the "childish prank" of putting "chemicals on the lawn"?

Paul had admitted to the inmate that he had "stolen some stuff out" of Debbie's house, but because she couldn't prove it, she had no right to not allow him to come back to her house. What kind of a sick kid thinks he is entitled to continue to enjoy the comforts and amenities of a home after he burglarized it? Furthermore, what is wrong with a kid who harbors anger and resentment to the level that he decides the victims of his burglary should be punished for simply denying him access to their home?

According to the inmate, it bothered Paul that his act of revenge went unnoticed. Paul never heard Jaredd or Dorsey or any of the neighborhood kids talk about the vandalism of the shed because they didn't know about it, so Paul thought his act of revenge went undetected. His scheme to "get her back" failed, so he needed another plan. A plan that would lead him to sneak into their home and attempt to stab them to death. Debbie shuddered at the thought of how sick and evil Paul had become.

At this point in her reading, Debbie looked around the courtroom. She was so angry that she wanted to stop the bail hearing and discuss the facts in the interview with Paul, his mother, and his attorney. How dare they try to get Paul out of jail when he so boldly had been bragging about being the perpetrator of the attack and the other violations against her family?

Paul was, by this time, seated next to his attorney on the right side of the courtroom. Debbie desperately wanted to talk to George about what she was reading, but he was seated at the table across from Paul talking with Detective Nelson. Judge Kleinfelter had not entered the courtroom yet, so she continued to read:

> A. I don't think Paul liked the daughter either. I think she might have had some words with him or something. But he said he called her a bitch, he said she's a real bitch, and he said, "I was planning on getting even with all of them." And I think he had feelings against the son because the son didn't come to his defense, and, you know, demand his mom allow them to still be friends.
>
> Q. Okay, so you're saying that Paul Ferguson told you that he went over there that night for— because he didn't like the family?
>
> A. That he wanted revenge, yeah.
>
> Q. Wanted revenge? Anything specific?

A. Well, also his intentions were—and then it seemed like he made this decision once he got there, was to assault the daughter, to rape the daughter, because he was—at one time he made it sound as if he went over there specifically to like, you know, to cut them. But then in another conversation he made it sound as if he went over still to rape the daughter.

Q. Well, what specifically did he tell you, as far as raping the daughter? Did he say I was there to rape the daughter?

A. Yeah, yeah, he said that she always liked me. He said so I don't even know why she turned against me, when the mom said that I stole something out of that house, nobody came to my defense. He said so I was gonna fuck her little white ass. That's what he said. So that was the second time he mentioned it.

Q. He said that he was gonna fuck her little white ass?

A. That's what he said.

Debbie's suspicions about why Paul took his pants and sneakers off in the kitchen were confirmed. She recalled asking Detective Nelson and Detective Hielig the day after the attack in her hospital bed if they thought Paul came there to rape Alisha. Although she heard her children telling their friends about the attack and explaining that Paul took his pants off because they were nylon and would make noise as he walked, Debbie never believed their theory. And thanks to the informant, she knew the truth: Paul took his pants and sneakers off in her kitchen and went right to Alisha's room because he intended to rape her.

Debbie began to cry as she imagined what would have happened to Alisha if she hadn't heard the floorboards creak and followed up on the dark hallway. As it turned out, Paul never got to Alisha, and Debbie was grateful that Alisha didn't have to wake up to that horror.

What she woke up to was bad enough. Debbie was not only wiping tears from her face, she was also shaking with emotions to the point that her family was beginning to wonder what was going on with her. She reassured them that she was all right and they would understand when they read the document she was reading.

When Debbie returned to the transcript, she knew she needed to skim the rest in order to be ready for the bail hearing to begin:

Q. Did he indicate which daughter?

A. No. I didn't even realize there was more than one. So he mentioned the daughter, and I assume—I don't know if he had assaulted her or not, he didn't say that he did, I mean as far as stabbing her, but he mentioned the daughter. And so I just naturally didn't question him about it.

Q. Okay, and what did he tell you about how he got into the house?

A. That he used a key. I didn't want—after he started talking about it, and I decided I was gonna say something to the detectives about it, I was trying to make an effort not to really question him, and get too specific, so I didn't—you know, 'cause I didn't want him to think I was gonna turn this information over. And I didn't want him to be suspicious, so I was, you know—I didn't even ask him what did he mean the front door or the back door, but he said he used a key to get into the house. So that was a comment he made about how he got in. He said they couldn't find any broken windows or anything like that. So he said this—then in a later conversation he mentioned that he had the key, and that he had gotten the key a long time ago to the house. He said I could have been in the house as many

times as I want. I could have—he said he was
even planning at one time to wait for them to
get home one day, and do something to them.
He even planned on setting their house on fire
at one time.

Q. Did he ever indicate to you anything about a
weapon?

A. He said that he had used a knife. He had a
knife that he got from a friend, and he made it
sound, because of his age, I'm assuming that it
was a friend at the school, or someone around
his age, that he knew. And he said that when
he got the knife he made a point of when the
guy gave him the knife he asked the guy, did
he have a knife? He was having trouble with
somebody in school, and he just wanted to
defend himself. So he said the guy gave him
the knife, and he made a point of not touching it, he just opened up his bag and let the
guy drop it in his bag. So he said he was making a point --he was making plans then not to
have his fingerprints on the knife.

No wonder Paul dropped the knife in Jaredd's room. He wanted
to leave it at the scene of the crime because it had the fingerprints
of another guy. According to the informant, "He was making plans
not to have his fingerprints on the knife." And if Detective Fox had
found prints on the knife, they would not have been Paul's prints.
That explained Paul's confident attitude about the evidence. He
planted false evidence.

Paul's premeditation to cut up or kill her family made Debbie
nauseous. The inmate's description of Paul "planning at one time to
wait for them to get home and do something to them," and planning
on "setting their house on fire" added to her sick feeling. As she finished skimming the transcript of the interview, she only grew more
ill:

Q. Did he say who he got the knife from?

A. He said either Donald or Dennis. It had a D sound to it.

Q. Donald or Dennis?

A. It was either Donald or Dennis, yeah.

Q. Okay, did he ever indicate what kind of knife it was?

A. No, again I was a little concerned. He spoke about this just most recently. And I was a little concerned, 'cause he's been to the preliminary and I didn't want him to think that I was trying to pump him for information. So I didn't even ask him about how the knife looked or how long was it, or anything like that. Okay. What, if anything, did he tell you about what happened inside that house that night? Well, once he had gotten—he said that once he had gotten into the house, he went upstairs, he knew where the daughter's bedroom was. Then again as I said, I didn't know there were two daughters, so I don't know which bedroom he might have been talking about, or if they sleep together or what. He wasn't that specific. But what he mentioned that he did do was, he went to the bedroom and she was lying on her stomach, or she was in a sleeping position where she couldn't see him, to look at him. And he got into the room, he closed the door behind him, but he said it must not have been closed, because the mother heard him in the room. He took his pants off, and he didn't mention his shoes, but for some reason I got the impression that he meant his pants and his shoes. He said he took his—he kept his top on, and took his stuff off on the bottom. Okay, let me slow you up there a second.

Let's talk about the pants and shoes business. Tell me about what he said about that. Why he did that? He said he did that because his intentions were to assault her, to rape her, so he took his pants off, and like the way he said it was, he said he took his bottoms off, he took everything off, he took, he—that's what made me think he said his shoes, because he said he took everything off of the bottom, he left his top on. That was his explanation later about why he had to get rid of the shirt, because there was supposedly some blood on it.

Q. Uh-huh.

A. But he took that off, and he didn't go from the stories—he went from that right to the point of the mother bursting into the room. I didn't ask him did he assault her, did he touch her, or did he even have sex with her, and he didn't say that he did. He said he went from that point, when he took his stuff off, right to the mother coming into the room. And he said he was trying to get out at the same time she was coming in.

Q. So from what he told you then, is he telling you he's walking around half naked, or—

A. It seemed like he said—I don't know how much time went by in between that, but it appeared as if he didn't have any pants on at the time, and she was sleeping when the mom came into the room. I don't know how long he was in the room, or if the daughter woke up, you know, while he was there, or when the mother came in the room, or how that happened, but he said what happened was when the mother came into the room he was trying to get around her, and by her, and at the same time, I guess when he went to go back into the room I guess, at that time he decided he was going to stab them, because he was trying to get back into the bedroom, and the mother was obviously trying to keep him out. I don't know either by pushing the door, or just with her hands. But she was like blocking him coming back into the room. And I assume, because he said her and the daughter. So that made me think that the daughter must have been up at that point. But he never mentioned her in any other way as far as knowing he was there until that point.

It occurred to Debbie, at that point in her reading, that the informant knew detailed aspects of the attack on her. He knew enough details that it would be obvious to any jury member that he was either telling the absolute truth about what Paul told him or he had been there and done the crime himself. Fortunately, he had been in prison since February, not present in her home on April 18, and, therefore, only aware of the details of the attack because of his conversations with Paul. Debbie was amazed and grateful that they would have a witness in court who could tell the details of the crime so well that no one could argue that Paul didn't commit the crime.

Debbie could not stop reading. She couldn't wait to see how much more she could learn and confirm from his interview:

Q. Okay, what did he tell you about as far as stabbing the mother?

A. That if he had got back in the room he was gonna kill them, because he said it was the only way he knew he could get away with it. So he said he knew his fingerprints weren't going to be on the knife.

Q. What do you mean that that was the only way that he would be able to get away with it? Are

you talking about—are you talking about—
was Paul Ferguson saying that—that's the
only way he could get out of the house?

A. No.

Q. Or is that the only way he could get out of
the charge?

A. That would be the only way—he made it
sound as if that was the only way that nobody
would ever know that it was him. It was his
contentions on leaving the knife there anyway he said. That was why he never touched
the knife when whoever it was that gave it to
him. He wanted a different set of prints on the
knife. So he said he knew this guy had never
been in trouble with the police or anything, so
nobody would ever have his fingerprints. So
he had calculated that from the time he got
the knife. He never said how long ago it was
that he received the knife from this guy, so I
don't know how long he had been planning on
doing this, but he was giving me that information, as if he had already been calculating how
he was gonna do it, as if he was actually having
the intentions of going into the house to stab
them up, and kill them, was the only way it
sounded to me.

Q. Okay.

A. So when he got rushed by the mother his—he
just went into a rage and he said he started
stabbing her.

Q. Okay.

A. 'Cause he was already out of the room, so I
guess he could have left if he wanted to.

Q. You said something about his prints wouldn't
be on the knife—

A. Yeah.

Q. Because of why?

A. Because whoever he got the knife from he saw them handle the knife, they handed it to him. They put it—they had it in their hand, put it in the bag. So he said he was making a point. I guess he had already scouted out this guy, and knew this guy had a knife, because he made it sound as if who he was getting it from didn't really know his real purpose. He lied to the guy, said he was using it for his own defense, and kids were after him, and he was making it sound as if what he was doing was making sure that, you know, his prints weren't going to be on the knife, yeah.

Q. Okay. Did he ever indicate anything about gloves?

A. He said that he had—he had some gloves at his house. He said he'd been doing some woodwork of some staining of a dresser or something in his bedroom, and they were like latex, I guess he meant rubber gloves, and those were the ones he had on when he handled the knife, and I guess –

Q. What did he say gloves, did he say latex gloves, what specifically did he say?

A. He said he had gloves on, but when he mentioned that when they came to the house to get the gloves—when they came to the house to search his house, he said, they found some latex gloves, he said, but they only found one pair. He said they never found the pair that I had on. Meaning that he used latex gloves. He was saying that they found a pair that he was using to stain wood in his bedroom, but that the second pair, obviously were the pair, another pair was what he used and had disposed of.

Q. Uh-huh. Did he indicate anything else to you about stabbing the mother?

A. Ah, his... his... his feeling and what he was saying when he said that she—he rushed out of the bedroom, is that he could have gotten away at that point. He said, but he thought she had saw his face, as he passed her, as he was trying to get out of the room. He said he knew she recognized her—recognized him, that's what he said, and that's what made him turn. And his intentions were to kill her. I mean there was no other way to read that, I mean if he went back into the room, because he knew she had recognized him. He said, he couldn't have left any witnesses, that was how he said it.

Q. Did he ever indicate anything that he did to carry out those intentions?

A. Ah, the stabbing, you know, like he said he actually had gotten passed her, because she rushed into the room, it was obviously—as an obstacle for him getting out of the room when he got past her, he knew that she had saw his face, and his stabbing was the intentions on trying to, I guess, kill her.

Q. Did he indicate anything at all about the daughter, or daughters?

A. Nothing, nothing more than the fact that once he had started stabbing the mother or stabbing at the mother, that they were awake, and that they were aware of what he was doing. And I had the impression that they were trying to keep him out of the room through a closed door or whatever they were doing, but they were conscious, because he said the daughter—because he said the mother and the daughter were trying to keep him out of the room, so she must have been up at that time. Again, like I said I didn't know if there were two or not. He mentioned a daughter. The same one that he was trying to assault.

Q. Okay, did he indicate to you anything as regards to the son?

A. That—he didn't say that the son was awake. But, I—like I said I didn't question him too in-depth about this. He was just telling his own story, the way he wanted to tell it, and it was sounding as if he went in—they must have gotten the door closed on him, when he got away from them, because he then went into the boy's bedroom, and slashed at the boy. He didn't make it sound as if the son was awake, and he didn't say if he was laying down or not, but he did say he cut him, and as he, I guess, it made it appear to me like he was going back past that bedroom, and saying goodnight, on his way out.

Q. Well, did he indicate why he would stab the son?

A. No. The way he was telling it, he was getting so excited just in telling it, he made it appear as if, you know, he either might have went in the wrong direction, and went into the boy's bedroom, and he could have either went there with the intentions of stabbing him, but like I said he knew—he said, that he knew he couldn't have left any witnesses behind. So he gave me the impression that he had talked about trying to kill the mother and the daughter once they had, had been awakened, and to me it sounds as if he had to do that to the son, but he only made a—he said he sliced at him. That's how he phrased it. So I don't know where he cut him or anything, but he said he sliced at him, and said goodnight, and ran out of the house.

Q. Why would he say goodnight to someone he sliced?

A. I don't have any idea. And I asked him the same question, I said why did you say that? He said I don't even know why I said it either. He said it was kind of funny, he said it came to mind. He said it was a funny thing to say.

Q. Okay, did he indicate anything to you what he did after he—after this stabbing is done?

A. Yeah. Well he realized—what he said what he had done that he knew he wasn't gonna run straight back to his house. I don't know why he said that. But, he said he wasn't gonna run straight back to his house. He was gonna take some sort of roundabout route. He said he went up toward 7th Street. He said he noticed he had blood on him, on his top, and he wanted to get rid of the gloves somewhere. His intentions were to put them in his pocket, and take them back home and flush them down the toilet.

Q. Take the gloves back and flush them down the toilet?

A. Take the gloves back with him. I don't know if he didn't because he didn't have pants on, or what the case was. But he said he realized he had blood on his top, he went up towards 7th Street, which he made it seem like it was a roundabout way to get back to his house. And he said yeah towards 7th Street, he didn't say

7th Street, he said towards 7th Street, and he said he ripped open somebody's garbage bag, plastic garbage bag in a trashcan and stuffed the shirt in it and the gloves. And then went home.

Q. Okay. Did he indicate anything at all about when the police came to his house?

A. Well, he said he knew—earlier he had been watching TV with his mom, and he knew that was going to be his alibi, so like I'm saying, he had already planned and plotted how he was going to do this. He said he was going upstairs. But he said what he did was sneak back downstairs and go out the front door and make sure the front door was unlocked. And went out the front door. and that was his way of getting back in the house. So, he said before the police even come he had went upstairs to his room, and I guess he… he said—what did he say, he said he put on some sweats, yeah he did, he said sweats. He said a workout outfit, but he said then, then the second time he said sweats when he talked about it, then he came back down stairs.

Q. Okay, are you saying that—are you saying that Ferguson told you he snuck out of the house without his mother knowing about it?

A. What he said the first time is that he snuck out without his mother knowing about it, but then when he talked about it the second time, the second or third time, when he mentioned about being in the house when the police came, then he said there was no way my mom couldn't have known that I was out. He said because she said something about—

Q. There's no way she couldn't have known?

A. Could not have known that he was... he was not in the house, he said, because she said— she asked him just before the police had came, "Where were you?" And he didn't say anything, so he said she knew that he wasn't in the house.

Q. Okay. What did he tell you, if anything, about when the police did arrive?

A. He didn't say what he said to them, but he said he wasn't worried. He said he knew that there was no way they could even prove or connect him to it. 'Cause I think he was thinking that his alibi with his mom was gonna be strong enough, and he's still saying to this day that he believes, you know, by his mom saying that he was home, that he's gonna be able to beat this case, plus with his fingerprints not being anywhere in the house.

Q. Okay. Did he indicate to you if his mother took any active measures to destroy evidence or is she fabricating evidence, or anything like that?

A. Just as recently as... as last Sunday, he spoke to me, he came down to my cell and spoke to me.

Q. Last Sunday would it be last Sunday, last Sunday is May the 5th?

A. Yeah.

Q. Yeah, okay.

A. Ah, it was—it was in the evening, he had obviously made a phone call home, cause all the phones are in the day room. He usually calls in the evening, and he said—he came to my cell, and said I'm really getting this thing rapped up. He said they're blowing it all kinds of ways, not only just the evidence, but he said I got something that's gonna work in my defense. So I asked him, what are you talking about? He said well I got some kids involved. He said some kids that I know have a recording of the son saying that I didn't do it. I said what do you mean, he's actually said on tape, like they put a tape in front of him, and he said it. He said no, what it was—then, you know, I was waiting for him to tell me that what it was is that they taped it without the guy knowing about it, without the kid knowing about it, but then he said no. He said what I did was have some kids, you know, with a male voice, say that Paul Ferguson didn't have anything to do with attacking our house or with stabbing me, and that it was some other kid.

Q. Now, just so I understand this, you're saying that he told you there is some kids, or some persona unknown that are—made a tape, pretending to be the son?

A. Pretending to be the son, they taped someone—I don't know if it's one of the group that has the tape, or if they got somebody else to do it, but they supposedly made a tape that said, you know, reporting to be the son, but really wasn't, saying that Paul Ferguson didn't really do it, I know it wasn't him because I saw who it was, and it wasn't him.

Q. Are you indicating then that Paul Ferguson's mother is—

A. She's aware that it's not a real tape, that—that it's son really the son, that's making this statement. That it's someone else, and he actually said my mom—the day before that he said my mom has a plan—this is what made me say – making me say his mom was involved. He said

136

my mom is making plans, you know, for my defense to make sure that they can prove that I was home at the time. I said well that's great if you can do that man and beat the charges, if you didn't do it, but all along he's telling me he's done it, so I'm just listening to what he's saying. And then the next day he tells me that these kids are making a tape and they're gonna give it to his mother, and he says she's gonna give it to the lawyer at the right time, to make it appear as if they have evidence now. So his mom is aware that it's not really the boy on the tape. And that it's really fabricated evidence, and this is what he said, and that his mom is gonna hold the tape to give to, I guess, their lawyer to present as evidence.

Q. Did Paul Ferguson ever indicate to you anything about any kind of scratches or wounds that he received in this struggle?

A. He said something about his face. When he first started talking about it, 'cause he mentioned the shirt, in the same breath that he was talking about some kind of scar he had on his face. I don't know if someone had scratched him, or he had cut himself or not, but what he said was, is that it's all healed now. And I think he has like a shadow, a long shadow on his face somewhere, but he wasn't talking about that, so I could still see the scar, what do you mean it's healed, he said no not there, and he motioned to like the bridge of his nose, or around his eye area. And I really couldn't see anything to be honest, you know, it didn't look like there were any scratches.

Q. He pointed to the bridge of his nose, or his eye?

A. Yeah, in that area. Like the scar he has—

Q. But you didn't see anything?

A. No, 'cause like I said, I didn't see Paul, and he didn't bring this up until like maybe three weeks, you know, following his like—maybe about a week ago he mentioned this. So it was like three weeks, I think, he had already been in the County, or close to that period of time. But I couldn't—you know, I wasn't like really trying to get in his face, like I was trying to examine him like a doctor; I was about maybe two feet away from him when we were talking. He was sitting at the desk, and I was sitting on my bed in my cell, and I said well I can see a scar, right, and he said well there's not any evidence—he said he thought he was cut a whole lot worse than that. That's why I wasn't sure if he meant he was cut by the knife, or someone had scratched him with their hands. But I said well I can still see a scar, and on one side of his face he has the shadow of a scar, that kind of like runs the length of the inside of his cheek, and it looks old, like an old scar. But he said, no, he said—

Q. Did he indicate that those places he was pointing at were scratched, or injured in—

A. Yeah.

Q. The attack?

A. What he said was is that he made a story up saying that his brother or somebody in his family had scratched him. I think he was saying with braces or something. Yeah, he did, he said with braces. But he said they came from—I think he said from the mother. I wasn't even sure whether he said the mother or not, but I know he said it happened when he was in the house. 'Cause that was where he thought the blood was coming from on his shirt, 'cause he said it was dripping, and he thought it was like, you know, his own blood. So he said he thought he could explain that by saying that his brother, or whoever it was in his house had scratched him with braces. 'Cause I'm quite sure he did say braces.

Q. Okay.

A. Yeah.

Q. Did he indicate to you anything else about, what he did afterwards, or—

A. Well, like I said he mentioned that he had gotten rid of the top, so I knew he wouldn't be running around with just underwear on, and that, and I'm assuming that he had on a T-shirt underneath.

Q. He got rid of the top, or his mother got rid of the top?

A. He said that he did before he got to the house.

Q. Okay.

A. Yeah, he said he got rid of the top and the gloves before he got to the house. And what he said he done he ripped open the bag, and a garbage bag and stuffed all the stuff inside someone's, you know, plastic trash bag, I guess to be picked up with the morning trash, or whenever the trash was being picked up.

Q. Okay. Is there anything else that you can remember?

A. Well, he's making a point all along that his mother really does believe that he did it, that his mother is just doing the best she can to defend him on this. And he said his mom is going to do whatever she has to do to help him.

Q. Okay, but he said that his mother knows that he is guilty?

A. Yeah, yeah. He said that his mother knows he is guilty, because he did mention that his mom asked him where was he, and he didn't—he didn't say anything to her. But this was like a little while after he got to the house. I guess she must have heard him upstairs or maybe she saw him coming into the house. But she asked him specifically where were you, knowing that he wasn't in the house. And he said he didn't say anything to her. And a little while after that, I think that's when the police came.

Q. Okay. That's all the questions I have about, you know, this information that you have concerning this incident, unless you can think of anything else, and you were gonna say something—

A. No, I just was gonna make the point, right, that his attitude was, and especially when he told me about the tape being doctored, that his mom obviously has some ideas about what she could do to get him out of this, and that they didn't have any problem manufacturing some evidence, or even lying in court. He said my mom will do whatever she has to do. She'll get on the stand and lie, he said. And whatever the lawyer says she has to say she'll say to get me out of this. He said that's why she didn't get on the stand at the preliminary hearing, for his defense to say that he was home, and it couldn't have been him, because they don't want to reveal saying one thing, and have to change it later on. He said so the lawyer told me she should hold back from saying anything until she's ready to make a statement at his trial, because they do plan on taking it to trial, cause he said, you know, he can beat it. He said he's threw enough—how did he say this, he threw enough bad evidence in the mix that you'll never be able to prove it was him. He said these people were hysterical, and they—they just said it was him, he said, but they'll be—the reason my lawyer will be able to break that down in court.

Q. Isn't it true that you came to me, you contacted me about this information?

A. Yes, I did. I called yesterday.

Q. Okay, and have I or anyone else in the police department, or any other agency, offered you any kind of deal, or offer, in return for your statement?

A. No one has, no.

Q. Okay, are you willing to testify against Paul Ferguson if necessary?

A. Yes, I am.

Q. Okay. I have nothing further to ask, so I'm going to end this interview. The time is now 1445 hours.

(Statement concluded at 1445 hours.)

Judge Kleinfelter entered the courtroom, sat down, and declared, "This hearing is now in session."

Debbie didn't want to miss any of his words, but she was so enraged at what she had just read that she could hardly see straight. Mrs. Ferguson sat directly across from her, with Paul's aunts, knowing full well that her son had attempted to kill her and her family, and she was trying to get him out of prison anyway. *What is wrong with this picture?*

Debbie held a document in her hands that could provide all the missing details of the case and that Mrs. Ferguson was a liar. She wanted to hand her the document and have her read all about her cocky, sick, evil son.

George Matangos called Detective Nelson to the stand. Detective Nelson described the attack and answered all of Judge Kleinfelter's questions. When Judge Kleinfelter asked Mr. Matangos for his next witness, he seemed a bit taken back when Mr. Matangos declared he had no more witnesses and that he rested his case. George was not putting Debbie and her children on the stand for the very reason Mr. Foreman did not bring Mrs. Ferguson to the stand in the preliminary hearing with one big exception. George didn't want Mr. Foreman to know the facts of their prosecution before the trial, and Mr. Foreman didn't want Mrs. Ferguson "saying one thing, and having to change it later on," as the informant put it, because her testimony was going to be lies.

When Mr. Foreman began his defense, he pleaded with Judge Kleinfelter to consider Paul's age and his dependency upon his family. He provided information that Paul's family was all located in the Harrisburg area to convince the judge that he was not a flight risk. He even included an admonishment of Justice Shugars for setting an "excessively high" bail and the hardship placed upon Paul's family to try to raise such a large amount of money.

Mr. Foreman went on with legal jargon about the true purpose of bail that sounded good for Paul but was meaningless to Debbie. He concluded his presentation by describing an elaborate plan that he and Paul's mother would arrange to maintain strict supervision of Paul to ensure he was in adult supervision at all times during his release from prison. The plan would also ensure Paul's presence for trial.

It was finally Judge Kleinfelter's time to make a decision. He began by concurring with Mr. Foreman that it was true that Paul was only fifteen years old. He agreed that raising bail placed an extreme burden upon the families of incarcerated individuals. Debbie and her family grew more and more nervous as Judge Kleinfelter continued to address Mr. Foreman.

However, when Judge Kleinfelter's tone changed, so did his message to Mr. Foreman. He was no longer agreeing with him, but instead, he proceeded to articulate the areas in which he and Mr. Foreman differed. He declared, for the whole courtroom, that he was not impressed with Mr. Foreman's plan to supervise Paul Ferguson outside of prison. He emphatically stated that no arrangement, short of incarceration, could provide the Bird family the sense of safety and security they deserved after surviving such a horrid attack in their home.

Even though Detective Nelson's testimony included the identification of Debbie, Jaredd, Alisha, and Ashley in the courtroom, Debbie was impressed and touched by Judge Kleinfelter acknowledgment of their presence and his obvious sensitivity to their ordeal. George was right when he said that he only needed Detective Nelson's testimony to convince the judge that what Paul had done to them on April 18 was horrible.

But what Judge Kleinfelter said next was worth a thousand words to Debbie and her family. He said, "I'm not only not lowering the bail for Paul Ferguson, I'm raising it from $100,000 to $210,000." He looked at Mr. Foreman and issued a warning in an angry tone that even George did not expect: "And if you bring this case back to trial with three eyewitnesses against a mother who says her son was home in bed sleeping, this young man stands to spend a good part of his adult life in prison." And with a stern rap of his gavel, Judge Kleinfelter announced, "This court is adjourned."

The left side of the courtroom was ecstatic. Debbie's family took turns hugging each other, and Mr. Matangos soon joined them. He was obviously elated by the outcome of the hearing, and anxious to get them all to his office to debrief. As they filed out of the courtroom and into the elevator, Paul's aunts passed by the elevator clutching their Bibles and chanting, "Lying lips will not prevail."

Debbie and her family were stunned and speechless. When the elevator doors closed, Debbie responded, for only her family and George to hear, "We're counting on it." Still struggling to control her rage over the truths contained in the informant's interview, she wrestled with not saying more.

In less than two minutes, George had Debbie, her parents, Marti, and the kids packed in to his office to tell them that he was shocked by Judge Kleinfelter's final warning to Mr. Foreman. According to George, Judge Kleinfelter essentially told Mr. Foreman that he had better plea-bargain this case.

Debbie was not clear what that meant for her and her family, but she was sure that George was very pleased. They not only prevailed over the bail issue, but they also succeeded in getting Paul's bail more than doubled. They all had a lot for which to be grateful. George promised to call Debbie regarding the informants's transcript, and Debbie was content to take her family home to their safe and secure house and neighborhood.

Chapter XXV

Pleas Don't Bargain

With a renewed sense of security and safety, Debbie and her children returned home. The next day had special significance as they celebrated the Fourth of July with a new appreciation of freedom and independence. Debbie shared the informant's interview with her family and friends as the ultimate confirmation of Paul's guilt. All their fears and anxieties about Paul being released from prison were gone—at least for the time being.

When George Matangos called Debbie, his intent was to discuss the possibility of a plea bargain. He reiterated the significance of Judge Kleinfelter's final warning to Mr. Foreman and proceeded to explain the plea bargain that he expected to get from the defense on Paul's behalf. Mr. Foreman would have Paul plead guilty to the charges in exchange for a sentence of eight to ten years in prison.

"Why would we accept such a deal?" Debbie challenged George.

"Because with a plea bargain, we're guaranteed that Paul will serve the specified years in prison," George clarified. He went on to explain that by going to trial, there is always a risk that a jury would find Paul not guilty and release him with no prison sentence at all.

The thought of Paul serving only eight to ten years in prison was almost as frightening and unacceptable as having him serve no time at all. George had, in prior meetings, explained to Debbie that Paul could get twenty to forty years for each count of criminal attempt homicide on her and Jaredd, ten to twenty years for aggravated assault on Alisha, and six to twelve years for burglary. The television and newspaper coverage of the attack continued to report that Paul could be sentenced to up to "eighty years in prison." How could George now be suggesting they consider only ten years altogether?

When Debbie told George she didn't believe in deals and that she felt individuals that do the crime should do the time, George reassured her that they would not accept a plea bargain without her consent, and that the decision to do so would ultimately be her decision to make. Suddenly she was not so sure of herself, and she didn't want all that responsibility. She ended her conversation with George by confessing that she hoped they would not get a plea bargain offer so she would not have to decide whether or not to accept it.

Burdened with the weight of such a decision, Debbie decided to call Detective Nelson to get his opinion on a possible plea bargain. Detective Nelson was thrilled about a plea bargain. "If we can put Paul Ferguson in prison for ten years on a plea bargain, I think we should take it," were his exact words, and Debbie was devastated. When Debbie argued that the newspapers claimed that Paul could get up to eighty years, Detective Nelson's response was, "There is no way that Paul will get the maximum sentence, and eighty years is out of the question." In an effort to keep Debbie from getting her hopes up, he cited numerous cases where people shot and killed each other on city corners during drug deals and got six years or less.

"My family and I were in our home when we were attacked," Debbie protested. "We were not on some street corner at night dealing drugs. We did nothing to deserve being attacked in our home, and Paul Ferguson had no right to enter our home and attack us."

Detective Nelson totally agreed with Debbie, and her outrage reminded him about how unfair the police and the legal system could be to innocent victims. He was sorry for Debbie and her children, and he didn't want to upset her. He just didn't want her to be misled into believing that maximum sentencing was a realistic expectation. He had been disappointed too many times himself to not want to protect her from the same disappointment.

146

Debbie felt the roller-coaster effect once again as she plunged from the height of optimism over their victory at the bail hearing to the depths of fear that even if Paul was found guilty at trial, he may only be sentenced to six years. The thought of Paul being back in her and her children's lives in six years was too frightening for her to even imagine. But despite her anxiety over a plea bargain, she was sure she was not going to accept it. She would have to trust in the legal system because she didn't believe in deals.

As it turned out, she did not have to reject a plea bargain from Attorney Foreman. According to George in a later phone call, there would be no plea bargain. Mrs. Ferguson rejected her attorney's advice, and Mr. Foreman was no longer handling the case. A Mr. Robert Tarman would be representing Paul, and he had already filed for a continuance of the trial date in order to provide him with sufficient time to prepare his defense. George was not surprised that Mr. Foreman was no longer Paul's attorney. He suspected that Mr. Foreman refused to take Paul's case to trial after Judge Kleinfelter's warning at the bail hearing, and Mrs. Ferguson was forced to seek other legal representation if she was unwilling to consider a plea bargain.

George was surprised, however, that Mrs. Ferguson was so persistent about going to trial. Surely Mr. Foreman had clearly explained to her the advantages of plea-bargaining versus the risks of going to trial. Debbie wasn't surprised that Mrs. Ferguson wasn't plea-bargaining. Debbie reminded George of the statements the informant claimed Paul was making in prison about his mother having "some ideas about what she could do to get him out of this" and having "no problem manufacturing some evidence, or even lying in court."

It was clear to Debbie after reading the informant's statement that Paul was confident to the point of being cocky about his mother lying for him and getting him out of this problem. Paul's own words echoed through her mind as she reflected upon the informant's statement. "They're not going to fry me because I'm a kid, so I'm not even worried about it. I threw enough bad evidence in the mix that they'll never be able to prove it was me. My mom will do whatever she has to do. She'll get on the stand and lie."

Debbie wasn't at all surprised that Mrs. Ferguson and Paul were prepared for a trial. And she was prepared for a trial as well. Each time she read Paul's words through the informant, she grew stronger and more determined to fight Paul and his mother to the finish.

Chapter XXVI

Back to Normal?

When the new school year started, Debbie and her children quickly got back into the routine of school, dance rehearsals, and fall soccer and field hockey practices. Although Debbie reflected often upon her days at home with meals delivered by her colleagues and neighbors during her recovery, she welcomed the return to her busy schedule and was grateful to be able to manage her own life again. Each day after work, she would drive across the Susquehanna River from work to her Susquehanna home to get Ashley. They would cross back over the Susquehanna River and make a quick stop at McDonald's for a Happy Meal for Ashley and a salad for Alisha en route to Ashley's dance classes in Enola.

Debbie would cross the river again and sit in the Susquehanna Township High School parking lot, waiting for Alisha to finish field hockey. When Alisha was finished, she would hop in the car and eat her salad as Debbie drove her back across the river to Enola for her dance class. Her dance bag was packed in the car and ready for her to leave her school bookbag in the car and report to dance.

Having delivered both girls, it was time to cross over the river again to pick up Jaredd from soccer practice and return home to make dinner. A return trip or two for dance pickups still remained on the evening schedule, and Debbie frequently counted the miles and the trips that she made daily over the Harvey Taylor Bridge just to provide opportunities that she felt were important for her children. She knew her life schedule sounded ridiculous to everyone who made the mistake of asking her what television shows she liked to watch in the evenings, but she had three children, and she was committed to them.

She was also committed to the fast-paced, bags packed taxi service she provided each night, which depended upon all parties being packed and ready to go. So when Ashley was not at home the first September afternoon of the new school year, Debbie grabbed the dance bags and followed her note to pick her up at Erica's house. No problem, Ashley was ready to go, and no time was wasted.

After a week of such notes, however, Debbie grew concerned that Ashley daily added another stop to an already-nearly-impossible transportation schedule. With each pickup at different friends' homes, Ashley would offer a new reason for not being at home. The afternoon that Debbie had made it absolutely clear to Ashley that under no circumstances should she be anywhere but home, Ashley was sitting on the curb in front of the house when Debbie arrived. Ashley had a book on her lap, and she was doing her homework. She had the dance bags by her side, and she was ready to go. She looked up and greeted her mom with a big smile and wave.

When Ashley hopped into the car, Debbie thanked her for being at home and ready as she had asked her to be. When Debbie asked her why she was sitting on the curb doing her homework, her heart broke with Ashley's answer: "I was afraid to be in our house by myself," she said sadly. Debbie realized in an instant that all the notes Ashley had left for her were about being somewhere else so she wouldn't have to be in their house alone. Debbie felt so sad and ashamed for pressuring Ashley to be at home alone. With the new school year starting and both Alisha and Jaredd being involved in high school sports, Debbie had not realized that Ashley was coming home each day to an empty house alone for the first time in her school experience. Despite her efforts to convince Ashley that her home was safe with their security system, she realized that all the technology in the world was not going to make Ashley feel safe in their home without her family. Ashley was very clear that she didn't mind sitting on the curb because she liked being outside where she had room to run if she needed to. As the tears rolled down Debbie's cheeks, she grieved the loss of innocence her children had experienced through this ordeal and worried about the total impact it would have on their lives.

Each time she was reminded of the traumatic effect Paul had had on their lives, she made sure she included it in their counseling sessions with Deb Salem. Deb agreed that she would continue to work with them through the trial and sentencing process in order to help them prepare for the trial and to process each post-attack trauma they experienced, such as Ashley's fear of being in their home alone. Deb was a tremendous resource for preparing for a trial, and Debbie was relieved that Jaredd and Alisha seemed more and more ready to testify each day. Ashley knew she would not have to testify, and she was perfectly content to only have to worry about the outcome of the trial rather than her participation in it.

George Matangos was a tremendous help as well in preparing them for the trial. He included all three children in the pretrial meetings and was patient and sensitive to all their questions and concerns. While many pretrial discussions were focused upon the statements of the informant, it soon became clear that he would not be testifying against Paul in court. Despite Debbie's arguments that he provided details of the crime that only Paul knew, she knew George was adamant that his testimony would only detract from an already strong case. "The defense would have a field day with an inmate convicted of over fifteen counts of forgery," he explained. "They would spend days on his criminal past of deception, and then challenge any jury member to believe his statements about Paul." As a prosecuting attorney, George could not allow such testimony to weaken or detract from his three eyewitnesses.

George had a lot of legal theories that he shared with a great degree of confidence with Debbie and her kids, and Debbie was grateful for his willingness to involve them in so many aspects of the legal process. She was disappointed that George did not agree that the informant would provide valuable testimony for their case against Paul. After all, his statements had provided all the missing pieces for her. She would have to trust that George knew what he was doing where the legal issues were concerned.

When Mr. Matangos informed Debbie that he was not planning to challenge Mrs. Ferguson's statement on cross-examination, Debbie was again concerned. "You mean she's going to testify that Paul was home in bed sleeping and present fake tape recordings and lies, and you are not going to challenge her?" she protested.

George's explanation was simple. "There is a theory that the more you hear a lie, the more it begins to sound like the truth. The defense attorney, Mr. Tarman, will have Mrs. Ferguson alibi all the evidence we have against Paul. Rather than have the jury hear the lies a second time during my cross-examination of her, I plan to ask her a couple of questions. The questions will be focused upon how much she loves her son and how she would do anything for her son. She will answer yes to each question in the series. I will end with the statement, "You will do anything for your son, including lie for him.""

Debbie liked the series of questions George had planned for Mrs. Ferguson, but she didn't like his plan not to challenge her on all the lies she anticipated Mrs. Ferguson telling on the stand.

While Debbie wasn't too sold on George's legal theories as they pertained to the informant and Mrs. Ferguson, she liked his theory on victims and children. He assured her that Mr. Tarman would not be aggressive with her because she was a victim and attorneys have lost jury support by being unsympathetic toward victims of violent crimes. Mr. Tarman would also go easy on Jaredd and Alisha because he knew that juries do not like it when attorneys are hard on children. For the same reason, George confessed that he would not be hard on Paul's sister, Natasha. It had become clear to Debbie through the pretrial meetings she had with George that jury selection and treatment play a significant role in the outcome of the trial. She wasn't sure that it should play such an import role, but she was convinced that it would.

Chapter XXVII

The Trial: Day 1

When the trial date of December 9, 1996, was set, the Bird family had waited nearly eight months to bring Paul Ferguson to justice. They had become quite a team with George Matangos, Detective Nelson, and Detective Fox. They knew there were more members of their team that they had not yet met but would meet at trial. With family and friends, they were ready for the trial of their lives.

The morning of the trial was a busy morning in the Bird household. Three kids and a single mother were getting ready while Debbie's mother, dad, sister, aunts, uncles, cousins, and Rainie were arriving at the house. Debbie dressed as she thought a mother of three children should dress, and her children all checked with her for her approval of their attire. "Wear something you would wear to church," was her best advice, and they each did their part getting ready without placing too many demands upon an already-stressed-out mom. They were all nervous and excited at the same time, but they each knew that their best friends would be there for them in the courtroom, and that was very reassuring.

It was hectic getting the fleet of cars into the city and parked in the parking garage. Debbie and the kids had to leave their support group for one last meeting with Mr. Matangos. When they left his office and boarded the elevator to the fourth floor of the courthouse, they were not prepared for the sight they encountered when the elevator doors opened. The hallways and corridors that had been quiet and empty during their previous practice sessions were packed with friends. Jaredd's baseball, basketball, and soccer team members were mixed in with Alisha's school friends, dance friends; Jaredd's girlfriends; Debbie's cousin Steve, and his wife, Ruby; Uncle John; and Aunt Martha. Coach Cook, Jaredd's basketball coach, was right there with team members offering support to Jaredd and his family. Reverend Roach, Deb McLamb, and John McGreevy were there from the neighborhood; and Deb Salem and Judy Calkin, Debbie's divorce attorney, checked in to wish them well. Debbie and her children were overwhelmed by the tremendous number of familiar faces and friends who took time from their work and school to attend a Monday-morning court session.

By the time they worked their way through the crowd to the entrance to the courtroom, they realized that their friends were in the corridors because they were unable to fit into the courtroom. Rainie greeted Debbie and her children at the door and led them to the front left pew where their closest family members and friends were already seated. Rainie explained her panic when she discovered that Jaredd's best friend, Dorsey, and his girlfriend, Mandy, were way back in the line of friends waiting their turn to get into an already-packed courtroom. She grabbed them each by the arm and led them to the front of the line, where she declared them family and led them through the metal detector. Rainie took charge in making sure Debbie and her kids had their closest friends and family by their sides through their next ordeal.

When Debbie was seated, she checked the right side of the courtroom—her opponents in the battle to follow. Mrs. Ferguson was seated next to Natasha, with the three aunts who prophesized that "lying lips will not prevail." Debbie wanted to ask them if they read the informant's statement and wondered how they would explain away all that Paul had confessed. Debbie was still angry at all of them and disappointed that the informant was not going to testify.

At the table in front of Debbie sat Mr. Matangos, Detective Nelson, and Detective Fox. Across from them was Mr. Tarman, Paul's new attorney. How could he defend Paul against her and her family who had been so brutally attacked? George had explained that defense attorneys make a lot more money, but Debbie wondered how they sleep at night knowing they are trying to keep evil people from suffering from the consequences for their crimes. Debbie realized she felt hatred for Mr. Tarman and Paul's family, but the real target of her rage was not in the courtroom.

When Paul was led into the courtroom, he had guards all around him. He wasn't in his orange prison suit; instead, he was dressed in a suit and tie. He had lost a lot of weight, and he had a big cross hanging over his tie for all to see. George had warned Debbie and her kids that Paul had lost a lot of weight at the advice of his attorney. He did appear smaller and less intimidating, which was the defense's plan to impress the jury. Debbie wasn't impressed, but she did fear that the jury might be swayed by Paul's innocent, God-fearing appearance.

Jaredd wasn't impressed either. He had his car keys in his hand and appeared to be holding them for all to see. Jaredd celebrated his sixteenth birthday six months ago and was proud of his used car and his ability to drive himself to school. Jaredd explained later that he and Dorsey had decided to rub it in to Paul that they were now driving while Paul celebrated his sixteenth birthday in prison. Debbie was surprised at Jaredd's actions, because it was not his nature to show off or be unkind to others. Debbie did not encourage her son to be so arrogant, but she knew he was still not over his anger at what Paul had done to him and to her, and perhaps he needed a way to express some of that anger. She would make sure she remembered to share this with Deb Salem in their next counseling session, just to make sure Jaredd's behavior was healthy; but for now it was the least of her concerns. She was rehearsing her testimony in her head because that was the way she intended to express her anger.

At 9:00 a.m., the judge entered the courtroom, and the proceedings began with Attorneys Matangos and Tarman approaching the bench together and privately discussing issues with the judge that remained unexplained to the audience waiting for the trial to begin. When the three of them appeared to be in agreement and ready to proceed, the potential jury members filed into the courtroom. The nameless faces who would determine the outcome of the trial paid close attention to Judge Kleinfelter. He introduced them to the Bird family and to the defendant, Paul Ferguson, and described for them the charges in the case of the *Commonwealth versus Paul Ferguson.* He informed them that the defendant was charged with burglary, which was the entry into the Bird home with the intent to commit a crime. He was charged with aggravated attempted homicide as well.

The judge's next question to all of them was whether they had any knowledge of the case from any source, whether it be the newspaper, television, radio, or simply from hearing about it from other people in the community. Several individuals raised their hands and described vague memories of seeing the defendant on TV. Each assured Judge Kleinfelter that their knowledge of the case had not caused them to have any fixed opinion as to whether or not the defendant was guilty of the crime.

When the judge was convinced that all potential jury members could base any decisions in the trial solely upon the evidence presented in the courtroom, he allowed the attorneys to begin the jury selection process. When the jury pool was asked if they knew the defendant or witnesses, Nancy raised her hand. Debbie recognized her as one of the chaperones who had joined her on a high school field trip to Germany when she was a teacher in 1975. Although they had not known each other prior to the trip and had not seen each other since then, they had spent fourteen days in Germany with seven other chaperones and approximately forty students.

Judge Kleinfelter challenged Nancy about a trip that took place over twenty years ago, clearly suggesting that such a length of time should surely not rule her out as a potential jury member. After clarifying questions, he asked her the one final question that ultimately required an affirmative response if she was to remain in the jury pool. "Do you feel you could serve on the jury in a trial that involves Debra Bird in an unbiased manner?"

As Debbie and Nancy exchanged eye contact, they both reflected upon their days in Germany. Debbie was sure she would not be unbiased if the tables were turned. She sensed the struggle in Nancy's face and wanted to tell her, *It's okay that you admit that even twenty years could not erase the fond memories enough to honestly say you could be a neutral, unbiased jury member for this trial.* Debbie smiled and gently shook her head no to let Nancy off the hook. She knew Nancy would not be unbiased when she heard the gory details of the attack on her.

Nancy seemed to know that too. After a long pause and eye contact between Nancy and Debbie that spoke volumes, Nancy answered Judge Kleinfelter with a heartfelt "No." She would not be able to hear the pain and horror Debbie and her children experienced, and not be sympathetic and unbiased. Nancy was excused from the jury panel, and Debbie was moved by having touched the life of another for fourteen days over twenty years ago in such a way that she would not be able to serve as a jury member in the trial of her life.

Mr. Matangos and Mr. Tarman continued asking questions of the remaining jury pool. They systematically took turns choosing the jury members until they had agreed upon twelve individuals and two substitutes to perform their civic duty. Judge Kleinfelter excused the remaining members of the jury pool who were not selected and offered the newly established jury a ten-minute recess to stretch and prepare for the trail.

During the recess, Mr. Matangos met with Debbie and her family to clarify the sidebar that resulted in Debbie and her children being sequestered for the trial. He explained that Mr. Tarman had requested that the Commonwealth's eyewitnesses be sequestered during opening statements. That suited Mr. Matangos because he wanted all witnesses sequestered for the trial. He did not want Tarman's witnesses to benefit from hearing his eyewitnesses' detailed accounts of the attack and the injuries sustained in the attack. Mr. Matangos made his request of the judge to sequester the witnesses for the entire trial. Mr. Tarman promptly objected, stating that he had not asked that witnesses be sequestered during the trial, just the opening statements.

Judge Kleinfelter had a solution to the conflict between the attorneys. Since they both agreed to the sequestration of witnesses during opening statements, he would grant their requests. As to the trial, defense witnesses would be sequestered, and the Commonwealth witnesses would not. Mr. Tarman quickly responded by stating that in order to avoid the sequestration of witnesses, mainly the defense witnesses during the trial, he would withdraw his motion to sequester them during opening statements.

The judge was growing tired of the games being played by Mr. Tarman and declared that he was considering each attorney's motion separately, and one's request would not be heard as dependent upon the other's request. "Right now the Commonwealth has requested sequestration of all defense witnesses from here on out, and I will grant that request. Now, what is your request, Mr. Tarman?"

It was clear to Debbie as George related the debate at the bench that Mr. Tarman was not getting what he wanted. For some reason, he did not want her or her children, the Commonwealth's witnesses, to hear his opening remarks, but he wanted his witnesses to hear their testimonies. She would never know what Mr. Tarman had to hide from her in his opening remarks, because she would never hear them. In turn, however, Mrs. Ferguson and Natasha would not be hearing her and her children's testimonies despite Mr. Tarman's whining to the judge.

According to George, Mr. Tarman went on record as objecting to having his defense witnesses sequestered for the trial and the debate between Mr. Tarman and the judge continued. Judge Kleinfelter asked him, "Why are defense witnesses better than Commonwealth witness?" He was referring to Mr. Tarman's objection on record.

"They're not," replied Mr. Tarman. "And I'm willing to level the playing field and have nobody sequestered, Your Honor."

Judge Kleinfelter ended the debate by clarifying for Mr. Tarman that the reason for sequestration of witnesses had nothing to do with whether one side or the other did it or not, nor did it have anything to do with leveling the playing field. The whole purpose of sequestration was to protect the integrity of the testimony by not having witnesses conform their testimony to that which has gone before them.

Essentially, from all discussions she had had with George prior to the trial, Debbie knew that was exactly what George wished to accomplish by his request for sequestration. The judge had made his final decision on the matter, and all the witnesses were sequestered from opening statements to the end of the trial.

When the jury panel was seated after the ten-minute break, the proceedings began without the Commonwealth and the defense witnesses present in the courtroom. The jury had been thoroughly prepped by Judge Kleinfelter as he delivered the following message to them:

"At the outset of the trial, each of the lawyers is given an opportunity to make an opening statement to you. First, the Commonwealth and then the defense have an opportunity to review the evidence as they expect it to develop from this witness stand during the course of the trial.

"It's important that you realize that what the lawyers tell you in their opening statements is not evidence in and of itself, and you should not consider any of it as such.

"Lawyers, as a matter of professional responsibility, should not represent to the jury that the evidence will show this or the evidence will show that unless they are really convinced that the evidence at trial will establish those particular points. But of course, they never know exactly the way it's going to come out, and so it's important for you to be able to distinguish argument from evidence in this case.

"It's helpful, though, that you have a statement from the attorneys at the outset of the trial, giving you the big picture of the case, so that when each witness testifies, you'll be able to fit their testimony into the big picture. You'll be able to consider it in that context. So it is good that you have this roadmap, so to speak, of the evidence—at least as the lawyers anticipate it.

"Now, after the attorneys sit down and have concluded their opening statements, I look to the commonwealth to call its first witness. The commonwealth gets to go first because they have the burden of proof in the case. By that I mean they have the burden of going forward with the evidence that establishes the contentions in this case that the defendant is guilty of the crimes with which he's been charged.

"So they get to call their witnesses first, and the district attorney will put questions to the witness on direct examination, and then the defense, likewise, has an opportunity to question each witness in a process we call cross-examination. We hope to elicit the facts that will enable you all to determine where the truth lies in this case.

"Now, the defense has no burden to put on a defense in a case, and the defendant has no obligation to testify. Nevertheless, if the defense should call witnesses in this case—and I have some belief that they intend to call some witnesses in this case—they too will be asked questions on direct examination by Mr. Tarman and be subject to cross-examination by Mr. Matangos.

"After all the evidence is in on both sides, you'll hear closing statements by the lawyers. They'll sum it up for you. Mr. Matangos will ask you to convict the defendant based on the evidence presented, and Mr. Tarman will very persuasively, I'm sure, argue to you that you should find the defendant not guilty based on some reasonable doubt that you might have about the evidence. Lawyers are permitted to argue the evidence to you in that manner, and then I will give you my final instructions on the law.

"I'll explain for you the principle of the presumption of innocence, burden of proof, what we mean by the term 'proof beyond a reasonable doubt,' and then I'll also explain for you the various elements of the crimes of criminal homicide, aggravated assault, and burglary. And then you'll have the case to deliberate.

"What is your role in this case other than to reach a verdict? Well, initially, you will be judge. Just as I am here wearing the black robe and I'm the judge of the law and the final word on the law—at least in this courtroom I am—you all will be the judges of the facts and the final word on the facts in this courtroom.

"How do you perform this role as judges of the facts? Well, essentially, being judges of the facts means to be the judge of the credibility. By that I mean the believability of the witnesses as they come before you.

"How do you do that, you might ask? Well, it's not all that difficult, and it's something that you're called upon to do in your everyday lives. Whether you're assessing what your son or daughter has told you about the broken cookie jar, or whether it's a coworker telling you about this or that in his or her private life; whether it's the used-car salesman; whether it's the commentator on television or an account you read about in the newspaper, you are all asked to evaluate lots of things that you hear.

"You don't believe everything you hear or all of everything you hear, and just because these witnesses come in here and testify and raise their right hand and swear to tell the whole truth doesn't mean they necessarily will. So you have to decide ultimately whom you're going to believe, what you're going to believe.

"Some of the obvious ways in which you'll perform those tasks, first of all, is that you have to pay very close attention to each witness as he or she appears before you. Observe their demeanor. Do they appear to be candid and forthright in answering the questions? Is their testimony evasive in any way? How well is the witness able to recall? Some witnesses may recall things differently because either they perceive them differently in the first instance, or, because of the passage of time, a witness may forget or recall incorrectly.

"Ask yourselves how well the testimony of one witness squares with the testimony of another witness and the facts in evidence. Is it corroborated by the other testimony, or, rather, is it contradicted? If there are contradictions, can those contradictions be explained? Does a witness have anything to gain or lose by your verdict? Any bias, prejudice, or other factor that might color that witness's testimony to cause them to shade the truth or put a certain spin on the truth, or even to outright lie to you? Consider those factors.

"As I say, in the final analysis, being the judges of the credibility of the witnesses is something that depends very much on the application of the common sense which you have gained throughout the years, and you don't leave that common sense outside the courtroom when you come in here. You bring it with you, and you apply it to this role as judge of the facts.

"Now, while you are to be judgmental, ultimately, we ask you to reserve judgment until the end of the case. It's human nature, of course, for people to begin to make up their minds as they're hearing something, and that's all right. But what would be a mistake would be if you were to make up your minds before you heard all of the evidence from the commonwealth, all the evidence from the defense, the summations of the lawyers, and my concluding instructions.

"As a famous baseball player once said, 'It ain't over till it's over.' And it ain't over in this courtroom until you've heard all of the evidence, the closing summations of counsel, and my final instructions on the law. Only then will you be able to make a reasoned judgment in this case, so do keep an open mind.

"In Pennsylvania, jurors are not allowed to take notes. That means you have to rely on your individual and collective memories as to what the testimony was. This isn't going to be that long, so you'll be able to remember the things that are important. And one of the beauties of the deliberation process is that while some of you will remember things that you think are important to you, others of you will remember points of testimony which you think are important to you, and when you're together in the deliberation room, you'll be able to share all of those things you think were important in the testimony. And through that process, you'll recall the testimony, which is relevant and material to your consideration in this case.

"Also, jurors are not allowed to ask questions in Pennsylvania. You have to rely on the questioning of the lawyers, and occasionally, I might ask a question if I think something needs to be clarified. Rely on the lawyers to ask those questions that are important to your ultimate role in this case. You may speculate in your own mind. You may have questions and ask them to yourself, what about this and what about that? Why did the lawyer ask a question about this, that, or the other thing? You count on these lawyers to ask the questions that are important to your consideration. If you start to speculate about other things, you're likely to conjure up who knows what in your mind. Don't allow any other thoughts about possible evidence to affect your decision or your role in this case.

"We want you to be comfortable during the course of the trial. We're going to take the opening statements here from each side, and then we're going to send you home for the day. But midmorning tomorrow, we'll take a recess about ten thirty and then again midafternoon. Now, if, during the course of the trial you feel the need for a recess and the clock says it's not time for a recess, you get my attention, and we will excuse you and accommodate you. We don't want anyone here distracted during the course of the trial. So if you need a recess, you just let me know. And I'll give it to you.

"You heard me say before you just recessed a few minutes ago that you're not allowed to discuss this case with anyone, including yourselves, certainly not the lawyers, or the witnesses in this case. You have this big stick-on badge that you were given that says 'Juror' on it. That's really so that the parties know that they shouldn't be having conversations about a case in your presence.

"You're going to be able to go home tonight, but as you walk the hallways or are on the elevators, you'll see some of these people. You shouldn't have any conversation with them, even about an innocent subject such as the weather or who is going to be in the bowl games coming up here on January 1. Any innocent discussion you may have may be misunderstood by someone watching you.

"Also, you'll go home, and there will be family members and friends there at the end of the day today, and they'll want to know about the case to which you've been assigned. They'll want to share that information with you. Before you know it, they'll be telling you how to decide the case. So you can't even discuss this case with friends or family members.

"Also, this case is likely to generate some publicity. I notice there's a reporter in the courtroom right now. This case is somewhat of a high-profile case. That's why we asked that question earlier during voir dire, if any of you have read anything of the story. In fact, I would avoid reading the newspaper at all this week if you are able to do so. I know there will be newspaper coverage, and perhaps even television coverage. We don't want you influenced by anything like that. So just avert your eyes from those news sources that might carry local news of the coverage. Now I think that's all I have to say to you by way of opening. Mr. Matangos, are you ready to speak to the jury?"

Mr. Matangos answered in the affirmative and delivered his opening remarks. Throughout his summary of the crime committed against his clients, he knew he had each member of the jury's full attention. His three key witnesses and the primary victims of the crime were sequestered and unaware of the contents of his opening address. Debbie, Jaredd, and Alisha waited patiently and nervously for their chance to enter the courtroom, knowing full well that when they were invited to return, it would be the time for them to take the stand and testify. They did not learn, until Mr. Tarman completed his opening statement, that Judge Kleinfelter had announced to the jury that his courtroom would adjourn following opening remarks by both attorneys so that the jury members could start fresh in the morning with the witnesses in the case.

That evening did not feel like any other evening that Debbie had ever experienced. Even though Jaredd left the courthouse in his own car to get to basketball practice, it did not feel like a Monday. It was odd for Debbie to have not worked during the day but have all the afterschool activities taking place as if there wasn't a life- impacting trial in session. The girls needed to get to dance, and the reality of life outside the courtroom hit Debbie like the cold air of winter as she left the courthouse with her family and hurried to her car. Thoughts of dinner were dwarfed by her concern for managing the evening activities.

When they arrived at home, Rainie helped Alisha and Ashley get ready for dance. She was always good at seeing where she was most able to help and offered to drive the girls to dance. Debbie accepted Rainie's offer without hesitation freeing Debbie to talk with her family and tune into the six o'clock news. They were all anxious to share their reactions to day one of the trial, and they were interested in hearing how the news reporter who attended the trial would describe the proceedings.

The Trial: Day 2

The headlines of the *Patriot Newspaper* on the morning of the second day of the trial read, "Slashing suspect misidentified, lawyer tells jury."

Debbie was shocked at the title and had instant flashbacks to the first time she heard the news of the attack on TV and thinking in anger, *This was not a burglary.* And now in anger, she struggled in protest of the word *misidentified* as she read on:

> The attorney for a 15-year-old Susquehanna Twp. boy accused of slashing a neighborhood family for no obvious reason told a Dauphin County jury yesterday his client is the victim of mistaken identity. In opening statements yesterday, Robert Tarman said Paul Ferguson was at home with his mother and sister when Debra Bird, 43, vice principal of East Pennsboro Area Middle School, and two of her three children were brutally slashed by an intruder in their Susquehanna Twp. home on April 18.
>
> Tarman said Ferguson's mother and sister would testify they were home watching television with him at the time of the assaults.

He also noted that there was no physical evidence linking his client, the first youth in the county to be prosecuted under a law that treats juveniles charged with violent crimes as adults.

"I have no reason to believe the Birds are trying to falsely accuse someone," Tarman told the jury, noting that it was dark and Bird and her children were in bed at the time of the attacks. "But these are a hard-working family too."

But Deputy District Attorney George Matangos told the jury the Birds endured a night of horror at the hands of a youth they all knew in an attack that no one can explain.

Matangos said he would play the jury the tape of the 911 call Bird made to police as she lay in her bed bleeding profusely from stab wounds to her head, neck and hands. Even at that point she told authorities Ferguson was her attacker, Matangos said.

Bird was preparing for bed about 10:23 p.m. that night when she noticed the door was closed to the room where her daughters, Alisha, 13, and Ashley, 10, were sleeping, Matangos said. As she reached for the doorknob, someone pulled it the other way and began stabbing her in the top of her head.

Matangos said she struggled with the attacker and grabbed the knife blade with both hands slicing through flesh and tendons.

As the struggle moved out into a hallway, Bird immediately recognized her attacker as Ferguson, Matangos said. He knocked her to the floor and stabbed her in the temple before slicing her throat.

Her daughter Alisha saw the struggle and screamed, distracting the attacker long enough for Debra Bird to knock him off her. The attacker chased the girl into her bedroom and tried to slash her as she jumped into a bunk bed and kicked at him. Alisha ran to her 15-year-old brother Jaredd's bedroom to try to wake him and Ferguson followed her there. He allegedly slashed Jaredd's throat from ear to ear, before saying "good night" and fleeing the home. He was apprehended in bed at his home a short time later.

Tarman told the jury Ferguson's mother let police into the home and allowed a search. He also said a hair found in the pants the assailant left in the home was from a Caucasian. Ferguson is Cuban.

But Matangos told the jury they would have no problem finding Ferguson guilty of attempted homicide and aggravated assault. "You're going to hear a case where the victims know who did this," Matangos said. "He rode the bus every morning with Jaredd and Alisha. He played on the same basketball team as Jaredd."

What started out as a concern turned out to be a pretty accurate description of Debbie's understanding of the case. Having missed the opening remarks from both attorneys, she was sure the reporter had done a good job of summarizing their presentations to the jury. She put the article aside and returned to the task of preparing her family for another day in court.

Day 2 of the trial began with the swearing in of the Commonwealth's first witness, Debra Bird. As she approached the bench, she reflected upon how she had changed from the last time she was called to testify against Paul at the preliminary hearing. She did not have splints on both arms, and her hands were healed. She had only scars to show for her injuries, scars that were not evident as she walked slowly past the twelve strangers who would soon re-experience her worst nightmare with her through her testimony. She had waited eight months, and she was ready.

Mr. Matangos led her through her history with Paul, being careful not to discuss what Paul had done to be banned from her home. The jurors could not be told about his previous crimes that got him to juvenile court two times before he attacked her family. They couldn't know Paul's prior crimes, so the jury was not prejudiced against him. He deserved a fair trial. She wondered how many fair trials it would take to put him away. Even though she didn't agree with it, she would avoid discussing Paul's past crimes.

She could tell the jury that Paul lived two and a half blocks away and that he used to be a friend of her son's. She could tell them that Jaredd, Dorsey, and Paul used to play Nintendo and Sega, swim, and play basketball at her house most summer days prior to two years ago. Paul's mother would be unable to tell the jury what Paul enjoyed at Debbie's house all those summer days because she didn't know. If Mr. Tarman had gotten his way, she could have learned the answer to that question from Debbie's and her children's testimonies, but Judge Kleinfelter preserved the integrity of the trial by honoring Mr. Matangos sequestration request. Mrs. Ferguson would have more trouble with that question than Debbie had.

Mr. Matangos established through his questions that February of 1994 marked a change in the relationship between Jaredd and Paul and the banning of Paul from his home. The boys shared the same school bus and the ninth grade basketball season, but were no longer friends after February of 1994.

Having established the past for the jury through Debbie's testimony, Mr. Matangos turned the jury's attention to the evening of April 18. Debbie described the activities in her home that evening, including the times her children and she went to bed. As she retold the details of the attack, from the floorboards creaking at 10:30 p.m. to Alisha chasing Paul from their house and the ambulance arriving, the sound of her voice was the only sound in the courtroom.

Mr. Matangos did not stop her as she retold the details of the attack as if it had occurred the night before. When Debbie finished replaying the attack verbally for the jury and Judge Kleinfelter, Mr.

Matangos asked her his first clarifying question: "Did you have an opportunity to tell Alisha that your attacker was Paul Ferguson?"

"No," Debbie responded as she continued to testify that she had not told Alisha anything but, "Go get John McGreevy." As she reflected upon the moment that she had directed Alisha to get help, she remembered her fear at the time that she was going to die and that she needed someone there for her children. In a more emotionally stable state, Debbie realized how unnatural it would have been at the time for her to tell Alisha that her attacker was Paul Ferguson. It would be like telling her who the person was whom they both saw, knew, and struggled with. No one does that.

She had not told Jaredd it was Paul that night either. Jaredd came to her room with a cloth against his bleeding face and said, "He cut me too. It was Paul, wasn't it?" He may not have seen Paul that night, but he knew it was him without her telling him.

Mr. Matangos asked more questions about the content of the 911 call, followed by details about the emergency room and her injuries. As Debbie offered details of her injuries, surgery, and follow-up treatments and therapy, Mr. Matangos placed Exhibit 1 on the easel next to her in plain view of the jury.

Exhibit 1 was a large floor plan of the downstairs of her home. Exhibit 2 was marked and displayed a large floor plan of her upstairs. With Debbie's assistance, Mr. Matangos pointed out each room for the jury to clearly see the scene of the crime. He wanted them to be able to relive the events of the attack as clearly as he had when he visited Debbie's home and interviewed her and her children over eight months ago. He had walked through the rooms and hallways and replayed the steps Paul had taken inside this home as he brutally attacked this innocent woman and her children.

Mr. Matangos could feel his adrenaline building as Debbie pointed out key areas of her home. Could the jury visualize how clearly Debbie could look from her bedroom to her daughters' room and notice their bedroom door closed in the dark that night? Could they imagine Jaredd sleeping in his bunk bed as his sister tried to wake him for help and how easily Paul slashed his face with the knife?

If they were not there with him yet, he was sure they would be when he got to the pictures of those blood-soaked beds and floors.

But Mr. Matangos instructed Debbie to leave her seat next to the judge and stand next to the easel. With a pointer, she traced the entire attack again for the jury members. She was careful to point out the table with the phone next to her bed that she chose not to use because she was afraid that whatever was blocking the light from her daughters' room would attack her in the dark. She showed them the window in her daughters' room that would have cast light on their doorframe had Paul not closed their bedroom door. And that blessed hurricane lamp that provided the short-lived reassurance that there was no large monster standing in her hallway between her and her daughters that night. The same light that ultimately provided the light necessary for her to see Paul as he attacked her in her bedroom.

Mr. Matangos chose at that point in Debbie's detailed recreation of the attack to interject the pictures. Judge Kleinfelter requested that Debbie return to the witness stand as Mr. Matangos lined up his next exhibits. The exhibits were a series of photographs of the upstairs rooms that were taken immediately after the attack by Detective Fox. The jury could see from the pictures that Debbie was knocked into her dresser and onto the floor when Paul tackled her. Her dresser was out of place, her wicker wastebasket crushed, and the wall ornaments knocked to the floor.

The pictures of her bed and nightstand were much more grue-some. Her phone was streaked with blood from her bleeding hands during the 911 call. She identified Exhibits 7 and 8 as "pictures of the knife Paul used." Mr. Tarman did not object to Debbie's direct reference to Paul, and Mr. Matangos continued. He cautioned her that his next four pictures might be difficult for her to see, but he needed her to identify them for the jury. They were the pictures that Lieutenant Fleisher had taken of her in the emergency room, and they were not hard for her to describe now. They were painful for her the first time she saw them, because she felt so sorry for herself for the condition she was in after the attack. She looked so weak, hurt, and vulnerable then. She was no longer frightened or weak now, and she wanted the jury to see just what Paul had done to her.

As George had predicted, Mr. Tarman had objected to the use of the pictures in the sidebar with the judge before the trial had begun. He had argued that he would "stipulate that it was serious bodily injury" in order to keep the photographs out. Judge Kleinfelter countered that the "defendant is charged with criminal attempt homicide" and "implied in that was an intent to kill. Are you willing to stipulate that the perpetrator of this crime had a fully formed intent to take the victims'—both victims' lives?"

Mr. Tarman: I can't say that, Your Honor. I can say that the photographs portray serious bodily injury. I think that would be overreaching for me to say that at this time.

Judge Kleinfelter: Then I'm going to stick to my ruling because I think the photographs are admissible to show an intent to commit murder, and that is one of the elements that has to be proven in this case, not simply that serious bodily injury has occurred.

The jury never heard those arguments, and the hearing proceeded as if Mr. Tarman's objections had never occurred. As Debbie stared at the close-up photograph of her face, Mr. Matangos asked her if she could tell the jury what the photo was.

"Yes. It's the right side of my head showing the big cut, stitched—sutured—and the part of the moon-shaped, deep cut in the back of my head, which was also sutured. I think my temple wound is sutured also," she continued.

"Do you recall when these photographs were taken?" Mr. Matangos probed further.

"In the emergency room," Debbie confirmed.

Judge Kleinfelter interrupted by asking Mr. Matangos if he was moving for admission of that exhibit.

"Yes, Your Honor." George was admitting them as evidence. Mr. Tarman interjected that he had already gone on record as objecting to the pictures, which Judge Kleinfelter promptly acknowledged and overruled.

Mr. Matangos continued with Exhibit 4, which Debbie identified as a profile of the right side of her face with the temple wound and side cut sutured. He moved for admission of Commonwealth's

Exhibit 4, followed by Mr. Tarman's objection and Judge Kleinfelter's overruling.

Exhibit 5 was handled much the same as Exhibit 4, but Mr. Matangos wanted the jury to be much more focused on Exhibit 6. He had it up for the jury and Debbie to see and pointed to a large cut on the side of Debbie's scalp. "Can you tell the jury when you received this wound?"

"Yes," Debbie answered without hesitation. She knew when each wound was inflicted upon her. "It was one of the later stab wounds to my head, when I started to get a grip on the blade, and he started to stab more on the opposite side of my head," she continued with a glance at Paul with a tone of anger in her voice. "Most of the stabs in the beginning of the attack were to the left side of my head." She still had trouble accepting that Paul repeatedly stabbed a sharp knife into her scalp.

"And the injury that we see here that I'm pointing to on your temple, when did that occur?" George was on a roll and very proud of Debbie's courage to continue viewing her grotesque injuries while explaining them so thoroughly and completely. He recalled how blessed he was to have such a "bright, articulate witness who was telling the truth." He remembered reassuring Debbie about how great she was going to be on the stand because she was "bright, articulate and telling the truth." She was a prosecuting attorney's dream and a defense attorney's nightmare. He couldn't help feeling a little smug as he showed off his star witness.

"When I had fallen to the floor and dislocated my shoulder and was on my side under Paul's body weight, he stabbed my temple."

That was perfect, George thought as he went on to point at an area of redness that extended across Debbie's neck and had sutures in the center. "When did you receive that one?"

"After Paul stabbed my temple and I rolled off my dislocated shoulder, he took the knife across my throat."

Of all Debbie's injuries, this one clearly illustrated intent to kill, and George intended to spend as much time as he could on this one. "It appears to be sutured over the cartilage of your throat. Is that correct?" George led Debbie into the description he wanted the jury to hear.

"There was a knife cut all the way across my neck," Debbie demonstrated by tracing her index finger across her own neck from ear to ear. "The only part of the knife wound that needed sutures was the area that the knife blade crossed my cartilage."

"How is it that Mr. Ferguson created that wound?" Mr. Matangos pressed.

"By taking the knife across my throat from this side to this side"—she again gestured with her hand—"when I was on the floor."

With that response, George had accomplished the visual he had intended, so he went on to present Exhibit 6.

Exhibit 6 captured a full view of Debbie lying in the emergency room with sutures in her neck and throat and a bandaged right hand. It provided a perfect summary of the injuries that Mr. Matangos had just presented to the jury. The bandaged hand in the picture created a smooth transition to Debbie's hand injuries. Pointing to Debbie's bandaged right hand in the picture, Mr. Matangos asked, "Is this what your son called Q-tips?"

"It was my son's friend," Debbie clarified. "Both of my arms were bandaged with my hands in fists creating an image of two giant Q-tips."

Mr. Matangos was more interested in what the bandages hid than the image they created. Exhibit 12 eliminated any guesswork on the part of the jury members as to what was under those bandages. The next photograph was a graphic close-up of Debbie's left hand. A large V-shaped laceration in the palm of her hand had already been sutured at the time of the photo, but the huge gash to her thumb was not. It exposed a bloody separation of her skin from the bone of her thumb knuckle. With George's prompting, Debbie explained to the jury that while she gripped the blade of the knife, the blade cut through the joint as Paul pulled it from her hands.

Mr. Matangos's next exhibits were more photos of Debbie's hand injuries. They clearly showed the gashes to three of her fingers that required surgery for lacerated tendons. Debbie was grateful for the prompt police work that preserved the images of the horror she experienced. The eight months had turned those gaping cuts and gashes into faint scars that were all she had to show for her horror, pain, and suffering. She was grateful for that as well.

Debbie wasn't sure where Mr. Matangos was going when he asked her, "What happened after you fell to the floor?"

The memories were etched so clearly in her mind that he could jump around with his questions and she could pick up wherever he started. "When I hit the floor, I had my left arm back in some way which caused a posterior dislocation of my left shoulder." She remembered the terrible pain in her shoulder that was instant and hard to ignore. Unlike the cuts to her head and hands, this pain screamed for relief. "While I was laying on my left side, he stabbed my temple. My shoulder hurt so badly that I concentrated on rolling off my shoulder and onto my back in an effort to relieve the pain. He took the knife across my throat, and as I lay on my back, I realized that he just stabbed my temple and slit my throat."

It was clear that George did not want her to stop when he asked Debbie, "What happened after that?"

Debbie was not going to stop. She was just recalling how her mind seemed to talk to her at this point in the attack. She remembered thinking *I'm going to die here on my bedroom floor if I don't fight for my life.* Fighting for her life amounted to jabbing the nails of her right hand into Paul's face. It was all she had since her left arm was dislocated at the shoulder and nonfunctional. "At that point," she testified, "I took my right hand into his face. He pulled back, and I pulled my feet through and started kicking him."

George had not fully established for his jury how Paul got the scratches on his face, so he was not yet ready for Debbie to be kicking Paul just yet. "Did you contact his face?" he asked.

"Yes, I jabbed the fingernails of my right hand in a clawlike position right into his eye level. Since the tendons of these two fingers"—she pointed out to the jury members her middle and ring finger of her right hand—"were cut, the two fingers could not flex. In my mind, all my nails contacted his face, but in reality, these two would not have bent to contact his face."

"So you're indicating that only your first and last fingers on your right hand made contact with Mr. Ferguson's face," Mr. Matangos repeated for emphasis as much as for clarification. "And how many times were you able to do this?" he continued.

"Once," Debbie answered. "He pulled back from my nails enough to allow me the room to pull my feet out from under him and start kicking him."

"With the light on, were you able to see what the defendant was wearing?" George was moving on to Paul's shirt.

"Yes. Paul wore a plaid shirt. The plaid was large squares of navy blue and white or black and white. It had dark buttons and short sleeves." Debbie could visualize the shirt as if it was in front of her face there in the courtroom.

Mr. Matangos continued, "Did you see anything else the defendant was wearing?"

"There was a white—looked like a white T-shirt that hung out below his plaid shirt. It was a very big, long plaid shirt, and I saw some white hanging out at the bottom of the shirt. That's it."

"Did you see any pants on the defendant?"

"I didn't see below his plaid shirt," Debbie testified, still recalling that Paul did not look naked from the waist down. Although the police account indicated that Paul had left his pants and sneakers in the kitchen, he did not look like he was missing his pants. Debbie could only justify not noticing he had no pants on the night of the attack by how large his shirt was and by it being warm enough that day in April for him to be wearing shorts. Actually, she was sure that her mind at the time of the attack was working too hard to understand why Paul was in her upstairs and eventually stabbing her to be analyzing his attire.

Mr. Matangos was back on the shirt when he asked Debbie, "Did you give the description of the shirt to any of the police officers?"

She promptly answered, "Yes."

When George asked her if she gave it to the 911 operator, Debbie could not recall all the questions the operator had asked her during the 911 call, so she responded, "If she asked, I would have told her. I was very clear on the shirt. It was in front of my face through the whole attack."

Mr. Matangos was again ready to change the direction of his questions. "The person we've been speaking about and identifying as the defendant, the person you call Paul Ferguson, do you see him in the courtroom today?"

Debbie looked directly at Paul as he sat in the courtroom in his new suit and with the large cross hanging over his tie. "He's seated at Mr. Tarman's table."

George asked questions about the changes in Paul from Debbie's description of him the night of the attack. He had lost weight and looked much smaller, thinner than he had been on April 18.

Judge Kleinfelter interrupted Mr. Matangos by announcing the need for a break. It was 10:26 a.m., and Debbie had been testifying for nearly an hour and a half. It was the fastest hour and a half she could ever remember.

When the jury returned to the courtroom, Mr. Matangos resumed his questioning of Ms. Bird with Exhibit 42, which was a large map of her neighborhood. The street map showed all the streets that connected Debbie's home and Paul's home. As Debbie traced a route from her house to Paul's house, it was easy for the jury members to visualize the two and a half blocks that separated their two houses. Mr. Matangos had her point out the location of John McGreevy's house, the Jewish Community Center, and the Susquehanna River on the map, which he knew would be reference points for later testimony.

Mr. Matangos used Exhibit 42 to paint a clear picture for the jury of the back entrance to Debbie's home and the alley behind her house. The members of the jury did not know it at the time, but Debbie was describing the route Paul took when Alisha chased him from their home out their back door and the alley he would use to return to his house prior to the police arrival.

Mr. Matangos felt satisfied that he had accomplished all of his objectives with his first witness, except for one important point. He wanted Debbie to establish one more fact clearly and firmly in the minds of the jury. "As you sit there today and you look at the defendant, is there any question in your mind?"

Debbie emphatically answered, "No," and Mr. Matangos continued, "That he is the individual with the knife—"

"None whatsoever—"

"Who did this to you?" he finished.

Her "No" grew even stronger.

"How can you be so sure?" Mr. Matangos challenged her, knowing that her commitment to the truth would not waver.

"Because I've known Paul Ferguson for a long time. And he was right"—and at this moment in her testimony, she looked directly at Paul in the courtroom to finish her statement—"we looked at each other eye to eye." And with all the power and rage she wished she had used against him that night in her bedroom, she concluded, "He was in front of me through the entire attack. There is no doubt in my mind."

Mr. Matangos thanked his witness with heartfelt confidence and admiration for her courage and strength on the stand. He had one more challenge for her to hold up to Mr. Tarman's cross-examination.

Not having heard Mr. Tarman's opening remarks, Debbie was unsure of how he would try to attack her credibility, but he did not intimidate her. In the short trial proceeding before her, she had grown to dislike Mr. Tarman almost as much as she disliked Paul and his mother. How could a man with any respect or integrity defend such evil acts of a now-sixteen-year-old boy and support the lies of his mother? She glared at Mr. Tarman with those distasteful thoughts about him as he approached her on the witness stand.

Mr. Tarman's questions immediately focused upon the light—or lack of light, as he intended to establish—that was available to Debbie to see her attacker on the night of the attack. "Ms. Bird, you already indicated that the upstairs hallway light was out, is that right?"

Debbie answered "That's correct" to a whole series of his questions. "That's correct," there was no light on in Alisha's room, Jaredd's room, the downstairs. "All lights were off," except for the hurricane lamp, which he made sure she agreed was closest to her bed and, therefore, the greatest distance away from the location of the "alter-cation," as he preferred to call the brutal attack.

Having exhausted all the questions one could possibly ask regarding lighting short of asking what the wattage was in the bulb in the hurricane lamp, Mr. Tarman went on to questions of time. "Ms. Bird, you indicated that you received a phone call at around 10:20 p.m., is that correct?"

Debbie was back to her "That's correct" responses to his questions.

"And then between 10:20 p.m., and 10:30 p.m., you were sort of drifting off to sleep, is that correct? Is that a fair statement?"

"Yes," that accurately described how she felt between 10:20 p.m. and 10:30 p.m. He must have been paying close attention to her testimony because she couldn't have described that feeling any better herself.

"And when we established this time of 10:30 p.m., do you know that time for sure? Did you actually look at your clock to see that?" His question suggested a coincidence that it was exactly 10:30 p.m. when he followed with, "So it wasn't 10:28 p.m. or 10:32 p.m. It was 10:30 p.m."

"Yes, I looked at the clock. It was 10:30 p.m."

His next question gave her flashbacks to the preliminary hearing and Defense Attorney Foreman's line of questions when Mr. Tarman asked, "Could you give me an estimate, or guesstimate, as to how much time elapsed between the time that you looked at your clock at 10:30 p.m. and when you were getting out of your bed until you placed the 911 call?"

That question did not require an estimate, for she remembered that the record of her 911 call indicated 10:35 p.m. She promptly answered Mr. Tarman's question with a precise "The 911 call was at 10:35 p.m. Five minutes."

"During the time period of the altercation with the assailant, how long do you think that took during your part of it?" Mr. Tarman continued to press the element of time for a reason that was unknown to Debbie.

"From the floorboards creaking until my 911 call was answered, I'd say four minutes of the five," Debbie guessed.

With no apparent transition of thought, Mr. Tarman asked, "Do you normally wear eyeglasses, Ms. Bird?"

"No," she said with pride in her 20/20 vision all her life.

Until he asked, "Do you own eyeglasses?"

Debbie had a sensation of panic because she did own eyeglasses and was sure Mr. Tarman somehow knew about her "splinter glasses" and was trying to trip her up on the stand. Shortly after the attack, she had difficulty with a stitch in her finger. Debbie's sister, Marti, noticed Debbie struggling to see the fine details of her recovering hands, and offered Debbie her reading glasses. Debbie was amazed at how clearly she could see the lines, creases, and stitches of both her hands. Her eyes were changing—a condition she would later learn was insensitively referred to as "old eye." She had not realized, until she put on Marti's glasses, that she could not see clearly close up. It was a shock to her because she had always prided herself on her needlework skills and her ability to remove splinters from her children without pain. She was so good her children brought their friends to her boasting that their mother had a "magic needle" that allowed her to remove splinters quickly and without pain.

Since her children had grown out of the splinter years and she had long ago traded her needlework time for the busy single-parent working-mother schedule, she was unaware of the changes that had taken place in her close-up vision. Being quite fascinated by the new look Marti's glasses had provided her, Debbie purchased a pair of magnifying eyeglasses at the drugstore.

"Do I own eyeglasses?" Debbie asked slowly in an attempt to fill the silence and overcome her fear that she answered Mr. Tarman's previous question incorrectly. "I have a pair of magnifying glasses I use to get splinters out," she confessed. "I can read, but I can't get the little splinters out or thread a needle, so I bought a pair of magnifying glasses."

Mr. Tarman must not have known about her splinter glasses since his next question was, "So you have never worn glasses, is that what you're saying?"

"I have never worn glasses," Debbie responded with a sense of relief that her splinter glasses did not seem to be an issue in the case.

"How about Alisha and Jaredd?" Tarman continued.

"Alisha does not, Jaredd wears contacts," Debbie answered with a renewed sense of confidence. Unless she was mistaken, Mr. Tarman just weakened his own defense by his line of questions regarding vision. He had just established that the two eyewitnesses that would testify to seeing Paul on April 18, both she and Alisha, had perfect vision. The eyewitness with the impaired vision, Jaredd, would testify that he heard Paul rather than saw Paul.

Mr. Tarman's next concern was the glove tips found in the hallway area of Debbie's upstairs. It only took him one question to establish that she did not see gloves on the assailant. Mr. Tarman then reminded Debbie that she had indicated that she scratched the assailant's face and asked her if she was sure of that, or if she just thought she scratched his face.

"No, I'm sure I dug my fingernails into his face," Debbie responded, and he immediately challenged her with his next question.

"Do you recall being interviewed by Detective James Nelson at the Polyclinic Hospital shortly after the attack?"

Debbie answered in the affirmative and knew where he was going with his next line of questions. "And you recall indicating to Detective Nelson that you weren't sure, that you thought maybe you scratched his face?"

She recalled her interview with Detective Nelson and Detective Heilig in her hospital bed right down to her denial when they asked her if she fought with Paul. She was overwhelmed at the time with frustration that she didn't kick him or put up more of a fight when she was on her feet and her hands were not cut up.

Her answer to Mr. Tarman's question in the courtroom that day was as honest as she could recall when she responded, "At the time, I wasn't sure. I hadn't thought through this and hadn't given any thought to the fight until I recalled laying on the floor and realized I was going to die if I didn't fight."

She wanted to tell him and the jury that she wasn't sure several hours after the attack in her hospital room, but she was sure now.

After she saw the pictures of the scratches on Paul's face and realized which two fingers of her right hand flexed and made those scratches, she was very sure she scratched his face. She wanted to tell them how she knew now what she wasn't sure about in her hospital bed, but Mr. Tarman was finished with his cross-examination.

It was Mr. Matangos's opportunity for redirect examination, and Debbie was relieved that Mr. Tarman was done with her. She felt comforted to be back to answering questions from George.

"You say you didn't see his fingers when he was attacking you," George asked. Apparently, he wanted to make it clear to the jury that it wasn't that Debbie didn't see the gloves on Paul that night—it was that she hadn't seen his hands or fingers at all.

"That's correct," she responded. "I didn't see his hands. His right hand was around the handle of the knife, and I was grasping the blade of the knife above my head. I don't recall ever seeing his left hand or the fingers of his right hand."

Mr. Matangos was finished, but apparently, Judge Kleinfelter was not. He was now asking the questions. "You say you locked the doors. Did there seem to be any sign of forced entry when you had a chance to look around afterwards?"

Debbie knew from the informant's account that Paul bragged in prison that he got into the house with a key he had stolen from Jaredd, and she wanted to satisfy the judge's curiosity by telling him that. Unfortunately, her attorney had decided the informant's information was not to be part of the trial, so she answered as honestly as she could. "I didn't get home from the hospital for three or four days, so I don't know what the house looked like the night of the attack."

"Are you one of those folks who would hide a key outside somewhere without telling us where it is?" Judge Kleinfelter pressed further.

"Yes," she always had a key in a key box under her car, and the children all knew where to find it. After talking with Jaredd after the attack, he admitted that his friends were with him anytime he needed to use the spare key to get into the house.

Judge Kleinfelter asked his next question as if he could read her thoughts. "Is that something you think the defendant would have been aware of?"

"Yes, I'm quite sure he was aware of that."

The judge was finished with his questions for Debbie, and he excused her from the witness stand. She was happy to return to her seat beside Rainie, but her new concern was for her children. Alisha and Jaredd still needed to testify, and they had been sequestered through her whole testimony.

As her sweet, innocent daughter entered the courtroom and took the stand, Debbie was overwhelmed by mixed emotions of sadness that Alisha had to experience this horrible crime and tremendous pride at her courage throughout the ordeal. She would do just fine because she too was "bright, articulate, and telling the truth." Debbie watched her daughter as if she had the lead in a two-actor play:

Mr. Matangos: Good morning, Alisha. I already introduced you to the jury panel yesterday, but could you please state your name for the court?

Alisha: Alisha Bird.

Mr. Matangos: Alisha, how old are you?

Alisha: I'm fourteen.

Mr. Matangos: And how old were you back in April at the time of this incident?

Alisha: I was thirteen.

Mr. Matangos: What grade were you in?

Alisha: At the time I was in eighth grade.

Mr. Matangos: Alisha, how long have you known the defendant?

Alisha: All my life.

Mr. Matangos: Alisha, I want to ask you about the night of April 18th. Do you recall—what's the first thing you recall?

Alisha: I woke up to my mom yelling for Jaredd, and I got out of bed and walked over to the door. Her room was pretty well lighted, and I could see my mom. She was lying on the ground with her hand up. It looked like she was trying—like something was going to fall on her, and then as I walked closer, I saw Paul looming over her. I called for my mom… I yelled for my mom. Paul got up and came after me. I turned around and ran back to my room, and I jumped into my bunk bed and made sure that I'd be facing him."

Judge Kleinfelter interjected, "Say that again. You got into your bunk bed and what?"

Alisha answered, "I jumped into my bunk bed so I would be facing him right away. I grabbed a pillow and put it up in front of me. And I started kicking to make sure—I just, like, kicked my leg, and I felt some pressure on the pillow. He was coming after me, and then I heard my mom's voice, and he went away."

Mr. Matangos resumed asking the questions. "What was your mom saying? Could you hear?"

Alisha: She was yelling for Jaredd.

Mr. Matangos: Could you see her at that point?

Alisha: No, I could not.

Mr. Matangos: Where was your face at that point?

Alisha: I was behind the pillow.

Mr. Matangos: When you say you felt pressure, did you hear anything? Was the defendant saying anything?

Alisha: No

Mr. Matangos: You couldn't tell why there was pressure on the pillow?

Alisha: I knew he was pushing on it; kind of just like coming after me.

Mr. Matangos: After you felt the pressure leave, what did you do?

Alisha: I put the pillow behind me, and I got up, and I was just standing there. My mom told me to get Jaredd, and I ran to my brother's room and opened the door. I jumped on him, once again making sure I was facing Paul because he was following me into my brother's room.

Mr. Matangos: After you jumped on your brother, what happened?

Alisha: I saw Paul coming in, and I kicked him. He lunged and said, "Good night," and then he ran out of the room. I followed him, and he ran down the hall to the steps and just ran down the steps, knocking over a picture. He ran through our kitchen and out the back door. I locked the door behind him. I turned the garage light on to see if I could see him cross past the sliding glass doors, and he didn't pass by. So then I went to the front door to see and turned on the light to see if Paul would go that way. I didn't see him. So I went upstairs and told my mom that he had left.

"She told me to go get our neighbor, John McGreevy. I got to the front door and hesitated a little because I wasn't sure if Paul was going to be waiting for me to step outside of the door. I was really in a panic and... because I thought—I was worried that Paul might be following me. John answered the door. He was eating. "And I just started, like—I was just like, 'John, John, hurry up. Paul stabbed my mom. Hurry up.' And he was kind of confused, and he came with me back to my house. I ran up the stairs, and my sister was awake then, and she was crying. John took the phone, and I went and checked on my brother, and he was in the bathroom.

"I saw his cut. It was really—it was a lot of blood. And then John told us all to go down to the living room, where we all sat. The police came and talked to us, and then we went to John McGreevy's for the night."

Mr. Matangos: And you told the police what happened?

Alisha: Yeah.

Mr. Matangos: Who did you tell them did this crime?

Alisha: Paul Ferguson

Mr. Matangos: As you sit there today and you look across the courtroom, do you recognize the individual who did this crime in the courtroom?

Alisha: Yes, he is right there.

Alisha pointed to Paul Ferguson.

Mr. Matangos: You are pointing next to defense counsel at the defense table. Is that correct?

Alisha: Yes.

Mr. Matangos: Is there any question in your mind that that's the person you saw leaning over your mother that night?

Alisha: No question.

Mr. Matangos: I'm showing you Commonwealth Exhibit 11, which was already presented once to Ms. Bird. I'm showing you a photograph. Can you describe what is in that photograph?

Alisha: That's my bedroom the night of the attack.

Mr. Matangos: How do you recognize that as portraying your bedroom on the night of the attack?

Alisha: The pillow that I used to cover me when Paul came at me is right there.

Alisha pointed to the pillow in the picture.

Mr. Matangos: Is there anything else you recognize on that photograph that would indicate it was from that night?

Alisha: The tissue box with the blood on it.

Mr. Matangos addressed the judge: Your Honor, I move for admission of Commonwealth Exhibit 11. If it was not previously admitted with Ms. Bird, I move for its admission now. Alisha, tell the jury again what you did with the pillow.

Alisha: I put it up in front of me to keep him—to keep Paul from hitting me.

Mr. Matangos: Did you see a knife in his hand?

Alisha: No, I did not see the knife.

Mr. Matangos: Did you ever see a knife in his hand throughout the entire attack?

Alisha: No, I never saw it.

Mr. Matangos went on to have Alisha identify more pictures of the crime scene. Exhibits 9 and 10 were photos of Jaredd's bedroom on the night of the attack, as evidenced by the blood and the knife on Jaredd's bedding and floor. Mr. Matangos presented the diagram of the upstairs floor plan and had Alisha retrace her actions during the attack. As Mr. Matangos had done with Alisha's mother, he had Alisha retell the details of the attack by pointing out where she was on the floor plan as each occurred.

When Mr. Matangos moved on in his questioning of Alisha to establish the lighting on the night of the attack, he continued to use the floor plan. Alisha pointed out the windows in Jaredd's room that provided additional lighting while she was in his room. She testified to the adequacy of the lighting from the hurricane lamp in her mother's room to enable her to clearly see her mother and Paul. Then Mr. Matangos's questions returned to details of the attack.

Mr. Matangos: Was Jaredd awake and able to respond to you?

Alisha: When I jumped on him, I could tell he was at least waking up.

Mr. Matangos: What were you saying to him, specifically, that you can recall?

Alisha: I was saying, "Jaredd, wake up!"

Mr. Matangos: And what tone were you using?

Alisha: Hysterical.

Mr. Matangos: And when the defendant came into the room, did you hear him say anything?

Alisha: Yeah, he said 'Good night' and lunged forward towards my brother's face.

Mr. Matangos: Did you know at the time what he had done to your brother?

Alisha: No

Judge Kleinfelter interjected again. "Let me interrupt and see if I understand. Who is he saying good night to, or who was he facing when he said good night?"

Alisha: My brother.

Mr. Matangos: Why did you follow Paul, the defendant, out of the house?

Alisha: Because it was Paul Ferguson. I mean, I know him. He's a jerk, but I didn't think he'd really hurt me. I didn't know he had a knife. I didn't exactly know why he was in my house. I just knew he shouldn't be, and I chased him out.

Mr. Matangos confirmed that Alisha followed Paul down the staircase that night and introduced Commonwealth Exhibit 25. Alisha identified the next exhibits:

"This is the stairwell, and that's my picture that he knocked down. This is the banister he broke when he was running down the stairs. He used it to stop at the bottom of the steps, and that is a picture of the part of the banister he broke off.

Mr. Matangos continued introducing photos of the hallway, kitchen, and laundry area that Alisha testified accurately portrayed her home the night of the attack. When he introduced Exhibits 19 and 20, Mr. Matangos needed Alisha to provide more details.

Mr. Matangos: Did Paul have to unlock the back door when you chased him out of your house?

Alisha: No

Mr. Matangos: You didn't go outside after him, right?

Alisha: No

Mr. Matangos: And when you first went in the kitchen, did you see anything left in the kitchen?

Alisha: No, I was just paying attention to Paul.

Mr. Matangos: When did you first notice something left in the kitchen on the floor?

Alisha: I think it was when we were waiting for the police to come. Either that, or they were already there and I just walked into the kitchen, turned on the light, and saw the pants and shoes and realized they were not anyone's in my family.

Mr. Matangos: What does the photo indicate?

Alisha: That's the pants and shoes that I found on the kitchen floor.

Mr. Matangos: And do you recognize that photo as depicting the condition of the pants and the shoes on the night that the incident took place?

Alisha: Yes.

Mr. Matangos placed Exhibit 1 back on the easel and had Alisha point out the back door of her house and the gate Paul most likely used to exit her yard. She described the alley that ran behind her house to Montrose Street. Having provided the jury with a visual of Alisha's last moments with Paul Ferguson in her home on April 18, he returned to the details of the rest of Alisha's actions that night.

Mr. Matangos: After checking on your mother and hearing her request to get John McGreevy, you left the house and ran to John McGreevy's house. How far away is Mr. McGreevy's house?

Alisha: There are three houses in between ours.

Mr. Matangos: When you got back to your house with Mr. McGreevy, what was your mom doing?

Alisha: She was on the phone with 911.

Mr. Matangos: Did you see your mom's injuries?

Alisha: I saw blood. I couldn't see the injuries, the actual punctures.

Mr. Matangos: What condition was your mom in? What did you see?

Alisha: She was kind of pale, and she was covered with blood.

Mr. Matangos: And where was she in the bedroom?

Alisha: She was lying on her bed.

Mr. Matangos: Were you with her when the paramedics came?

Alisha: No, we were down in the living room when the paramedics arrived.

Mr. Matangos: Were you there when the paramedics took your mom out of the house?

Alisha: I don't know… I don't know when they took her out.

Mr. Matangos: Alisha, other than the blood on the tissue box, was there anything else found in your room or that you saw in your room that shouldn't have been there?

Alisha: There was blood on the floor and a flashlight.

Mr. Matangos informed the judge, "Your Honor, I am approaching with Commonwealth's Exhibit 30 for identification purposes." He turned to Alisha. "Alisha, can you tell me what this photo is?"

Alisha: That's the flashlight found in my room.

Mr. Matangos: Do you own a flashlight like that?

Alisha: No.

Mr. Matangos: Alisha, before you left the house when you first talked to your mom, did she tell you it was Paul Ferguson, the defendant?

Mr. Tarman spoke up. "Your Honor, that is a straight leading question, and that's very leading, and I'm objecting.

Judge Kleinfelter said to Mr. Matangos, "Will you rephrase it?"

Mr. Matangos readily obliged. "What did your mother tell you the first time you spoke to her before you left the house for Mr. McGreevy's?"

Alisha: I came up and told her that Paul was gone. I said, "He's gone." She said, "Go get John McGreevy," And that's all. And then I went out of the house.

Mr. Matangos: After the incident, have you and your family done anything else to receive treatment or any other medical attention?

Alisha: My mom spent a long time in hand therapy for her tendons. My brother is still undergoing a procedure to cover his scar. Other than that, we had counseling. We did that about once a month.

Mr. Matangos: What type of counseling, Alisha?

Alisha: Family counseling.

Mr. Matangos: What is that for? What do you do in counseling?

Alisha: We just talk about our feelings and our fears and how we were as a family before and after the attack.

Mr. Tarman: Your Honor, I really think that's going just a little bit out of the scope of what really belongs in front of the jury. We've already heard they had counseling. To go into the counseling, I would object.

Mr. Matangos: I'll withdraw the question.

Judge Kleinfelter: I think she's basically covered it anyway in her answer. I don't know of any need to go further than that.

Mr. Matangos had no further questions of Alisha. The two-character play was over, and Debbie was so proud of how perfectly Alisha's memories of April 18 complimented her version that Alisha had not been present in the courtroom to hear. Unlike Act 1 of the drama, Act 2 would have an antagonist, Mr. Tarman. Debbie felt the same strong need to protect her daughter that she felt the night of the attack. Only this time, the enemy did not have a knife and she had George to help her protect Alisha.

Mr. Tarman, the antagonist in the play that was unfolding before Debbie, approached the stand for cross-examination:

Mr. Tarman: Alisha, you had gone to bed in your bedroom, where you sleep with Ashley, sometime before you were awakened, is that right?

Alisha: Yes

Mr. Tarman: Let me ask you this. Were you asleep when you heard your mom screaming?

Alisha: No, I was awake.

Mr. Tarman: Can you recall being interviewed by Detective Nelson, who is seated at the next table, shortly after this happened?

Alisha: That night or the next day?

Mr. Tarman: The next day.

Alisha: Yes, I remember.

Mr. Tarman: Can you recall telling him that you were asleep in your room and then were awakened by the screams?

Alisha: Yes.

Mr. Tarman: So—

Alisha: Well, she yelled more than once.

Mr. Tarman: But you were asleep when this all started, is that right? I know you were awakened.

Alisha: Yeah.

Mr. Tarman: Certainly, after you got out of your bed, you were awake. But before that, you had been asleep, is that right?

Alisha: Yes.

Questioning Alisha was not going to be as easy for Mr. Tarman as questioning Debbie. It had taken all the dialogue thus far between Alisha and Mr. Tarman just to establish that Alisha was asleep when Paul began attacking Alisha's mother, a concept they both agreed upon. And Mr. Tarman was not even interested in whether Alisha was asleep or not. He was merely setting the stage, so to speak, for his "lack of lighting" theory. Mr. Tarman would have to phrase his questions more precisely:

Mr. Tarman: And at that particular time when you awoke, Alisha, there was no light on in your room, is that right?

Alisha: That's right.

Mr. Tarman: And you didn't turn any light on in your room, is that right?

Alisha: Correct.

Mr. Tarman: And there was no light on in the hallway either, correct?

Alisha: That's correct.

Mr. Tarman: So the only light that you know of—let me ask you this: was there any light on in Jaredd's room?

Alisha: No.

Mr. Tarman: When you ran in there, did you turn any light on in Jaredd's room?

Alisha: No.

Mr. Tarman: When you awoke, Alisha, you went to your door. You were then looking into your mother's room, is that right?

Alisha: Yes.

Mr. Tarman: And you can remember seeing the attacker on top of your mother, is that right?

Alisha: Yes. I saw Paul on my mother.

Debbie smiled inside at Alisha's feistiness. She knew just what Alisha was thinking and feeling when she changed Mr. Tarman's term *attacker* to *Paul*. Debbie and Alisha did not fight for their lives against an attacker or an assailant. They took turns saving each other from Paul Ferguson. It was personal for them, and they would continue to keep it personal for the jury throughout their testimonies.

Mr. Tarman: At that point, you could see the person's back, is that correct?

Alisha: No, they looked at me. Paul looked at me.

Mr. Tarman: When you first looked, you could see the back; is that correct?

Alisha: No. When I first looked, I saw the profile of Paul.

Mr. Tarman: Did you see your mother?

Alisha: Yes, I saw her first.

Mr. Tarman: And did she have blood on her at that time?

Alisha: Not on her face at that time, because I looked at her face.

Mr. Tarman: Did you remember seeing blood on her face?

Alisha: No, not at that time.

Mr. Tarman: When did you see blood on her face?

Alisha: When she was lying in bed on the phone.

Debbie was amazed at how clearly Alisha remembered the details of that night. She thought back on the moment she realized that it was blood in her right eye from her head wounds that caused her inability to see when she thought she was blinded from the stab wound to her right temple. While she was on her back on the floor fighting for her life, her head wounds were bleeding onto the floor under the back of her head. That was why she had no blood on her face when Alisha first saw her lying on her bedroom floor. After Paul got up to chase Alisha, and Debbie got up from the floor, her head wounds began to bleed onto her face and into her eyes. When Alisha returned to her room after chasing Paul from their home, the blood would have been all over her face as she lay in her bed making the 911 call. If only she could offer the clarification to support her daughter on the stand. Alisha was absolutely right, and there was a simple explanation.

Mr. Tarman continued to grill Alisha.

Mr. Tarman: "Can you recall giving a statement to a female officer who talked to you that night—actually, one of the officers who came to your home?

Alisha: No, I don't remember talking to a female officer.

Mr. Tarman: At all?

Alisha: There was a female officer who was with a male officer.

Mr. Tarman: Can you remember telling either one of them that when you first saw your mother, she had blood on her face?

Alisha: I don't really remember those conversations very well.

Mr. Tarman: In your first story to the police, Alisha, you left out the part that the person came to your room and you had to hold up your pillow?

Mr. Matangos: I object, Your Honor. I don't know what he's cross-examining with, but if it's a police report, I'm sure Alisha never saw a police report. I never asked her if she said anything to the police officers.

Mr. Tarman: I'll rephrase it. When you first gave the story to the officers that came to your home, Alisha, you didn't indicate to them—

Mr. Matangos: Objection once again, Your Honor.

Judge Kleinfelter: Let me hear the entire question. May I have the question again?

Mr. Tarman: Yes. The police officers that came to your home, when they interviewed you, can you recall telling them the part of your story about running to your room and holding the pillow over your face?

Alisha: I told him I don't recall what I said to them. I got interviewed by a lot of policemen.

Mr. Tarman: All right. When you were talking to the policemen who came to your home, can you recall telling them the words you heard the attacker say were, "You're done"? Can you recall that?

Debbie knew that this would be the most difficult part of Alisha's cross-examination. George had discussed with Debbie and her children a report by a police officer named Champaign that contradicted many aspects of all the other police reports. George further explained that Officer Champaign had entered their residence on the night of April 18 with a preconceived notion that he was responding to a domestic violence incident as opposed to an attack by an intruder. He immediately assumed that Debbie and Jaredd injured each other in a mother-son altercation.

George explained how Officer Champaign conducted his interviews with Jaredd and Alisha with skepticism and doubt about their honesty. Debbie had a flashback to a brief discussion she had had with an officer who was not nice to her. She recalled being surrounded by emergency technicians in her bedroom involved in various medical emergency procedures when a police officer entered her bedroom and seemed to challenge her. He asked her if she was sure her attacker was Paul Ferguson. Her affirmative response to his question was not sufficient.

"Police officers have confirmed that Paul Ferguson is home in bed sleeping. Are you absolutely sure it was him?" he asked firmly.

"Yes," Debbie remembered saying with increased assertiveness, "I'm sure it was Paul."

It was when Officer Champaign challenged her with his disrespectful statement of disbelief that "Paul Ferguson's mother insists that her son has been home all evening" that Debbie snapped back in a tone of utter rage. "I don't care what Paul Ferguson's mother has to say. I'm telling you that Paul Ferguson was here and attacked us."

George reassured her during their meeting that she had responded exactly how a convinced witness would answer such interrogating questions. An uncertain witness would weaken with each response by statements like, "It looked like Paul," or "I think it was Paul." But

Debbie got stronger with each response rather than weaker. He was proud of the way she had taken on Officer Champaign, but disappointed that she had to under those circumstances. At the moment she was most in need of medical care and emotional support, a police officer was questioning her account of the perpetrator of an attack upon her.

Debbie felt bad for her children as she reflected upon what they must have gone through that night with Officer Champaign. They were herded into the living room while their mother lay in her bed covered with blood, to be interrogated by a policeman who thought Jaredd and his mother cut each other and were trying to frame a neighborhood boy.

George's point in discussing Officer Champaign's police report with Alisha, Jaredd, and Debbie was to clarify the inconsistencies. Alisha and Jaredd had both heard Paul say "good night" after he slashed Jaredd's face. Officer Champaign's report indicated that Alisha claimed Paul said "You're done." Alisha explained to George that the one police officer was not very nice and seemed to be argumentative. He pressed for a reason why Paul said, "good night" and what he meant by it.

Alisha could only surmise he meant good-bye in the sense that "it's over," or "you're going to die." In other words, "You're done." Those words became part of Officer Champaign's report, and Alisha would do her best to correct the officer's error by continuing to answer Mr. Tarman's questions:

Alisha: I don't recall saying that to the officer. I know I told him that it was 'good night.' It was something that stuck out in my head, because I didn't understand why Paul would say something like that. I know he didn't say 'You're done.' I think the officer took it as I heard something and thought it meant that, but I did say I heard Paul say 'good night.'

Mr. Tarman: But you can't remember Paul saying 'You're done?' You can't remember saying that?

Alisha: No, I don't remember saying that.

Mr. Tarman: Alisha, you've already told us throughout this testimony that you never did see a knife, is that right?

Alisha: That's correct.

Mr. Tarman: Can you remember seeing any gloves on him?

Alisha: No

Mr. Tarman: How about did you ever give any description to the police officers as to clothing?

Alisha: No, I don't remember.

Mr. Tarman: Can you remember the clothing that the person had on?

Alisha: A shirt, a large shirt.

Mr. Tarman: Anything else?

Alisha: I don't remember anything else.

Mr. Tarman: Thank you, Alisha.

Judge Kleinfelter: I wanted to ask you this: during those times when you would see Paul on the school bus, and perhaps at other times, did you have any conversations with him on the way to school or at school?

Alisha: No, I didn't have conversations with Paul.

Judge Kleinfelter: Did he attempt to have conversations with you?

Alisha: No

Judge Kleinfelter: All right. You may step down.

Alisha was finished, and her mother breathed a sigh of relief. She made room on the seat between her and Marti for Alisha to join them. Debbie was so proud of her daughter's courage and poise on the stand, and she told her so. Alisha was smiling and very proud of herself as Marti praised her. Debbie's mother reached out from the seat behind Alisha to commend her granddaughter for her strength, and Pappy gave her an "All right, Lishy" in a proud tone that was slightly louder than he should have been in the courtroom.

As Alisha joined the spectators in the courtroom, the bailiff was directing Jaredd from sequestration to prepare to take the stand. After a brief sidebar involving the two attorneys and Judge Kleinfelter, the judge announced a lunch break for the jury from 11:57 p.m. to 1:30 p.m., so Jaredd's testimony would have to wait until after lunch.

Despite the tenseness of the courtroom and the uncertainty of the trial outcome, lunches were a welcome break. Debbie's children and best friends enjoyed lunchtime at the courthouse cafeteria while Debbie and her family walked to the corner of the block to dine at the Hilton Restaurant. In the relaxed atmosphere, they could discuss the intricacies of the trial and the untold aspects of the case. Debbie's Uncle John and Aunt Martha did not hear well, so they had more questions about what they didn't hear properly than what they did not understand. Debbie's cousin Steve's wife, Ruby, attended each day of the trial but lacked the details of the case. At lunch, she was always trying to fill in the gaps from what she learned in the courtroom and what could not be told to the jury members.

With each lunch break, Ruby would get the answers to questions such as what Paul did to Debbie's family to be excluded from their house two years prior to the attack and many of the details of the informant's jailhouse statement about Paul. Debbie loved Ruby's enthusiasm for the case and enjoyed hearing the thoughts of a person who would have similar questions as the jury members who were hearing about the case for the first time.

John McGreevy was helpful with keeping the adults up to speed on the trial details. Initially, he told Debbie that he did not think that her father, Oscar, would want to make the hour-long trip to Harrisburg each morning for the duration of the trial, but he was wrong. Oscar talked about the trial all the way home each day and all the way back to Harrisburg each morning, according to Debbie's mother. During the breaks in the trial, he frequently engaged in a friendly banter with the bailiff who was close to his age. Debbie's mother was grateful for Oscar's interest in the trial because she needed to be in the courtroom each day supporting her daughter and grandchildren, and she appreciated his support.

When the lunch break ended, the jury was seated in the jury box at 1:37 p.m. Judge Kleinfelter greeted the members of the jury and directed Mr. Matangos to proceed with his next witness, who was already in the stand:

Mr. Matangos: Jaredd, I already introduced you yesterday to the jury, but could you please state your name for the record?

Jaredd: Jaredd Bird.

Mr. Matangos: How old are you, Jaredd?

Jaredd: Sixteen.

Mr. Matangos: Back in April of this year, how old would you have been?

Jaredd: Fifteen.

Mr. Matangos: Jaredd, tell us a little bit about the relationship, the extent of the relationship you had with the defendant. How long have you known him?

Jaredd: I've known him since probably fourth grade, probably elementary school. I think our friendship began because my friend Dorsey was friends with Paul. That's how Paul and I became friends. He lived relatively close to my house, and we had been friends from elementary school all the way up to 1994.

Jaredd's initial responses to Mr. Matangos's questions centered on his friendship with Paul prior to 1994. It was understood between Jaredd and Mr. Matangos that there would be no discussion about what caused the relationship to change in 1994. The jury could know that the friendship changed, but not that Paul cut school one day in February of 1994, entered his house without permission, and stole items from his home. Jaredd also had to avoid mentioning Paul's juvenile criminal record.

While Jaredd described the summer days of basketball and swimming at his house with Dorsey and Paul, Mr. Matangos focused upon the frequency of Paul's visits to Jaredd's house and, specifically, his room upstairs. After Mr. Matangos had clearly established through Jaredd's testimony that Paul was very familiar with Jaredd's bedroom and the bedrooms of his sisters and his mother, his questions turned to the details of the attack.

Mr. Matangos: Jaredd, let me ask you about April 18 of this year. After you went to bed, what's the first thing you recall that night?

Jaredd: The first thing I recall after I went to bed was noise. I don't remember what time it was. I just remember hearing noise.

Mr. Matangos: Could you make out what the noises were?

Jaredd: I do remember hearing what sounded like something being knocked off a dresser and hitting the floor. I heard what I thought at the time was like a voice, but I couldn't make anything out. I remember lying on my right shoulder and my door opening. I remember the light coming in, and that startled me. I felt pressure on my body.

Mr. Matangos: Did you know what was causing the pressure at that point?

Jaredd: Not at the time, but then I realized it was my sister who had jumped on me. She was screaming, "Wake up, Jaredd, wake up!" She rolled onto my legs, and I remember the defendant saying 'Good night.' I immediately felt a warm—like a hot water feeling on my face.

Jaredd indicated the left side of his face with his hand.

Mr. Matangos: Did you see the defendant come into your room?

Jaredd: No

Mr. Matangos: What is it that makes you say, then, that it was the defendant who said that to you?

Jaredd: Because I heard his voice, and I recognized it. I used to hear his voice a lot when we were kids, and I heard his voice every day on the bus. It's like one of those things you just don't forget. I mean, you don't forget friends' voices. You know how you get a phone call, you pick it up, and you immediately know who it is by just hearing them say "hey" or "yo." One word, and you know exactly who it is.

Mr. Matangos: There's no question in your mind that the voice you heard make that statement was the defendant's?

Jaredd: No, I'm positive it was the defendant.

Mr. Matangos: After you felt the hot water feeling on your face, what happened?

Jaredd: Well, I put my hand up to my face. In the light that came into my room, I saw that it was a liquid—it was my blood. I got out of bed and walked down the hall to the bathroom and looked into the mirror. I could see inside my face. I had a puddle of blood—

Mr. Matangos: What do you mean you could see inside your face?

Jaredd: When my face was cut, it opened like a book. I could see down into my jaw.

Mr. Matangos: What did you do when you saw that?

Jaredd: I turned directly around, and I opened the closet door. I got a hand towel out of the closet and immediately put it against my face.

Mr. Matangos: Did you see where your sister had gone?

Jaredd: No, I didn't see.

Mr. Matangos: After you put the towel against your face, do you remember what happened?

Jaredd: Well, I remember when I put it against my face, I pulled it off to see if it slowed the bleeding. I put it back on my face, and then I turned and exited the bathroom. I walked down to my mother's room and stood outside the door.

Mr. Matangos: Could you see your mother?

Jaredd: Yes, I saw my mother. From the door, I didn't have my contacts in, but it looked like she was lying on her back. I noticed she had the phone up against her shoulder.

Mr. Matangos: Do you remember any discussions you had with your mom after you got out of your room?

Jaredd: After I got out of my room, I went to the bathroom. After I left the bathroom, I went to my mother's room. When I saw her, I said, "He cut me too, Mom. It was Paul, wasn't it?"

Mr. Matangos: Why did you say that?

Jaredd: I said that not so much, that I didn't know who it was, because I knew exactly who it was. I just somehow—friends just don't do that to other friends. And even if he was a past friend, I couldn't understand why he would do that.

Mr. Matangos: After you were at your mom's doorway, what do you remember happening after that?

Jaredd: I proceeded back down the hall. At that time, my sister was coming up the stairs, and we passed each other without saying a word. I was going back to the bathroom to look at my face. I went downstairs and had a look around. I walked back up the steps to my mother's room. By this time, my sister was there with John McGreevy. I walked into the room and stood next to my sister. At the time, my mom was on the phone with somebody, and I think it was 911, but I learned that later. She told me to come over to her and check for major bleeding. When I went over to her, I saw canals of blood streaming down her face and all over her and her nightgown and pillows. I tried to move her arm so I could see her throat that she said had been slit. When I touched her arm, she winced with pain and said, "Don't, don't." I told her it was going to be okay, and not to move.

Mr. Matangos: Do you recall when the police arrived?

Jaredd: I don't know exactly what time.

Mr. Matangos: Do you recall if you were downstairs when they came?

Jaredd: Yes, I was in the living room.

Mr. Matangos: Jaredd, the individual you've indicated who said those words to you in the bedroom, do you see him here in court today?

Jaredd: Yes, I do. He's sitting over there. May I point?

Mr. Matangos: Yes.

Jaredd: Right there.

Jaredd pointed directly at Paul Ferguson.

Mr. Matangos: You're pointing to Paul Ferguson seated next to the defense attorney at the defense table?

Jaredd: Yes.

Mr. Matangos: Is there any question in your mind as to that voice?

Jaredd: No.

Mr. Matangos continued to ask questions of Jaredd concerning his trip to the emergency room and his medical treatment. Jaredd described for the jury his immediate care, followed by meeting Dr. Stratus, the plastic surgeon who repaired his injury with forty-eight stitches to his face.

When Mr. Matangos was sure the jury was well apprised of the injury to Jaredd's face, he presented Commonwealth's Exhibit 2 for Jaredd to describe. Jaredd pointed out the relevant aspects of the second-floor diagram as he relived the parts of the attack that he remembered. He pointed out the two windows in his room that shed enough light that night for him to see that the warm-water feeling was his own blood. He clearly illustrated how his bottom bunk bed stuck out perpendicular to the top bunk bed, exposing his face to Paul on the night of the attack.

Mr. Matangos used Exhibit 44, the aerial photograph of Jaredd's house to illustrate for the jury Jaredd's backyard and the location of the basketball net, swimming pool, and the gates in the fence surrounding the pool. He also had Jaredd point out the garage window he left unlocked so he could enter the house if he forgot his key and was locked out of the house. Jaredd went on to explain that he would use the extra house key that his mother kept in a magnetic box under her car if he was locked out and her car was at home. He recalled specifically a time that he used the key from underneath his mother's car when Paul was with him.

Exhibits 9 and 10 were presented for Jaredd to identify pictures of his room on the night of the attack. The knife used in the attack appeared in each of the two photographs. Jaredd testified that he never saw the knife until after the police found it. After hearing his account of the attack, he never returned to his bedroom after he left it to go to the bathroom to see his cut face. Mr. Matangos made sure Jaredd stated that the knife did not belong to him or anyone in his family.

Mr. Matangos presented Exhibit 23 for the first time in the court proceedings. It was a photograph of Paul that was taken by the police on the night of his arrest. Jaredd identified Paul on the photograph and testified that he had lost a lot of weight since that picture was taken. Mr. Matangos wanted to establish for the jury that the picture presented Paul as he appeared in April of '96.

Mr. Matangos concluded his questions for Jaredd by presenting Exhibits 27 and 28. Perhaps he wanted the jury's last image of Jaredd to be the most gruesome because the photos were of the bloody bathroom on the night of the attack.

Mr. Matangos: On Exhibits 27 and 28, how did that blood get on the floor?

Jaredd: That was from the puddle of blood in my hand. It took me a few seconds to run to the bathroom. That much blood was in my hand. I spilled it into the sink. There was probably three times that amount of blood that I washed down the sink.

Mr. Matangos: What else did you do in the bathroom besides washing that blood down?

Jaredd: I washed my hands and knees off because they had blood on them, too.

Mr. Matangos: Thank you, Jaredd. Nothing further at this time.

Judge Kleinfelter: Cross-examine.

It was Mr. Tarman's turn and Debbie's last time to be nervous. She knew that having her children testify was a lot to ask, but the whole ordeal was something she would have wished to avoid for them. George promised her that Mr. Tarman would not be hard on her children because that tactic would not be well received by the jury members. She wanted Mr. Tarman's questions of Jaredd to be over quickly and to have Jaredd back with her for the rest of the trial.

Mr. Tarman: Jaredd, we've already agreed there was never any light on in your room, is that right?

Jaredd: That's true.

Mr. Tarman: And you never saw the assailant?

Jaredd: No, I hadn't.

Mr. Tarman: You couldn't give any description of clothing then, could you?

Jaredd: No.

Mr. Tarman: Jaredd, we've heard that earlier in the evening you participated in some sports, is that right?

Jaredd: Yes.

Mr. Tarman: And so you were fairly tired when you got home?

Jaredd: Yes.

Mr. Tarman: And you went to bed?

Jaredd: Yes.

Mr. Tarman: About what time did you go to bed?

Jaredd: I don't recall exactly what time, but if I had to put an approximation on it, I'd say maybe nine thirty or nine, somewhere in there.

Mr. Tarman: So by the time of this incident we're here for today, you were sound asleep, is that right?

Jaredd: Yes.

Mr. Tarman: You've earlier testified that you heard noises but you couldn't make anything out, is that right?

Jaredd: Yes, that's true.

Mr. Tarman: And I take it from that, that you couldn't hear the voice of your mother or of your sister, is that right?

Jaredd: That's correct. Well, I could hear them, but I couldn't make them out.

Mr. Tarman: Couldn't make them out?

Jaredd: That's correct.

Mr. Tarman: When your sister came in and jumped on top of you, it took you a while to get awake even after that, is that right?

Jaredd: Well, actually, when she opened the door, some light came into my room, and that startled… that, like, startled me. I guess that's when I began waking up.

Mr. Tarman: You began to wake up then?

Jaredd: When she jumped on me, I was getting up. I was pretty close—I was conscious.

Mr. Tarman: Do you remember her jumping on you and saying 'Get up, get up,' and her having trouble getting you up?

Jaredd: Yes.

Mr. Tarman: Do you remember hearing the assailant, the attacker, saying the words—not yelling—but saying the words "You're done."? Did you ever hear that?

Jaredd: No.

Mr. Tarman: When you went downstairs briefly, where did you go, Jaredd?

Jaredd: I went down to the bottom. I grabbed hold of the banister. I turned around, and I looked down the hallway both ways, and then I turned around and proceeded right back up the steps.

Mr. Tarman: Was the banister broken at that time?

Jaredd: I don't recall.

Mr. Tarman: Back when you and Paul were friends and it was pre–February 1994, you played sports together, is that right?

Jaredd: Yes.

Mr. Tarman: And at that time did you ever share sneakers, like during a basketball game or anything like that?

Jaredd: No.

Mr. Tarman: Aside from these words, "Good night," you heard nothing else?

Jaredd: Nothing else.

Mr. Tarman: Jaredd, do you remember coming in the night before or the night of this incident with your bicycle, and maybe coming in one of the back doors?

Jaredd: I don't remember.

Mr. Tarman: Do you recall making—do you recall speaking to Detective Nelson here to my left after the incident, shortly after the incident?

Jaredd: No.

Mr. Tarman: You can't remember speaking to him at all?

Jaredd: I don't remember seeing him. I didn't have my contacts in. What do you mean by 'shortly after?' The following day or right after?

Mr. Tarman: The next day at ten fifteen in the morning over at your girlfriend's. Do you remember being interviewed?

Jaredd: By two officers, yes.

Mr. Tarman: Do you remember telling the police officers that the night before the night of the incident, you may have left the back door open when you brought your bike in?

Jaredd: I don't remember saying that, but if it's on the paper, then I must have said it.

Debbie's heart sank as she recalled how guilty each of her children had felt about somehow being responsible for Paul's presence in their house the night of the attack. Each one thought they left something open in an otherwise locked home that allowed Paul to enter and attack their mother. She was sure that each one of them would have answered the police in the same way if they had asked them how they thought Paul had gotten into their home that night. They would have blamed themselves for leaving a back door or a window unlocked. It wasn't until they read the informant's statement that they learned that Paul entered their home with a key he had stolen years prior to the attack. Debbie wanted to interrupt the court proceedings and share with everyone the guilt Paul had put her children through, but the questions from Mr. Tarman continued.

Mr. Tarman: And when you were just shown a photograph of Paul Ferguson that was taken the night of his arrest, you made the comment, 'He obviously lost a lot of weight'?

Jaredd: Well, till now. Looking at him now, he obviously lost the weight because he looks a lot bigger in the pictures.

Mr. Tarman: Do you recall him being a lot bigger back then?

Jaredd: I recall him weighing more than all my friends.

Mr. Tarman: If I were to give you a weight of 230 to 235 pounds, would that be about right?

Jaredd: That's possible.

Mr. Tarman: This is the first that you've seen Paul since back before the time of the incident, is that right?

Jaredd: No. I saw him at the preliminary hearing.

Mr. Tarman: Other than that, this is the only time?

Jaredd: That's true.

Mr. Tarman: Thank you, Jaredd.

Jaredd was finished with Mr. Tarman's cross-examination. Debbie was relieved and anxious to have Jaredd back with his family in the courtroom.

Mr. Matangos had just a couple of facts to clarify for the jury in his redirect examination:

Mr. Matangos: Jaredd, what size sneaker do you wear?

Jaredd: Ten and a half… ten and a half, eleven.

Mr. Matangos: What size pants do you wear?

Jaredd: Thirty-two, waist, about maybe a 32 length.

Mr. Matangos: Thank you. Nothing further, Your Honor.

Judge Kleinfelter: All right. You may step down.

Jaredd: Thank you.

Jaredd was grateful that his testimony was over. He was ready to join his family in the spectators' section of the courtroom. The next witness was his neighbor, John McGreevy. John had been sequestered throughout Jaredd's testimony and, essentially, had been absent from over a day of courtroom proceedings.

Although John had not heard the testimonies of Debbie, Jaredd, or Alisha, his testimony fit perfectly into their accounts of the evening of April 18. When Mr. Matangos asked him if he remembered where he was at approximately ten thirty that evening, his version of that horrific night began:

John: I heard a knock on the front door. My doorbell does not ring. I heard a knock, and then I heard Alisha Bird's voice say, 'John, let me in.' I opened the door immediately and let her in, and then she said something like, 'Paul... Paul Ferguson. My mother is all bloody.' And then she said, 'Come on.' And I picked up a flashlight, and I turned the TV off, and then we went down.

Mr. Matangos: When you went back with Alisha, did you see Mrs. Bird?

John: I did see her subsequently, but when we walked in the front door, Jaredd was coming down the stairs, and he had a big white towel on his cheek, holding it there, and then I think someone said to me that, you know, the mother was upstairs. And of course, when Alisha had said her mother was all bloody, I said, "Let me go up and see."

Debbie recalled, as John testified, the day she learned that John McGreevy, the chief executive of Polyclinic Hospital, was her neighbor. On the day after Jaredd was born at the Polyclinic Hospital, Mr. McGreevy stopped by her room to introduce himself and congratulate her on the birth of her first child. She learned from the nurses after Mr. McGreevy's visit that she was a very special patient to be visited by the head of the hospital. Little did she know at that time that John's grandson, Jolion, would be born four days later in the same hospital and move in with John, who lived just four houses away.

Debbie would become friends with her neighbor John McGreevy for years to follow that first meeting, because Jolion and Jaredd would become best of friends and spend countless hours playing together under John's and Debbie's supervision. John's daughter and Jolion moved in with John so Jolion and Jaredd grew up having birthdays and homes just four days and four houses apart.

As John continued to testify on the stand, Debbie reflected on how fortunate she was to have had a friend like John for all those years and for having him there to help her and her children on the night of the attack. After her brief reflection, Debbie returned her attention to John's testimony:

John: And I went upstairs and in the hallway to the entrance to her bedroom. I saw that she was lying in bed and talking on the phone, so I stood there for a second. I figured she was talking on the phone, and I didn't want to interrupt. Then she somehow kind of motioned me into the room, and I went into the room. I didn't know who she was talking to, but in a low voice, she asked me if I'd take the phone. I took the phone, and it was a 911 operator. The operator asked me if I could tell where the blood was coming from, if there was any blood gushing. I said to the operator, 'She's just all blood,' and I think I said, 'We need an ambulance.'

Debbie and Alisha looked at each other and smiled as they recalled laughing over John's request for an ambulance. Debbie recalled how they all needed a reason to laugh after the attack and Jaredd's reflection of John's request for an ambulance and Alisha's description of the time it took John to get ready to leave his house to help them the night of the attack provided the first comic relief after their nightmare was over. That quickly, George's next question ended Debbie's pleasant thoughts.

Matangos: Where did you see blood on Mrs. Bird?

John: Oh, it was all over her face and it was just—just all over her face.

Matangos: Did you see any other injuries on Mrs. Bird?

John: No. That's the only thing I could see, except she was kind of holding her head in a peculiar way, and I didn't know exactly why at the time. And then I found out subsequent to that, that she apparently had dislocated her shoulder. She was kind of in pain, so she must have been holding the shoulder as such so as not to move it.

Matangos: After you talked to the 911 operator, did anything else happen?

John: Well, when she said that there's an ambulance on its way, I could hear people coming in downstairs, and I assumed that it was the police. I went down the stairs, and the police and the ambulance personnel were coming in. They took Jaredd and sat him down on the couch in the living room and started giving him intravenous therapy. And then one of the crew, a policeman, said something about, 'You'd better get upstairs.' One of the crews went upstairs, and one of them handled Jaredd's IV therapy downstairs.

Matangos: Were you present when they took Mrs. Bird out of the house?

John: I don't think I was because we were sitting on the—there was Alisha, Ashley, and myself, and we were sitting on the couch in the living room. Corporal Champaign from the Susquehanna Police was kind of coordinating things that were going on. He was trying to interrogate Alisha. There were so many interruptions. Ashley said she had to go to the bathroom, and Corporal Champaign said he couldn't interrupt the crime scene. He asked me if I would take Alisha and Ashley down to my house and keep them there until he called.

Debbie played the phrase "trying to interrogate Alisha" over and over in her mind after John mentioned Corporal Champaign. He was the police officer who treated her and her children like criminals instead of victims of a violent attack. She thought it was profound that John used the word *interrogate* instead of *interview*, and she was convinced that he wasn't mistaken. She and her kids had been interrogated in their own home that night, and she worried that his reports might jeopardize their case.

George asked John if he took the girls to his house as directed by Corporal Champaign, and his testimony continued.

John: I did.

Matangos: What was the condition of the two girls?

John: Alisha was—I would say she was visibly upset, but she handled herself very well. Even though she was upset, she was very good. Ashley was kind of—you know, she was upset, but not to the degree that Alisha was because Alisha had seen her mother, I think.

Matangos: Did the girls stay at your house that night?

John: They slept at my house until the next morning. I had to go once around ten minutes to five because Corporal Champaign called and said he couldn't get the door locked. And I said I'd be right down. It was just a way of locking it that he wasn't familiar with.

Matangos: And other than that, you stayed with the girls the rest of that night?

John: I stayed there.

Matangos: Thank you, sir. Nothing further at this time, Your Honor.

Judge Kleinfelter: Mr. Tarman?

On cross-examination, Mr. Tarman asked John how many police cars had arrived at the Bird home as he left to take the girls to his house. John described a sea of floodlights, yellow tape, and possibly TV cameras as he stepped out of the Birds' residence. With the bright lights shining right into his eyes, he could only be sure he saw two ambulances. He couldn't tell how many police cars, but he estimated "a lot."

Mr. Tarman was finished with his questions for John before Debbie could figure out where he was going with his line of questions. He thanked Mr. McGreevy, and his cross-examination was over.

When Mr. Matangos called his next witness, Officer Daryl Brubaker, Debbie could not recall ever seeing or meeting him. In fact, she could not even remember George mentioning his name in all their meetings prior to the trial. She was curious about who he was and what role he played in the investigation.

Matangos: Officer Brubaker, you were involved in this incident that took place on April 18 of this year involving the injuries to the Birds, is that correct?

Officer Brubaker: Yes, I was.

Mantagos: Can you tell us, do you recall what time you arrived or what time you first began your participation in this incident?

Officer Brubaker: We were advised through county communications at 2236—10:36 p.m. I believe my arrival was 10:38 p.m.

Matangos: And where did you end up going to?

Officer Brubaker: The Bird residence, 3323 North Third Street, I believe it is. I'm not sure at this time.

Matangos: When you arrived at the Bird residence, what happened?

Officer Brubaker: Corporal Champaign had arrived there shortly before myself, and there were several Harrisburg Police officers there already as well. Upon my arrival, I was advised there were victims inside that were stabbed repeatedly around the face. I'm not sure. I did not actually see the victims. We searched around the residence to make sure that the suspect had already departed, which we ultimately found out that he had. At this time, I was advised by Corporal Champaign of the name of Paul Ferguson as a possible suspect, and he asked me to respond to the residence to see if I could locate him there, that residence being 110 Bergner Street.

Matangos: What did you do?

Officer Brubaker: It was about ten of eleven when I responded there.

Fourteen minutes after my 911 call, Debbie thought.

Officer Brubaker: Upon my arrival, I and several other Harrisburg police officers who went along to assist me, began surrounding the house. As we did so, a lady identified as Ivonne Ferguson opened the garage door and said, 'What are all the police doing here?' At this time, I explained we had an incident, and I needed to speak—or if her son, Paul Ferguson, was at the residence. She said that he was, and I asked if I could speak with him. She took me inside the residence and up to the second-floor bedroom. I went inside the bedroom. She had positively IDed him as Paul Ferguson, her son.

Matangos: Was there anyone with you that went into the house with you?

Officer Brubaker: Officer Kyle from Harrisburg City Police.

Matangos: He was also present when Mrs. Ferguson came out to talk to you, is that correct?

Officer Brubaker: Yes.

Matangos: Do you recall what time you arrived at the Ferguson residence?

Officer Brubaker: It was ten minutes of eleven.

Matangos: So you went immediately to the room?

Officer Brubaker: Yes. She led us right up to the second floor to his bedroom. I went inside. He was—Paul Ferguson was lying under the sheets, under the covers. I immediately asked him to show me his hands, which he did. After I saw his hands, I asked him to get out of the bed, which he did voluntarily. He got out. I searched him, patted him down to make sure he wasn't concealing any weapons. At that time, he had on a white shirt and dark-colored sweatpants, as I recall. Upon looking at him, I noticed he was sweating around the forehead and temples, beads of perspiration. I just explained to him that we had an incident going on, that we needed to speak with him; and I immediately took him out of the house, downstairs to the driveway. I stood by there until I was instructed by Corporal Champaign over my portable radio at ten after eleven to take him into custody, which I did.

Matangos: After you left the residence with the defendant, Ferguson, who was still inside the house?

Officer Brubaker: When we initially came outside, several of the other city officers had to leave the scene. It was just Officer Kyle and me. Mr. Ferguson might have gone back inside; however, there was a fourteen-year-old daughter in there and two twin toddlers, as I recall, that were still in the house at the time. I did my best to secure the area with the limited manpower that I had.

Officer Brubaker sounded a bit apologetic at this point in his testimony. It was becoming clear that he needed more help. He took custody of Paul in time to witness beads of perspiration on his forehead, but he was too short-staffed to properly secure the residence. Debbie recalled George being convinced that Mrs. Ferguson had time inside her home to gather the evidence against Paul. He even theorized that she knew from past searches of her home that she could put Paul's bloody shirt in her car and it would not be searched. He believed that was why she opened the garage door that night instead of her front door. She was in the garage hiding the evidence. George's next questions of Officer Brubaker would attempt to establish the lack of police supervision of Mrs. Ferguson and the Ferguson home:

Mr. Matangos: Did you spend any amount of time in the room at all, the defendant's, Mr. Paul Ferguson?

Officer Brubaker: No, it was brief. I wanted to get him up and outside.

Mr. Matangos: After you patted him down, did you take him immediately out of the house?

Officer Brubaker: Yes, I did.

Mr. Matangos: You stated you saw beads of perspiration on Mr. Ferguson. How do you know they were beads of perspiration?

Officer Brubaker: Through my experience at chasing people down or sweating myself. I've seen perspiration on foreheads before.

Matangos: What did you do when you got to the police station?

Officer Brubaker: Once he was back in the station, we put him in the holding cell. I believe I got together a search warrant to the residence at 110 Bergner Street.

Matangos: What did you put together to get a search warrant?

Officer Brubaker: The elements that took place, the exact structure, the interior, and its surroundings.

Matangos: Did anyone search the home after you left and before this search warrant was executed?

Officer Brubaker: No one searched the home at all. I know it was secured by the two Lower Paxton officers who arrived on the scene. Before I could transport Paul Ferguson back to the office. They did that. They stood by and secured the residence.

Mr. Matangos: When you say, "secured," what do you mean?

Officer Brubaker: They stand by inside to make sure the people inside don't tamper with anything, don't move about, and make sure nobody goes in and out of the residence from that point.

Matangos: They weren't with you, the Harrisburg officers, when you first arrived?

Officer Brubaker: No, they weren't.

Matangos: Between the time that the Harrisburg officers left and you and Officer Kyle came outside with the defendant, between then and the time the Lower Paxton Police entered, who was watching the house?

Officer Brubaker: It was myself, as best as possible.

Matangos: And you were standing outside by your car?

Officer Brubaker: Right, because Officer Kyle had to depart soon afterwards. I don't know if they had an incident, but I do know he said, "If you don't mind, I got to break from here." I said, "Not a problem. It's not your jurisdiction."

Matangos: So it wasn't even you and Officer Kyle after you got outside. It was just you and the defendant?

Officer Brubaker: Later on it was just myself until Lieutenant Fleisher arrived.

Matangos: Did you have a description at the time you went to the house?

Officer Brubaker: Yes. I have to say that I… that I know Paul Ferguson just because we learn people over the course of my career in Susquehanna Township. Not personally, but names come up.

Yeah, Paul's name came up in two incidents resulting in juvenile court. And who knows how many other police incidents had Paul's name been involved, Debbie thought as she wondered if it would be a problem that the officer made his last comment and if the jury members caught it.

Officer Brubaker continued: "I was told at the scene to be on the lookout for a black male, approximately fifteen years of age, five nine, from 175 to 200 pounds. He was supposed to be wearing—the only thing I knew was a plaid shirt at the time."

When Mr. Matangos finished his questions for Officer Brubaker, Mr. Tarman picked up where he left off. He focused immediately upon the description that had been given to Officer Brubaker.

Debbie knew her inaccurate estimation of Paul's height and weight would be an issue for the defense to scrutinize. Having repeated the description several times in his formation of questions to Officer Brubaker, Mr. Tarman had made his point and moved on. He highlighted Mrs. Ferguson's cooperation with the police and the speed at which the officers arrived on the scene.

While Mr. Matangos used Officer Brubaker's testimony to emphasize the lack of police help to secure the Ferguson residence, Mr. Tarman saw Officer Brubaker's situation as a break for the defense. It was obvious through Officer Brubaker's prior testimony that, as the only Susquehanna Township Police Officer to arrive at the Ferguson residence, his primary responsibility was to take custody of Paul Ferguson. He did that quickly, resulting in him paying very little time or attention to details while he was inside the Ferguson residence.

Mr. Tarman was prepared with lots of questions about those details:

Mt. Tarman As you observed the defendant, and I take it you were fairly close to him, you got him out of the bed and told him to put his hands up, is that right?

Officer Brubaker: Yes.

Tarman: Did you notice any markings or blood on his hands at that time?

Officer Brubaker: No.

Tarman: Did you attempt to check the clothing at all or—for blood or for any kind of markings on the clothing?

Officer Brubaker: Other than just plain view looking, no, I did not.

Tarman: You didn't see any blood on the white shirt there, did you?

Officer Brubaker: No, I did not.

Tarman: And did you not observe any blood on the pants, did you?

Officer Brubaker: No, I did not.

Tarman: And when he got out of the bed, he was under the covers. So obviously he had to take the covers off, or did you remove the covers?

Officer Brubaker: No. He had his hands—I had him show his hands, and I said, 'Get up out of bed.' And with that, he might have moved the covers or moved his legs, but I didn't assist him.

Tarman: Did you observe any blood or markings on the bed, either the blankets or sheets or pillow or anything?

Officer Brubaker: No, I did not.

Tarman: And you've already stated you didn't notice any cuts or injuries on him, is that right?

Officer Brubaker: Not at the time, no.

Tarman: Did you—did either you or Officer Kyle make at least a cursory check of the room?

Officer Brubaker: Other than briefly looking around, no. My intent was to get him out of the residence, outside, until I found out from my supervisor what's going to be happening here.

Tarman: While you briefly looked around—I realize it wasn't extensive—you're saying that you didn't notice any blood or markings on the floor or anywhere else, did you?

Officer Brubaker: No, I did not.

Tarman: You allowed him to put on a pair of sneakers, is that correct?

Officer Brubaker: I believe so. I know he was in bare feet, so he put the white sneakers on that were in the pictures.

Tarman: Did you notice anything unusual about his feet—markings, blood or anything like that?

Officer Brubaker: No.

Tarman: Did you see any short-sleeved plaid shirt in the house?

Officer Brubaker: No, I did not.

Tarman: The white sneakers that you allowed him to put on, where did they come from?

Officer Brubaker: I'm not sure. I don't recall.

Tarman: The Lower Paxton Township Police officers who arrived to secure the scene, they arrived within minutes, is that correct?

Officer Brubaker: No. They didn't arrive until five minutes past twelve. As soon as they arrived is when we went back to the station.

Tarman: And you don't know—did you go back inside at all yourself?

Officer Brubaker: No, no, I did not.

Tarman: And you're not sure about Officer Kyle?

Officer Brubaker: No, I can't recall.

Tarman: The clothing that he had on that you found and the sweatpants that we just looked at and the shirt—particularly the sweatpants—did you search them?

Officer Brubaker: I patted him down.

Tarman: Did you find anything at all?

Officer Brubaker: No.

Tarman: The pockets were empty?

Officer Brubaker: To the best of my knowledge. I would have pulled it out if I found something.

Mr. Tarman seemed to successfully use Officer Brubaker's short-handedness on the night of the attack to rule out any evidence of Paul's involvement in a bloody attack. It seemed obvious to Debbie that blood would not be found at Paul's residence unless they found his bloody plaid shirt, the disappearance of which could only be explained by George's theory that Mrs. Ferguson had time to get the shirt into her van parked in their garage or Paul's story to the informant in prison that he stuffed it into a garbage bag on his way home. Either way, the shirt was gone, and Mr. Tarman knew it. Officer Brubaker could not account for any details about Paul or the inside of his house because he focused on getting Paul out of the house quickly and safely.

Debbie was beginning to worry that the police work that night was not as thorough as she had thought. When Mr. Tarman's questions for Officer Brubaker turned to the issue of the search warrant, her fears worsened. She was amazed to learn that the search of Paul's house was not conducted until 4:15 a.m. on the day after the attack, over five hours after Officer Brubaker had arrived at Paul's house. When Mr. Tarman presented the search warrant for Officer Brubaker to identify, he asked him to read the items he had listed to search for which included "any bloody clothing, muddy or gravel-coated clothing, muddy or gravel-coated footwear, black nylon top, and any bloodstained knife."

Mr. Tarman then proceeded to systematically eliminate each one of the items from Paul's home or possession. He pointed out that the bloodstained knife was found at the Bird's residence, apparently in the event that Officer Brubaker was not aware of that fact. Mr. Tarman seemed to take pleasure in having Officer Brubaker count in his report all the policemen who conducted the search of Paul's residence and pointing out that at least nine officers were involved in the search. His emphasis upon the number of officers seemed to underscore the fact that they found none of the items listed on the search warrant in the Ferguson home.

In an almost mockery of Officer Brubaker, Mr. Tarman moved on to the inventory of what was seized from the Ferguson residence. One single item appeared on the inventory: a pair of latex gloves. And to ensure that those gloves were not confused with the glove tips found at the scene of the crime, Mr. Tarman posed his last question of his cross-examination to Officer Brubaker: "Are you aware of the fact that those gloves are not the same type of gloves or not the same gloves as were found at North Third Street?"

Officer Brubaker responded with, "I'm not aware of that."

And Mr. Tarman was finished cross-examining this witness.

By this time in Officer Brubaker's testimony, Debbie was feeling like Nicole Brown Simpson's mother must have felt during the cross-examination of Detective Mark Fuhrman during the O. J. Simpson murder trial. She wanted to give Officer Brubaker credit for apprehending Paul, but she was so concerned about the details left unchecked inside the Ferguson residence, that she couldn't help but feel that the police, in this case, were more help to the defense. When George stood up to begin his redirect examination of Officer Brubaker, she had a renewed sense of hope and confidence.

Matangos: Officer, before you stated in response to Mr. Tarman's question that all of the Harrisburg officers left after you came out of the house with Mr. Ferguson.

Officer Brubaker: To the best of my knowledge, yes, they had departed.

Matangos: It is also to the best of your knowledge that Officer Kyle, at some time after you came out of the home with Mr. Ferguson, left as well?

Officer Brubaker: Yes.

Matangos: You didn't—did you call Corporal Champaign immediately after coming out of the house?

Officer Brubaker: I didn't want to sit in limbo there. I was trying to do as best I could with the limited manpower, so I had called to see how the situation was going and what he wanted me to do. It was at ten after that he told me to take Mr. Ferguson into custody.

Matangos: Ten after 11:00 p.m.?

Officer Brubaker: Correct.

Matangos: At the point, you're essentially alone at the scene with the defendant, is that correct?

Officer Brubaker: To the best if my knowledge, yes.

Matangos: His mother, you indicated in direct, went inside the house sometime thereafter?

Officer Brubaker: Yes.

Matangos: Do you recall when?

Officer Brubaker: It would have been the time while I was standing outside. I do not know the exact time, no.

Matangos: Between 11:10 p.m. and 12:05 p.m., when Lower Paxton police officers arrived, you're alone with Mr. Ferguson at your vehicle, is that correct?

Officer Brubaker: Correct.

Matangos: No one else is there. You're outside of the home?

Officer Brubaker: Correct.

Matangos: You indicated to Mr. Tarman that you didn't see Natasha or the two toddlers?

Officer Brubaker: No, I did not, at any time.

Matangos: Did you see into the room that's across the hall from the defendant's bedroom when you went into that house?

Officer Brubaker: No, I didn't. She was pointing up to the bedroom door saying 'That's the door,' or 'That's where we'll be going back to his room.' I kept my eyes on that area in case he came running out of the room.

Matangos: Did you notice whether the other bedroom door was closed or open?

Officer Brubaker: I did not notice.

Matangos: For the fifty-five minutes that no one else was there securing the scene, was that garage door left open, or was it closed?

Officer Brubaker: I think it was closed.

Matangos: When you came down the steps, did you go right out that front door to your vehicle?

Officer Brubaker: Correct.

Matangos: When you left to go to the station at 12:05 a.m., when Lower Paxton police officers arrived, did Mrs. Ferguson accompany you?

Officer Brubaker: No. It was just me and Ferguson, who was then my prisoner, and Lieutenant Fleisher, who was an escort in the vehicle behind me.

Matangos: You indicated on direct that Paul had perspiration on his forehead. How do you square that with the fact that Mr. Tarman asked you what he told you at the time, and he said he was in bed sleeping?

Officer Brubaker: He was hot or warm for some reason. He was perspiring.

Matangos: Mr. Tarman approached you and showed you the clothing when you apprehended him. Did you ever ask him while you were at the house or in the transport to take his shirt off or pull his pants down?

Officer Brubaker: No.

Matangos: Did he ever roll up his sleeves at any time?

Officer Brubaker: Not to the best of my knowledge.

Matangos: Did he ever pull up his pants legs above his knees?

Officer Brubaker: Not to the best of my knowledge.

Matangos: So you never saw his arms?

Officer Brubaker: No.

Matangos: And you never saw his legs?

Officer Brubaker: No.

Mr. Matangos focused his redirect examination on clearly establishing that no police officers were inside the Ferguson residence from 10:50 p.m. to 12:05 a.m. while Officer Brubaker had Paul in custody outside his home. This left plenty of time for Mrs. Ferguson to clean up and hide the bloody shirt if Paul returned home in it after his attack, as George theorized. He even seemed to suggest in his redirect questions that the garage door was closed, and therefore out of sight of Officer Brubaker while Mrs. Ferguson was inside unattended. George also succeeded in his redirect in ending with the jury focused on the perspiration on Paul's forehead.

Debbie was feeling better, but Mr. Tarman still had his opportunity for recross-examination of Officer Brubaker.

Mr. Tarman's last questions for Officer Brubaker were designed to put some doubt into his testimony that Officer Kyle left before the

Lower Paxton Township Police arrived by suggesting that he didn't know for sure when Officer Kyle left. Officer Brubaker conceded that he didn't know for sure. Mr. Tarman also wanted Officer Brubaker to testify that Mrs. Ferguson followed right behind him to the station when he took Paul there. Officer Brubaker could not testify to her following him or arriving later at the station.

George Matangos had told Debbie that Mrs. Ferguson had not gone directly to the station. In fact, his theory about the missing shirt included Mrs. Ferguson having the shirt hidden in her van and dropping it into a dumpster on her way to the station. Debbie could not remember how George knew that, but according to Officer Brubaker's testimony, George had not gotten that information from him. Obviously, he was not aware of Mrs. Ferguson's actions while he had Paul outside their residence, let alone after he took Paul to the station.

When Mr. Tarman finished his questions for Officer Brubaker, Judge Kleinfelter asked one question of him. The judge asked Officer Brubaker for his opinion as to how long it would take someone to walk, jog, or move quickly from the Bird residence to the Ferguson residence.

Officer Brubaker's answer was quick and simple: "Within a minute."

Judge Kleinfelter had his answer and was ready for Mr. Matangos's next witness.

As Detective Kevin Fox was sworn in, Debbie was looking forward to his testimony. He was part of their prosecution team, and she thought she knew all he would be telling the jury. As soon as Detective Fox's testimony began, Debbie was fascinated by all she hadn't heard before. Detective Fox began by explaining how the evidence at the Bird residence had been collected by the We Team, of which he was a member.

The We Team was comprised of evidence technicians from different police departments who have specialized training in gathering evidence. When Detective Fox testified that he was called to process the crime scene at 3323 North Third Street, Mr. Matangos asked him, "What does that mean, process the crime scene?"

Detective Fox defined it as fingerprinting, photography work, and gathering evidence one at a time. Marking it, numbering it, and photographing it before putting it into a bag to take from the crime scene. When he added, "We mostly do homicide scenes, rape scenes, and any serious crimes, Debbie was reminded again of how serious the attack on her family was by police standards.

After Detective Fox provided the introductory information that Mr. Matangos felt was necessary for the jury to understand his role in investigating the crime, Mr. Matangos asked Detective Fox to describe the crime scene from the beginning as he recalled first entering the Bird home. It was eerie and chilling for Debbie to relive the night of the attack through the eyes of the detective in charge of recreating the crime by the evidence left behind. He saw Alisha's picture on the staircase and the broken banister as he went up the stairs. He looked into the bathroom and saw the bloody sink. He found the assault knife lying on Jaredd's floor right where Paul dropped it as he said "Good night" and fled the scene. A wave of sadness came over Debbie as Detective Fox described her bedroom as having "quite a bit of blood on the bed and blood-soaked pillows, blankets, and sheets." The horror was over, but those images were permanently imprinted in her mind.

As Mr. Matangos moved Detective Fox onto the specifics of the evidence he collected, Debbie was amazed and impressed with the thoroughness and professionalism of Detective Fox's work. Mr. Matangos used the photographs he had already entered as Commonwealth exhibits to interject the new evidence Detective Fox had provided. Exhibit 10 was the picture of the knife on Jaredd's bedroom floor. Detective Fox testified that the photograph accurately portrayed the location and position that the knife was found at the crime scene. Then Mr. Matangos instructed Detective Fox to open his first evidence bag and describe its contents.

Detective Fox presented the knife pictured in Exhibit 10, which had a six-inch blade and a six-inch handle. When he described it as a "folding knife, or pocketknife, that comes together," Judge Kleinfelter interjected, "That's a pocketknife?" to express his skepticism that a knife that large could be called a pocketknife.

Detective Nelson was quick to pick up on the judge's challenge and responded, "A big pocketknife," providing a moment of levity in an otherwise-sobering testimony. The knife was marked as Commonwealth Exhibit 32 and admitted as evidence.

Detective Fox and Mr. Matangos soon established a pattern of presenting photograph exhibits followed by the matching actual item from the evidence bag. The flashlight Paul dropped in the girls' laundry basket was admitted as Exhibit 33. It was not found until "0802 hours on the 19th of April," according to Detective Fox's detailed records. He explained that the flashlight was actually found the morning after the incident.

Commonwealth Exhibit 19, the picture of the pants and sneakers found on the kitchen floor, provided a perfect segue to the admission of the pants as Exhibit 34 and the black sneakers as Exhibit 35. Mr. Matangos made sure to have Detective Fox read the size of the pants (XL) and the size of the black sneakers (size 13) to the jury, knowing full well that the sizes matched the defendant perfectly.

As Mr. Matangos's questions for Detective Fox regarding the evidence moved from general items to items more specific to Paul Ferguson, Debbie focused carefully on every detail of the testimony:

Matangos: Detective, you've already indicated that you were present at the Susquehanna Police Station when you ordered photographs to be taken of the defendant, is that correct?

Detective Fox: That's correct.

Matangos: Commonwealth's Exhibit 23 is a photograph of Mr. Ferguson. Do you recognize it?

Detective Fox: Yes, I do.

Matangos: How do you recognize it?

Detective Fox: I was present when the photograph was taken.

Matangos: Is that the clothing he was wearing when he was brought to the police station?

Detective Fox: Yes.

Matangos: Detective Fox, I'm showing you Commonwealth Exhibit 23-A for identification. What is the photograph of?

Detective Fox: That's a photograph of Paul Ferguson without his shirt.

Matangos: Were you present when that photo was taken?

Detective Fox: Yes, I was present when all photographs were taken of Paul Ferguson.

Matangos: And when did this take place?

Detective Fox: I believe it was around one o'clock in the morning on the day after the incident.

Matangos: And, again, where was it taken?

Detective Fox: At the Susquehanna Township Police Station.

Matangos: Showing you Commonwealth's 23-B for identification purposes.

Detective Fox: That would be the photograph showing part of Mr. Ferguson's right arm.

Matangos: Anything significant about that photograph?

Detective Fox: Yes. I would describe his arm as having four distinct scratch marks on his arm below the elbow, sort of on the forearm.

Matangos: Again, 23-C for identification purposes. Do you recognize it?

Detective Fox: Yes. This is also a photograph of Mr. Ferguson. It's his leg.

Matangos: Is there anything significant about that photograph?

Detective Fox: Yes. There are some obvious scratches on his leg.

Matangos: Detective, showing you Commonwealth's Exhibit 23-D. Could you describe that?

Detective Fox: Yes. Those are also scratches on Mr. Ferguson, his arm. Looks like it might be a slight scratch on his torso on his right side.

Matangos: Commonwealth Exhibit 23-E and 23-F for identification. What are those photographs of?

Detective Fox: Those are photographs of Mr. Ferguson's leg just above the right knee and towards the inside of the thigh. There's an obvious abrasion or wound on that part of his leg.

Matangos: And, Detective, Exhibit 23-G for identification purposes, what is that?

Detective Fox: Another photograph of Mr. Ferguson. His arm. And there are scratches on that and a ruler also indicating the length of the scratches.

Matangos: And, finally, the last of this series, Commonwealth Exhibit 23-H for identification, what is that?

Detective Fox: That's a photograph of Mr. Ferguson's right foot. It shows an injury to one of his toes.

Detective Fox testified that all the pictures were taken at the same time, at approximately 1:45 a.m. on the nineteenth of April. He admitted that he was present for all the photographs and that they fairly and accurately depicted the condition of Mr. Ferguson at the time the pictures were taken. He had several of the photographs blown up at Mr. Matangos's request, and they were ready to present them to the jury.

Matangos: Detective, I'm approaching you with Commonwealth's Exhibit 14 for identification. I'm going to ask you to tell us what that is.

Detective Fox: It's a photograph taken of Mr. Ferguson's face, showing some scratches on the forehead and one across the side of his nose and close to his left eye.

The scratches she put on his face, Debbie thought. George wanted the jury to see a blown-up picture of the defense wounds she made on her attacker. She was so grateful for George and Detective Fox.

Matangos: I'm approaching with what's marked Commonwealth's Exhibit 15 for identification. What is it?

Detective Fox: Mr. Ferguson, on his legs, the area of the knee and just below the knee indicating—I would describe it as an abrasion.

The abrasions on Paul's knees when he tackled her and landed his 240 pounds onto her hardwood bedroom floor. Debbie wondered if the jury members were seeing and understanding why George chose certain pictures to blow up for emphasis.

Matangos: Commonwealth Exhibits 16 and 17 for identification—can you tell us what those are?

Detective Fox: Exhibit 16 is a picture of Mr. Ferguson's—of one of his legs, I believe his right leg. It shows scratches on his leg and some blood—looks like a blood smear.

Matangos: And Commonwealth 17 for identification—what does it indicate?

Detective Fox: This is a picture, a blown-up picture of Mr. Ferguson's legs from the thighs down to the ankles, a frontal view of his legs indicating the bruises and abrasions on his knees.

Debbie was sure George was displaying the scratches her toenails made on Paul's thighs after she jabbed her nails into his face and pulled her legs through his straddled legs and started to kick. In retrospect, she wished she had realized that her nails in his face and her kicks in his thighs had left scratches in time to have had the contents under her fingernails and toenails analyzed. She realized she was beating herself up again for not doing more and remembered Deb Salem's words: *You did everything you had to do to survive.* She would survive without the DNA evidence under her nails.

As Mr. Matangos finished clearly displaying his blown-up pictures of Paul to the jury, he came full circle back to Mr. Tarman's questions of Officer Brubaker regarding Paul's injuries:

Matangos: Detective, were any of these wounds visible when the defendant appeared at the police station and you first saw him?

Detective Fox: Just the one on his nose and on his forehead.

Matangos: The others were not evident until you had him remove his clothing?

Detective Fox: That's correct.

Matangos: Approaching you now, Detective, with items marked Commonwealth Exhibit 38 and 39. Showing you Commonwealth Exhibit 38 first. What is that?

Detective Nelson: This is the right shoe that Mr. Ferguson was wearing when we photographed him.

Matangos: And what is Commonwealth's Exhibit 39?

Detective Fox: That would be his left shoe.

Matangos: Those two items that you're holding are the sneakers that Mr. Ferguson was wearing in the photograph, is that correct?

Detective Fox: That's correct.

Matangos: Is there any indication of a make or model of those sneakers?

Detective Fox: These are Reebok sneakers.

Matangos: What color are they?

Detective Fox: They're white.

Matangos: And is there a size indication in those sneakers?

Detective Fox: Yes, they're size 13.

Did the jury make the connection? Debbie wondered as George so brilliantly revealed that the sizes of the white sneakers Paul put on to go to the police station and the black sneakers left in her kitchen by the attacker were both 13. She could only hope as she wondered just how much longer Detective Fox would be on the stand.

Mr. Matangos left the pictures of Paul and his personal items and quickly focused Detective Fox's attention on the glove tips found on the floor at the entrance to Debbie's bedroom. Detective Fox described the gloves as those commonly used to wash dishes. They were yellow on the outside and beige on the inside. Since his investigation indicated that the glove tips did not belong to any members of the Bird family or the emergency medical technicians, Detective Fox concluded that "the perpetrator may have been wearing gloves, and during the struggle, the tips may have been pulled off of the glove."

Mr. Tarman had not objected to any aspect of Mr. Matangos's direct examination of Detective Fox until he asked Detective Fox if he had an opinion as to how the glove tips had gotten to the floor of the entrance to Mrs. Bird's bedroom:

Detective Fox: Yes, I do have an opinion.

Matangos: Could you state that, please?

Detective Fox: During the struggle with the defendant, Mr. Ferguson, the victim, Mrs. Bird…

Mr. Tarman: Your Honor, I would object to the defendant being named as the guilty party. We're not to that point yet in the case."

Judge Kleinfelter: Well, we'll substitute *perpetrator*.

Detective Fox: As the perpetrator and Mrs. Bird struggled, as she indicated, she grabbed the knife at least on one occasion and had a real strong grip on it. I believe her words were that she wasn't going to let it go, or she was going to pull it from his hands. I believe that when she grabbed the knife, she actually had part of the glove also. As she indicated, it took him a lot of effort to pull the knife from her hands. Had she not had hold of those gloves, I don't think it would have taken a lot of force to pull a knife blade through somebody's hands that were wet with blood, no matter how hard she was gripping it. I believe the assailant had gloves on at the time, and as she was grabbing for the knife to pull it out of his hand, she was grabbing the tips of the glove, and I think the tips came off then.

Matangos: Your Honor, that's all I have on that.

It was 4:25 p.m., and a good time to recess for the day. Judge Kleinfelter reminded the jury not to discuss the case or permit anyone to discuss it with them. They were directed not to read any news accounts of the trial or watch any television. "Put the case out of your mind, and we'll see you here tomorrow at 9:00 a.m. Have a nice evening," were Judge Kleinfelter's parting words to conclude the second day of the trial.

With day 2 of the trial behind her, Debbie wanted to put the case out of her mind and have a nice evening. She needed to focus on the evening activities, and she knew she'd be too busy to read the paper or watch TV. After she took Alisha and Ashley to dance practice, Debbie went to Jaredd's home basketball game. She sat in the bleachers feeling like she somehow didn't belong there. She was at such an important and critical point in her life, yet she was sitting at a basketball game trying to focus on her son and his team's success. Winning or losing a basketball game seemed so trivial when compared to winning or losing the trial that consumed her every waking thought.

As she looked around her, life seemed to be normal for the other parents who came to watch their children. She was sure they had no idea what her family was experiencing until Reggie Guy, the star of the varsity team, saw her and made his way up the bleachers to talk with her. He wanted to know what he missed that day at the trial. He apologized with sincere regret that he could not attend the second day. Having attended on Monday and missing school, he had to get back to classes. Debbie could tell by his interest in hearing all the details he had missed that he wasn't just being kind. He really wanted to be there.

Debbie thanked him for coming to the trial the previous day and took the opportunity to share with Reggie her appreciation for his visit to see her in the hospital. She told him how much her mother was touched by the caring and compassion he expressed on that visit. Reggie was a sweet guy who, once again, went out of his way to express his concern for Debbie and her family.

Before the game ended, Debbie had experienced many gestures of support, the most significant being Reggie's and Dr. Holtzman's, the superintendent of Susquehanna Township School District. It was not unusual for Debbie to have a conversation with the superintendent, Tom. They were on a first-name basis as fellow school administrators, neighbors, and friends. Tom's wife, Dolly, and Debbie had been in the same neighborhood babysitting coop for the years when their children were small. In fact, Debbie had babysat for the Holtzmans' children, Jessica and Zack; and Dolly had baby- sat for Debbie's three children in the past.

Tom would acknowledge Debbie whenever they ran into each other at school events, but this visit from Tom had a definite agenda. He wanted to see how the trial was going, but more importantly, he wanted to share an unusual call he had gotten from Mr. Tarman on Monday after the first day of the trial. He confessed that he knew Tarman personally, having shared some real estate investments with him. Debbie tried not to hold that against Tom as he continued his discussion. He stated that he was not surprised to hear from Mr. Tarman, but he was shocked when Mr. Tarman asked him why he had allowed so many Susquehanna students to attend the trial. Mr. Tarman complained that they were all supporters of the Bird family, suggesting further that Tom was somehow responsible for encouraging the support.

Tom was diplomatic and had a personality and nature that was loved by all. He explained to his friend that this incident had a serious and profound impact on his student body, staff, and community. As far as the students' need or choice to attend the trial, the district attendance policies permitted students, with parental permission, to be excused from school to attend a trial of this significance. He further reminded Mr. Tarman that the level of support for the Bird family was a tribute to the character and quality of the family.

Debbie thanked Dr. Holtzman for his support of her and her family throughout his conversation with Mr. Tarman. She appreciated his friendship and the time he took to be positive with her children when he saw them in school and at school events. As far as Mr. Tarman was concerned, she continued to find his actions and demeanor distasteful. Unfortunately, she would be seeing him at 9:00 a.m. the next day for day 3 of the trial.

Chapter XXIX

The Trial: Day 3

The third day of the trial began with Detective Fox on the stand and Mr. Matangos resuming his direct examination. Detective Fox explained the process used for fingerprinting items collected as evidence. He presented the glove tips and indicated the black powder that still lingered on the tip surfaces. He testified that they were unsuccessful at finding any fingerprints on them. He admitted that their lack of findings was not surprising since the rubber surface did not lend itself well to the fingerprinting process.

Mr. Matangos presented a picture of Paul's bedroom and referred to it as Exhibit 24-1. Detective Fox identified the picture as accurately portraying the room at the time the search warrant was executed. The picture showed Paul's bed, hardwood floor, several balled-up tissues, and a pair of latex gloves. Detective Fox indicated that they decided to take the gloves as evidence. He went on to describe smaller items on the floor of Paul's bedroom that could barely be identified on the picture as a kitchen spoon, an empty chip bag, a can of Behold dusting spray, and a dead mouse. Referring to the dead mouse, Detective Fox said, "It appeared to be—it had been there for some time and was in a decomposed state."

Just as Debbie was thoroughly grossed out and confused about the significance of the dead mouse, Mr. Matangos moved on to a totally different subject of evidence. He asked Detective Fox to explain how he measured the distance between the Bird residence and the Ferguson home. Detective Fox described a device used by the Traffic Safety Unit to investigate traffic accidents. He testified that the device measured twelve hundred and seventy feet, or two-tenths of a mile, between the two residences. He walked the distance and timed it to take four minutes and fifty-three seconds. He then described taking a "semi-fast jog" from the victim's home to the defendant's home, resulting in a time of one minute and fifty-three seconds. Mr. Matangos asked Detective Fox a series of questions that resulted in another objection from Mr. Tarman.

Matangos: Would you describe that you ran at the speed, say, a perpetrator would, leaving the scene of the crime?

Detective Fox: No.

Matangos: Did you run slower or faster?

Detective Fox: A lot slower.

Matangos: And these, again, are personal observations from your own experience?

Detective Fox: From my own experience.

Matangos: You had an opportunity to observe Mr. Ferguson that night when you got to the police station?

Detective Fox: Yes, I did.

Matangos: Do you have an opinion as to how long it would have taken Mr. Ferguson to get from the Bird house to the Ferguson house?

Mr. Tarman: Your honor, I think we're going a little bit too far. I mean, my goodness, this is really subjective.

Judge Kleinfelter: I would have to sustain the objection. You would not have any foundation for that unless he timed the defendant running at some point.

Debbie started to see a pattern to George's questions. He would push an issue as far as Mr. Tarman would allow him to go without an objection. When Mr. Tarman's objection was sustained by the judge, George moved on to a new subject. He was revisiting the pants and sneakers in the kitchen. When he asked Detective Fox if he had an opinion as to why the perpetrator had left his pants and sneakers in the kitchen, Mr. Tarman immediately objected. Debbie was sure Detective Fox would have speculated that Paul took his pants and sneakers off in the kitchen prior to going upstairs because he intended to rape Alisha, consistent with the informant's statement; but Mr. Tarman was not going to let that happen. Without his testimony, the theory of rape as a motive would not be presented to the jury. George tried, but could not get that by the talented and alert defense attorney.

Mr. Matangos was finished with Detective Fox's direct examination, and Debbie was so proud and grateful for Detective Fox's expertise and careful and thorough handling of the evidence. Little did she know, but Mr. Tarman was about to destroy her confidence in the thoroughness of the police work.

Mr. Tarman began slowly and pleasantly with his cross-examination of Detective Fox. He used Detective Fox to confirm that Mrs. Ferguson was cooperative throughout the search of her residence. Detective Fox did recall that she had asked them not to wake the children, that one of the two toddlers had been ill, and he was really careful not to wake them. Mr. Tarman seemed to jump on the statement and made sure that Detective Fox repeated that Mrs. Ferguson had told him that one of the toddlers was ill.

Mr. Tarman proceeded to have Detective Fox attest to the thorough search of the Ferguson residence, that all the areas of the Ferguson residence were searched, including the garage and the basement. Mr. Tarman made sure that Detective Fox testified that no evidence of value was obtained from the Ferguson residence during the search. In fact, the latex gloves that were recovered from the defendant's bedroom were not like the glove tips found in the victim's residence, and Mr. Tarman had Detective Fox repeat that fact several times throughout his cross-examination.

Mr. Tarman made sure the jury was not misled by the latex gloves taken from the Ferguson residence by suggesting that the police had no reason to take the latex gloves from the residence.

By the time Mr. Tarman moved on to the items Detective Fox had sent to the Pennsylvania State Police Crime Lab, he was coming off as arrogant. Detective Fox had to continue to admit finding no evidence that pointed to the defendant despite his efforts to send the evidence to a higher level of examination. Detective Fox's testimony turned into a series of questions from Mr. Tarman resulting in a negative response.

"Were there any signs, markings, or tears on the defendant's white sweatshirt?"

"No."

"Did they find dirt on the defendant's white Reebok sneakers that matched the dirt on the soles of the black sneakers left by the perpetrator?"

"No."

"Did they analyze the dirt around the Ferguson residence to see if it matched the dirt found on the black sneakers?"

"No."

"Did the analysis of the blood at the crime scene match the defendant's blood?"

"No."

"Did they try to determine the maker or manufacturer of the glove tips found at the scene of the crime?"

"No."

Mr. Tarman moved systematically through his questions, knowing full well that the police found no fingerprints or blood analysis to link his client to the crime. Even though Debbie knew that Paul didn't leave fingerprints because he wore gloves, and that there was no blood evidence because he only sustained scratches at the crime scene, she was concerned that Mr. Tarman was succeeding in making Detective Fox and his evidence analysis look incomplete, inconclusive, and inept. Should the police have attempted to try to locate the manufacturer of the glove that matched the glove tips, the flashlight, or the knife? Did they do a thorough-enough job if they couldn't find fingerprints on any of the doorknobs, the broken banister piece, and the staircase wall that Paul clearly touched on his way out of her house without tips on his glove? When Mr. Tarman finished his series of questions of Detective Fox with, "So you have nothing—no fingerprints, no blood evidence, and no DNA analysis done," Debbie was back on the roller coaster of emotions. She just went from the high excitement over Detective Fox's responses to Mr. Matangos to the low of what appeared to be a failure of the police to obtain any evidence against Paul Ferguson. And Mr. Tarman was not finished yet.

Detective Fox testified that he found no blood on the pants and shirt Paul was wearing at the time he was taken into custody. And oddly enough, Mr. Tarman began to have Detective Fox state the brands of the items he had confiscated as evidence. Paul's shirt was a Nike, and his white sneakers were Reeboks. Mr. Tarman made a point to revisit the pants and the black sneakers left at the crime scene in order for Detective Fox to establish for the jury that they were not brand-named items.

Just when Debbie felt that it couldn't get any worse for the prosecution, Mr. Tarman presented evidence that Detective Fox had collected and used it in the defense of his client:

Mr. Tarman: Detective Fox, I'm putting in front of you two photographs—the photographs being Defense Exhibit 4 and Defense Exhibit 4-A. Could you identify what those photographs are, please?

Detective Fox: Yes. 4-A is a photograph of Paul Ferguson's hands, the palm side of both hands, left and right.

Mr. Tarman: And the other photograph also is of his hands, is that correct?

Detective Fox: That's correct. That's the backside of his hands.

Mr. Tarman: So you took photographs of both hands on both sides and they show every finger. Is that right?

Detective Fox: That's correct.

Mr. Tarman: Are those the same photographs we heard about that were taken by yourself and Patrolman Cuckovic at the Susquehanna Township Building on Linglestown Road?

Detective Fox: Yes. They appear to be the same photographs.

Mr. Tarman: I believe we heard they were taken shortly after his arrest around 1:00 a.m., is that correct?

Detective Fox: That's right.

Mr. Tarman: What was the purpose of taking the close-ups of the hands on both sides?

Detective Fox: To see if there was any injuries to his hands or any blood on his hands.

Mr. Tarman: And did you examine Paul Ferguson's hands in addition to taking the photographs? Did you do a visual examination of his hands?

Detective Fox: Yes.

Mr. Tarman: And did they reveal any kind of blood, scratch, or any kind of a marking that would be out of the ordinary?

Detective Fox: No.

Mr. Tarman: As a matter of fact, they're perfectly clean on both sides; isn't that correct?

Detective Fox: Yes, they're very clean.

Mr. Tarman: When I say clean, I mean no scratches or marks, is that right?

Detective Fox: They're clean.

Mr. Tarman: Was there an attempt to do any kind of an examination of his fingernails to see if there would be anything under his fingernails?

Detective Fox: No.

Mr. Tarman: Did there appear to be anything under his fingernails to your examination?

Detective Fox: No. They looked normal to me.

Mr. Tarman: And clean?

Detective Fox: Clean.

When Mr. Tarman declared that his cross-examination of Detective Fox was concluded, Mr. Matangos did not hesitate a moment to begin his redirect examination.

Mr. Matangos: Detective, regarding the search at the defendant's residence, did you at any time take the babies out of the bed and search the beds they were sleeping in?

Detective Fox: No.

Mr. Matangos: Did you ever search under the mattress or under the sheets that were on the babies' beds?

Detective Fox: No.

Mr. Matangos: Did you ever search the vehicles that were parked in the garage?

Detective Fox: I did not.

Mr. Matangos: To your knowledge, were those vehicles ever opened and gone through by any of the officers at the scene?

Detective Fox: Not to my knowledge.

Mr. Matangos: Regarding fingerprinting and the pants, why didn't you fingerprint those pants?

Detective Fox: They aren't conducive to producing fingerprints, in my opinion.

Mr. Matangos: And the hair that was found on the tip of the glove, you indicated you weren't sure whether that was from inside or outside the tip of the glove?

Detective Fox: No, I'm not.

Mr. Matangos: You are aware, are you not, that the Birds have a cat?

Detective Fox: Yes, I'm aware of that.

Mr. Matangos: And you heard Mrs. Bird testify that the cat occasionally pushes open the doors on that second floor?

Detective Fox: Yes, I heard that testimony.

Mr. Matangos: From your visual observation, were you able to tell whether that was a human hair or animal hair?

Detective Fox: Actually, there are two hairs in that envelope. One appears to be animal hair.

Mr. Matangos: Just from your own personal opinion as to what that is?

Detective Fox: Yes.

Mr. Matangos: Regarding the source of the blood and why there were no blood tests, DNA-type tests done on any blood found at the Birds' residence—why there was no testing on any of the blood smears or anything like that—why was there no comparison testing done?

Detention Fox: It was my opinion, and other investigators' opinions, that it was obvious that most of the blood left at the Bird residence was the victims' blood. And when I photographed Paul Ferguson and took his clothing off, none of the injuries on him, in my opinion, would have produced any dripping of blood or smears of blood. They were just merely scratches.

Mr. Matangos: So was there any need, whatsoever, to test the blood?

Detective Fox: I didn't feel there was.

Mr. Matangos: Was there any need, whatsoever, to find the maker of the knife found?

Detective Fox: No.

Mr. Tarman: Your Honor, these are all very leading questions.

Judge Kleinfelter: Oh, I don't think that's a leading question. Was there any need to find the maker of the knife? That's not a leading question. Your answer was no?

Detective Fox: That's correct.

Judge Kleinfelter: Why not? Why don't you explain your answer?

Detective Fox: Well, there were no knives found at the Ferguson residence that were similar that we could have compared knives and maybe manufacturers. I'm quite familiar with knives. I hunt and fish, and there's no model number or serial number on knives that I'm aware of. Maybe a brand name, but how that could help us in this investigation, I wouldn't know.

Mr. Matangos: The flashlight itself you indicated has some type of plug. Could you demonstrate again how the recharging takes place?

Detective Fox: It has the male end of a charge plug. It pops out from the flashlight, and you plug it into a wall socket. There's no separate charger for it. You don't have to put it into another charger to charge this flashlight. You put it into the wall socket. I could plug it into any wall socket in this room, and it would charge.

Mr. Matangos: And that flashlight was recovered where again?

Detective Fox: It was recovered from the daughters of Mrs. Bird, in their bedroom.

Mr. Matangos: Do you know where in the bedroom specifically?

Detective Fox: I don't know where specifically. I personally didn't take it from the room.

Mr. Matangos: Is it noted on your inventory?

Detective Fox: I think it's on the outside of the bag. It says inside the door, southeast corner of the girls' bedroom.

Mr. Matangos: The maker of that flashlight is listed as First Alert?

Detective Fox: Yes.

Mr. Matangos: Did you search for any receipts or... for either the knife, the flashlight—for either of those items at the Ferguson residence?

Detective Fox: If we had seen any receipts—well, the flashlight itself—when we were doing the search warrant, we weren't aware. I wasn't aware of the flashlight at that time, so I wouldn't have looked for a receipt for the First Alert flashlight.

Mr. Matangos: It wasn't a part of your search, was it, as indicated by the search warrant?

Detective Fox: As I said, I wasn't aware there was a flashlight recovered. It was brought to our attention by one of the daughters, I think, that the flashlight didn't belong to them. It was recovered later.

Mr. Matangos: The print that was found on the knife, could you tell us again where that was found, the partial print?

Detective Fox: It was found on the blade of the knife, as opposed to the handle.

Mr. Matangos: You indicated to Mr. Tarman that that print, whether it was partial or full, was compared to Mr. Ferguson's, and it did not belong to him?

Detective Fox: It couldn't be compared to—it was compared to Ferguson's print, but there was not enough identifiable markings on the latent print from the blade that could be identified to his or anyone's.

Mr. Matangos: So that print, you're saying it couldn't have been compared to anybody's no matter whose print you had to compare it to?

Detective Fox: That's correct.

Mr. Matangos: Did you take Mrs. Bird's fingerprints?

Detective Fox: No.

Mr. Matangos: Why not?

Detective Fox: Her hands were in too bad a shape to have that done.

Mr. Matangos: That's why no comparison was done with Mrs. Bird's prints?

Detective Fox: That's correct. That's partly correct, because the print that was from the knife couldn't be compared to anybody's print. It wasn't—the print itself wasn't good enough to compare with another print.

Mr. Matangos: The clothing that the defendant had on when he was at the police station, that was the clothing he put on in his house or that he had on when found, the white shirt indicated to have the Nike logo and purple pants—those were not sent to PSP for any type of lab work to be done on them?

Detective Fox: No.

Mr. Matangos: The only inspection you did was visual?

Detective Fox: Just the visual inspection by myself.

Mr. Matangos: And finally, Detective, Mr. Tarman asked you about looking under the fingernails of Mr. Ferguson, the defendant, for any evidence. Were there any—what type of wounds were on Mrs. Bird?

Detective Fox: What type?

Mr. Matangos: Were there any scratch wounds on Mrs. Bird?

Detective Fox: I was never made aware of any scratches.

Mr. Matangos: What type of wounds did you photograph? What type of wounds were they?

Detective Fox: They were slash wounds.

Mr. Matangos: Thank you, Detective. Nothing further, Your Honor.

Debbie was amazed at Mr. Matangos's ability to pull all the loose ends together. He managed to have Detective Fox elaborate on his answers to more clearly be understood, and the police work no longer seemed incomplete. Even when Detective Fox did not know where George was going with his questions, George was able to reformulate the question to get the answer he wanted. She realized she was extremely biased, but Debbie felt Detective Fox's occasional confusion made him seem more honest and unrehearsed. When George wanted Detective Fox to explain why the police did not check under Paul's fingernails, he just wanted Detective Fox to testify that the victims had no wounds that were inflicted by fingernails. George accomplished getting the answer he wanted in a roundabout fashion that made the testimony seem very genuine. She just hoped Mr. Tarman would not ruin the good feeling she was experiencing after Mr. Matangos's redirect examination of Detective Fox.

Mr. Tarman: Detective Fox, I don't mean to belabor this, but even if there are slash wounds and blood is flying around, it's not uncommon in cases like this where a victim's blood will end up underneath the fingernails of the defendant, isn't that correct? It's not uncommon? A lot of blood?

Detective Fox: I would say it's uncommon to end up under an assailant's fingernails. I never came across that, Mr. Tarman.

Mr. Tarman: We do know blood appeared on the glove tips, don't we?

Detective Fox: Yes, we do.

Mr. Tarman: Drawing from that, it's not a whole lot further for blood to appear on a person's hands or underneath their fingernails, is it?

Detective Fox: That's correct.

Mr. Tarman: All right. There is nothing to prevent you from— you looked at the clothing, the white shirt and purple pants. You looked at it, you saw nothing, and that's why you didn't send it to the Pennsylvania State Police, is that right?

Detective Fox: That's part of the reason, but any blood I would have found on his clothing, I would—or could—have assumed it was from him himself, his own injuries.

Mr. Tarman: And you did not find it, and therefore, you didn't send it to the Pennsylvania State Police Lab, is that right?

Detective Fox: That's correct.

Mr. Tarman: But there was nothing preventing you from doing so, was there?

Detective Fox: There was nothing preventing me from doing it, no.

Mr. Tarman: You've been asked if the car was searched. You have no knowledge as to whether the car was searched or not, do you?

Detective Fox: I don't have any personal knowledge of that.

Mr. Tarman: It certainly—we've already heard there was no resistance. There certainly wouldn't have been anything to prevent any one of those ten officers from searching that car, is that right?

Detective Fox: I don't think there would have been.

Mr. Tarman was finished with his questions for Detective Fox, but Mr. Matangos was not. When George stood up to further question Detective Fox, Debbie was surprised that he was permitted to ask more questions of the witness. With no objections, George began to further question Detective Fox.

Mr. Matangos: Mr. Tarman made mention again of blood on the glove tips, and you made mention of 'transfer.' What did you mean by that?

Detective Fox: Transfer? Meaning that blood came from one source and ended up on another source. It was transferred. It was taken from one area and placed on another area.

Mr. Matangos: In relation to those glove tips, what were you indicating by that word?

Detective Fox: That the blood from the victim ended up on the gloves of the assailant.

Mr. Matangos was finished with Detective Fox's testimony. Judge Kleinfelter excused him from the stand. Debbie wondered if the time went as fast for him on the stand as it had for her. As she looked over the jury, she wondered what they were thinking and how the prosecution was doing. He was their team's evidence expert, and the details he provided regarding the evidence seemed overwhelming.

Chapter XXX

Ajax, a Family's Best Friend

When Mr. Matangos called Keith Ocker to the stand, he introduced him as Officer Keith Ocker of the Derry Township Police Department in Hershey. Debbie thought he was another police officer whom she hadn't met until he described himself as a "canine handler." She knew immediately that he was the dog trainer George had told her about. She knew his dog had followed a trail to Paul's house. She also knew that Mr. Tarman had tried to keep him from testifying because the dog was a German shepherd rather than a bloodhound and, therefore, not suitable for tracking services. Debbie quickly became totally absorbed in Officer Ocker's testimony.

Mr. Matangos: And by canine handler, you mean you work with a dog, your partner is actually a dog?

Officer Ocker: Yes. I classify him as my partner.

Mr. Matangos: What is your partner's name?

Officer Ocker: Ajax.

Mr. Matangos: How long have you had Ajax?

Officer Ocker: Since '94.

Mr. Matangos: How does this work with officers that have canines? Does this animal become your personal animal as well?

Officer Ocker: Yes. He stays at my residence when we are off duty and we develop a strong bond as a result of that because he basically is with me twenty-four hours a day.

Mr. Matangos: What is your background in regards to your patrol duties with the canine unit? How long have you been doing that?

Officer Ocker: A little over two years.

Mr. Matangos: And has it been strictly with your partner, Ajax?

Officer Ocker: Yes.

Mr. Matangos: What kind of dog is Ajax?

Officer Ocker: Purebred German shepherd imported from Czechoslovakia.

Mr. Matangos: How were you put together with Ajax?

Officer Ocker: There was a selection process for the position of canine handler within our department. I was chosen to fill that position. Our dogs are purchased through a master trainer, Bill Castle. He gives the dog to the handler who would suit that handler as far as his motivation and training aspects.

Mr. Matangos: Before you were chosen for the program, what kind of qualifications were necessary to be a canine handler?

Officer Ocker: Mainly an interest in that aspect of law enforcement and previous background with animals, whether you had pets before, because the care and maintenance of the dog is very intensive.

Mr. Matangos: And did you have previous contacts with dogs or animals of that nature?

Officer Ocker: Yes. I have had pets since childhood, and my father-in-law is a trainer and field trial judge for hunting dogs.

Mr. Matangos: Is the German shepherd the usual breed chosen for canine usage?

Officer Ocker: Within our department, yes. Other breeds are used, depending on what they're used for. Our patrol dogs are cross-trained, so they are trained in tracking, drug detection, all the aggression aspects, handler protection, and article searches.

Mr. Matangos: Do you know how old Ajax was when you first came into contact with him?

Officer Ocker: Thirteen months.

Mr. Matangos: Prior to your receiving him, do you know what training or what type of structure the dog had before you became partners with him?

Officer Ocker: Yes. Our trainer purchased the dogs through dog clubs in Europe. While they are in Europe, they receive training, which is known as Schutzund training. While they're over there, they go through obedience, tracking, and the aggression work. They have competitions to see which kennel club has the superior dog in those aspects. From that point, the trainer has a person over in Europe who looks for the qualities that would make good police dogs. After being selected for the position, the trainer assigns you a dog.

Mr. Matangos continued to lead Officer Ocker through the details of the guidelines, standards, and hours of training required to certify a dog.

Judge Kleinfelter: This is all very interesting, but you're going to ultimately offer that the dog performed some tracking in this case?

Mr. Matangos: Yes, Your Honor.

Judge Kleinfelter: Is there any question about the competence of the dog and dog handler to track?

Mr. Tarman: Well, Your Honor, that remains to be seen. I've been given a report that indicates that there may be some question as to that, yes. And I'm not willing to accept this dog.

Mr. Matangos: All right. So we'll hear all about the background, then. I apologize, Your Honor. That's why I was getting into it. We discussed this previously.

Judge Kleinfelter: You had had a conversation about this already. I know the jury is very interested in dog training, but if we could have cut through some of that and moved the trial along, I'd have preferred that. However, you were somewhere in the classroom.

Mr. Matangos: Yes, the classroom training.

And Mr. Matangos returned to his series of questions for Officer Ocker:

Mr. Matangos: In order to be certified in tracking, what does the dog and yourself have to accomplish?

Officer Ocker: They have to be able to follow a track for any given distance, and there has to be several surfaces that the dog has to track across.

Mr. Matangos: What do those include?

Officer Ocker: Hard surfaces—meaning roadways, grass areas, and dirt roads.

Mr. Matangos: And what types of items is the dog able to track?

Officer Ocker: Human odors and ground disturbances. If there is an article dropped from the person we're tracking, we will stop and alert to that article.

This dog would have stopped and alerted at the trash can that Paul stuffed his bloody shirt in if he really had done so, Debbie realized from Officer Ocker's testimony. *Perhaps George was right and Paul wore the bloody plaid shirt home and his mother helped him get rid of it.* Debbie had been so sure the police had failed to search the alley lined with trash cans behind her house and that the shirt was lost to the trash collection the day after the attack. *Could Ajax have found that shirt if it was there as he tracked Paul to his house?*

Mr. Matangos: Human odors, I think, are kind of self-explanatory. What does 'ground disturbances' mean?

Officer Ocker: When you walk across a ground surface, mainly grass or dirt, you disturb the surface. Specifically, when you crush grass, there is a liquid in the grass that gives off a different odor than grass that has not been disturbed. It's the same with dirt. If you scuff across dirt, it's going to give a different odor than ground that is not disturbed. Hard surface tracks are a little more difficult because you can't scuff asphalt. So they rely mainly on the odor of the human.

Officer Ocker testified that Ajax was successful in his training and certified in tracking by the North American Police Workdog Association in August of 1994, and recertified on November 21, 1995. While recertification is required every two years, Officer Ocker testified that he takes Ajax for certification yearly. Mr. Matangos had to be proud of this witness, and he continued to show him off to the jury.

Mr. Matangos: Other than tracking, was your dog certified in other types of police work?

Officer Ocker: Yes. He's certified in drug detection, which includes marijuana, hash, cocaine, crack, heroin, and methamphetamines. He's trained in obedience, agility, article search, area search, tracking, building search, aggression control, and police utility.

If the jury was not impressed with Ajax yet, Debbie didn't know what else they needed to hear. She looked over at Mr. Tarman as he sat next to Paul in the courtroom and was sure he was wishing he had allowed Judge Kleinfelter to direct George to skip over Ajax's competence for the job.

As it turned out, George had a lot more examples of Ajax's suitability to display for Mr. Tarman and the jury.

Mr. Matangos: During the course of your working with Ajax, how many actual tracks have you done with Ajax?

Officer Ocker: Training tracks or duty related tracks?

Mr. Matangos: Well, training tracks first. Let's get them out of the way, if you know?

Officer Ocker: Several hundred. I couldn't tell you, offhand, how many, but initially, within the first year that I had the dog, I trained with him every day.

Mr. Matangos: Did you keep a log, or is there any recollection on your account of how successful he was at those training tracks?

Officer Ocker: Yes. I have a file cabinet full. Any time I do a training log, I do a report, whether it's on my own or in front of a master trainer, so I have a file cabinet full of all those training logs.

Mr. Matangos: Any recollection on your account of how many of those have been successful?

Officer Ocker: Since we received our first certification, almost all of them have been successful. There are certain areas of the track that he needs work on. Because of weather or other factors, he would stray from the track. However, I would say he's been successful 98 percent of the time.

Mr. Matangos: Now on duty tracks, do you have an idea of how many there were?

Officer Ocker: I've done ten.

Mr. Matangos: Of those ten, we're talking about human tracking?

Officer Ocker: Yes.

Mr. Matangos: Tell us how Ajax is used on these tracks and essentially what happened on those ten tracks.

Officer Ocker: We're called whenever the department has a suspect that has fled from the scene of a crime. There have been two that have led to either collection of evidence or the discovery of the suspect. During our classroom instruction, our instructor who taught that aspect of training said that if we succeed 10 percent of the time—

Mr. Tarman: Your Honor, I would object to whatever somebody told him.

Judge Kleinfelter: Overruled.

Mr. Tarman: I don't think that's necessary.

Mr. Matangos: Sorry. Continue, Officer.

Officer Ocker: If we successfully complete 10 percent of our tracks, then we're doing a good job as far as on duty, because there are so many factors that come into play when we are called to the scene.

Mr. Matangos: What kinds of things—when you say "factors," what kinds of things play a part on these tracks?

Officer Ocker: A lot of departments don't have access to canines, so the officers, when they respond to the scene and someone flees, their initial instinct is to try to find them themselves. A lot of times when we get called to the scene, we'll have ten to fifteen officers walking the same area that the suspect fled, so that causes contamination of that area. Also, weather plays a key role in tracking.

Mr. Matangos: What are considered the unfavorable conditions for tracking?

Officer Ocker: Torrential downpours, extreme heat where the dog would become exhausted if the track continued a great distance, strong wind, and then if it was a hard surface or not. Hard surfaces are more difficult and require that the canine be called to that location sooner.

Mr. Matangos: What about time of doing the track? How soon does it need to be, or when you're called to the scene, what are considered favorable or unfavorable circumstances in that aspect?

Officer Ocker: It depends on the circumstances, whether there has been a disturbance or contamination of the area, and the weather conditions. There have been successful tracks that have been done twenty-four hours after.

Matangos: Other than these human trackings that you've done while on duty, there have been other instances where you've been called in to either do article searches or some of those other activities that you and your canine do, is that correct?

Officer Ocker: Yes.

Matangos: Have you and your dog been involved in any drug detection?

Officer Ocker: Yes.

Matangos: How many times have you been involved in drug detection?

Officer Ocker: If I can look at my notes? For drug detection, he's been involved with eighteen vehicle searches, seventeen building searches, seven locker searches, and three money scams for a total of forty-five drug searches.

Mr. Matangos: And how successful was he in any of those instances?

Officer Ocker: He's detected 74.8 pounds of marijuana, 36.5 grams of cocaine, 41 grams of heroin, 5 grams of methamphetamines, and total money scam for money that he's detected narcotics on $41,837.

Mr. Matangos: And you have also been involved in one area search. What is an area search?

Officer Ocker: Area search is when we know the suspect fled the scene and is in a certain area and is contained in that area. Rather than risking officers' safety, we will send the dog in on command and let him find the suspect himself rather than me holding on to the leash and actually following. So he's at work on his own rather than pulling me along.

Mr. Matangos: What occurred during the one area search that Ajax was involved in?

Officer Ocker: Ajax alerted to the suspect who fled the area of a burglary attempt and was hiding in a wooded area and conducted what we call a revere. A revere means that when we turn him loose to find the suspect, he is going to react to how the suspect reacts. If the suspect makes a move where he is going to attack the dog, the dog is going to bite. If the suspect tries to flee, the dog is going to bite. If the suspect stands still, he's going to bark and hold. On this occasion, Ajax did not bite him. He barked and held the guy there until the guy was ordered out.

Debbie was overcome with emotion at the thought of sending Ajax after a suspect who was too dangerous for officers to trail. The image of Ajax pursuing a criminal who might shoot him, and doing so out of loyalty and devotion to his partner was too much for her to bear. She didn't want Ajax to get hurt. When Officer Ocker added, "On this occasion, Ajax did not bite him. He barked and held the guy there until the guy was ordered out," Debbie sobbed quietly out of relief that Ajax was unharmed and an overwhelming sense of gratitude for such a special dog. She had not yet heard what Ajax had done in his tracking at her crime scene, and she was already in awe of him.

Officer Ocker continued to praise his dog by testifying that during that same incident, Ajax was sent back into the wooded area to conduct an article search for burglary tools. He located a crowbar and gloves.

Having determined that he had provided the jury with enough background to establish Ajax's credibility as a tracker, Mr. Matangos pressed right on to the night of the attack. Officer Ocker recounted being called by Derry Township's Dispatch Center at one minute after midnight, making it the morning of the nineteenth of April. He, with Ajax by his side, accepted the request, picked up his canine vehicle with all his equipment, and arrived at the Third Street residence at approximately 1:00 a.m.

Mr. Matangos: And what was your recollection of events after you got there?

Officer Ocker: When I pulled up to the scene, Detective Fernsler, Detective Weidensaul, and Corporal Champaign met me. They advised me what they had there, what had happened at the residence.

Mr. Matangos: And when you say, 'what had happened,' what were you told had happened?

Officer Ocker: They basically told me that someone entered the house, there was an altercation, and that the suspect fled. Detective

Fernsler took me inside the residence and showed me an area in the kitchen where there were articles of clothing lying on the floor. I believe it was shoes and pants. At that point, that's where I began my track, inside the residence.

Mr. Matangos presented Commonwealth's Exhibit 19 to Officer Ocker, who identified it as the articles of clothing that were lying on the floor at the point where he and Ajax started their track. As Officer Ocker described his partner, Ajax, Debbie couldn't help but love this dog, and she wondered if the jury members, too, loved him.

Officer Ocker: I give Ajax a verbal command and motion with my hand. We've been doing this long enough that as soon as I put that lead on, he tracks fast, faster than most dogs. I use a fifteen-foot leather lead, and to slow him down, I run the lead under his front leg, and oftentimes between his rear legs. When I do that, he basically knows what he's going to do, but I give him a command, which in Czechoslovakian is *Stupa,* and he knows what he is supposed to do.

Mr. Matangos: Before you began the track, did you know of the suspect?

Officer Ocker: No, I didn't.

Mr. Matangos: Did you know where the suspect lived?

Officer Ocker: No, I didn't.

Mr. Matangos: Were you in any manner, fashion, or form told where the suspect lived?

Officer Ocker: No, not until after my track was completed.

Excellent questions, Debbie thought. She knew that the dog tracked from her house to Paul's house, but she didn't know that the policeman in charge of the dog did not know Paul, was not from the Susquehanna Township Police Department, and was not even told the suspect's name or address prior to the tracking. She felt that anger again toward Mrs. Ferguson and Mr. Tarman that she had felt so many times since the attack. How could anyone defend a son or a client against such damning evidence? Did the jury note the significance of Officer Ocker's statements that he had no preconceived ideas about the direction his tracking would take? Did they see the coincidence that Ajax led his trainer to the house of the same person that she had named as her attacker as she made her 911 call on the night of the attack?

Mr. Matangos: What happens after you give Ajax the command?

Officer Ocker: He smells the area, takes in the odors, and then starts the track in the direction of the odors.

Mr. Matangos: Now, if this was one o'clock, did you know about when the incident occurred?

Officer Ocker: I wasn't sure. Later, they told me, and I believe that I indicated in my report that there was an approximate two-hour delay.

Mr. Matangos: Was that significant in any way in your opinion?

Officer Ocker: No, because there were no adverse weather conditions, and I was informed by the officers at the scene that none of the officers went out looking for the person, that they stayed inside and didn't walk the area for evidence or anything like that. They stayed in the residence, I believe.

Mr. Matangos: Is that what you were referring to when you talked about contamination?

Officer Ocker: Yes

Mr. Matangos: The weather conditions, did you document those?

Officer Ocker: Yes, I did.

Mr. Matangos: What did they indicate?

Officer Ocker: There were no adverse conditions such as rain. The temperature was approximately fifty to fifty-five degrees, and there was a slight breeze from north to south.

Mr. Matangos: And in any of those conditions that you noted or anything that you took notice of that night, was there anything that was adverse regarding the weather?

Officer Ocker: As far as the climate, no. There was no contamination that I was made aware of by officers at the scene. In fact, I was informed that they had really no knowledge as far as the path that the person would have taken.

Matangos approached the bench and had Commonwealth Exhibit 50 marked. Officer Ocker identified it as a diagram of the route that the track led from the crime scene to the end point of the tracking. He indicated that he prepared the diagram as he does for every track regardless if the track is done for duty or training. When Mr. Matangos moved for the admission of Exhibit 50, Mr. Tarman went on record as objecting as "previously stated on the record before the trial." When Judge Kleinfelter indicated that he could not recall the basis of the objection, Mr. Tarman requested a sidebar to discuss it.

In the private meeting with Judge Kleinfelter, Mr. Tarman, and Mr. Matangos, Mr. Tarman restated his argument against the admission of any of the dog tracking evidence on the grounds that "in this particular case, the defendant was not apprehended, and he did not go right to the defendant's house." When he further argued the relevance of the tracking evidence that did not go to the defendant or his house, Judge Kleinfelter countered that if that was the case, the evidence wouldn't hurt his defense.

Mr. Tarman persisted with his objections, as all good defense attorneys do to keep incriminating evidence from juries. He maintained that the prosecution would use the evidence to say that Ajax tracked "towards the defendant's house," and he preferred not to have the evidence presented at all. Judge Kleinfelter turned to Mr. Matangos and asked him what the evidence would indicate.

George said, "The diagram, itself, Your Honor, will depict the officer's course of travel with the dog out of the rear of the residence to the alleyway to Bergner Street, down Bergner Street to the intersection of Bergner and Second Street, which is the intersection that Mr. Ferguson's, the defendant's house is on. Right across the street is where the officer will indicate that the track was unsuccessfully completed. The dog picked up the scent of a dead rabbit, and the officer was unable to re-scent the dog to get a complete track."

Judge Kleinfelter said, "So the relevance, then, is that the track leads towards the defendant's residence but stops short of it. While it's not conclusive, it's probative, and it does show that the perpetrator at least fled in the direction of the defendant's residence. It's a bit of circumstantial evidence, which would have been more powerful if the dog had gotten all the way, but he stopped short, and so it has limited relevance. And, Mr. Tarman, you can argue just how limited you think it is."

Mr. Tarman gave up his objection, making sure that it remained on the records. Mr. Matangos continued with his Exhibit 50, which he placed in plain view of the members of the jury. Officer Ocker continued his testimony by tracing and describing the trail Ajax took from the victims' kitchen, out the back door, through the side gate of the fenced-in backyard, to the alley behind the residence.

Officer Ocker described Ajax taking an abrupt left turn in the grass at the alley and moving in the grass along the alley toward Bergner Street, Debbie visualized Paul running barefoot in the grass along her swimming pool between her yard and her neighbor's yard. He avoided running in the alley because of its gravel surface and stayed on the grass at the end of the four properties on her block until he got to Bergner Street. Officer Ocker noted the shrubbery along the alley, which probably caused the scratches Paul had on his arms when he was photographed at the police station.

Officer Ocker testified that Ajax "cut the corner short" at the intersection of the alley and Bergner Street by turning left in the grass of the last property. Tracking along Bergner, Ajax remained on the grass of the last yard until he reached Third Street. Officer Ocker noted for the jury that the end of the block had no sidewalk. He did so to explain why Ajax was tracking with his nose to the ground, which was consistent with his previous testimony, that tracking dogs track differently depending upon the various surfaces.

When Ajax moved across Third Street along Bergner, he raised his head from the ground with his nose in the air and his tail erect. His body posture indicated to his trainer that he smelled the air scent, which was given off by the person he was tracking. More specifically, Officer Ocker described, "If someone went that direction, they lose skin cells from their body, and that is what he is picking up here. When he smells ground surfaces, his nose is on the ground, and again his tail is erect and he won't pick his head up. And, typically, when he gets on a hard surface, he will raise his head and air scent. When he's on the grass or dirt area, he will ground-scent and keep his nose on the ground," which was what Ajax was doing until he got to Third Street.

When Ajax crossed Third Street, he raised his head and air-sniffed across the hard surface across the street. He immediately lowered his nose to the ground in the grassy area between the curb and the sidewalk that ran along the entire block of Bergner to Green Street. Ajax crossed Green Street with his nose in the air again consistent with tracking on hard surfaces, but returned his nose to the grass between the sidewalk and the curb of the next block.

Debbie suddenly realized why Ajax stayed on the grass on a direct route to Paul's house. Paul ran on the grass as he fled the scene of the crime to avoid the rough surfaces of the sidewalks and the streets. He had no shoes, so he ran in the grass as much as he could on his way home. She wanted to make her discovery known to the jury, as she was sure they were not seeing the significance of the surfaces Ajax sniffed on his track to Paul's house. She wasn't even sure that the jury could see how Officer Ocker's diagram led directly to Paul's house.

When Ajax led Officer Ocker from the grassy area of the block between Green and Second Streets, he crossed the intersection of Bergner and Second with his nose in the air and continued air-sniffing along Bergner Street when he stopped at a dead rabbit that had been hit by a car. Debbie could not see Officer Ocker's diagram from her seat in the courtroom, but she could visualize the dead rabbit lying right in front of Paul's house at the corner of Bergner and Second Streets

Officer Ocker gave Ajax a physical correction to override the natural instinct that was guiding Ajax when he encountered the dead rabbit. Officer Ocker explained, "When we utilize a canine for a lot of different areas of law enforcement, we rely on the instinct of the dog. Eighty percent of what we use the dogs for is based on the animal's instinct. There's actually only 20 percent of what we do with the dog that we train him to do and want him to do, whether it's against his instinct or it's not pleasant for him." In an effort to further clarify for the benefit of the jury, he stated, "An animal's instinct would be, of course, to stop and smell a dead rabbit because it depicts food. Another thing that would cause him to stop would be a female dog that was in heat. They are two areas that would stop him from what he's doing, and I would have to remotivate him or get him concentrated on the task we're trying to perform."

Officer Ocker continued to describe the tracking from the time Ajax got distracted by the dead rabbit. He gave Ajax a correction by pulling on his choker, saying "no" and repeating the "Stupa" command to continue tracking. Ajax responded immediately to his trainer by lifting his head to air-sniff the hard surface of Bergner Street. Ajax returned to the grass area where he had been ground tracking, which was directly across the street from Paul's house. He again came back into Bergner, air-scented, and continued back in the opposite direction. He turned around and Officer Ocker knew Ajax couldn't smell on the ground anymore because of the amount of hard surface and was relying on air scent.

As Officer Ocker had pointed out in prior testimony, the wind was blowing from north to south on the morning of the tracking, he reminded the jury when Ajax air-scents, he may not be right on the exact location where the person stopped. He would be downwind from the exact location due to the wind conditions, and he would work his way back up to that area where the odor was strongest, and that was what Ajax was trying to do. Due to the delay in getting there and the air direction, he stopped the track in the area of Bergner Street just west of the Bergner and Second Street intersection. Officer Ocker further noted for Mr. Matangos and the jury members that his tracking report indicated that there wasn't any traffic on these streets, with the exception of Front Street, and he had noticed that the majority of the traffic was moving north to south, which would again cause the air current to move the scent in a north to south direction.

What a coincidence Ajax stopped his tracking right in front of Paul's house. Allowing for the slight movement of the air scents from north to south, the trail ended at Paul's front door, according to Debbie's calculations. At that precise moment, Mr. Matangos was about to make sure the jury was fully aware of the location where Ajax stopped tracking.

Mr. Matangos: And to this point, and even to where you are at the corner of Bergner and Second Streets, did you know where the defendant's house was?

Officer Ocker: No.

Mr. Matangos: Were there any police cars or anything out in front of the defendant's house that would have indicated to you that was his house?

Mr. Matangos pointed at Paul's house, which was the only house on either side of Bergner Street where the tracking ended.

Officer Ocker: No.

Mr. Matangos: Do you know where his house is located on that diagram?

Officer Ocker: After I told—I believe it was Detective Weidensaul who followed behind me about fifty feet—that I was going to stop the track because Ajax couldn't pick up any more ground odors, I was then informed that the suspect's residence was right here.

The officer indicated Paul's house on his diagram.

As Officer Ocker pointed out Paul Ferguson's house on his diagram at the precise location that his tracking ended, Mr. Matangos ended his questioning of Officer Ocker. It was noon and a perfect time for Judge Kleinfelter to declare a recess for lunch. He reminded the jury members not to discuss the case during their lunch break. His warning did not apply to Debbie's family and friends and discussing the testimony of Officer Ocker consumed their lunch conversation. It was clear to Debbie that her father and her cousin Ruby were as fascinated by the details of dog tracking as she was. The time had flown by as quickly over lunch as it had in the courtroom; and in no time, the lunch break was over and it was time for Mr. Tarman to try to discredit Officer Ocker.

After the jury was seated in the jury box and Officer Ocker returned to the witness stand, Mr. Tarman began his cross-examination. He reviewed Ajax's certification by emphasizing that he only had to complete one track successfully to be certified. He made sure Officer Ocker agreed that Ajax was cross-trained to do other tasks and, in fact, was used more often for drug detection than suspect tracking. When Mr. Tarman attempted to minimize Ajax's ability to track, he found Officer Ocker a bit more defensive.

Mr. Tarman: Is it not true that the tracking is the most difficult task that a dog like this has to perform?

Debbie was waiting for Mr. Tarman to begin his attack on the use of a German shepherd rather that a bloodhound for tracking. She wondered if he would be successful in planting doubt in the minds of the jury regarding Ajax's abilities. She was so proud of Ajax and was beginning to feel angry already with Mr. Tarman. Officer Ocker would help relieve her tension as he confidently responded to each challenge by Tarman.

Officer Ocker: It depends on the dog. I don't think you can make a broad statement by saying tracking is more difficult. Some dogs pick it up much easier than other dogs.

Mr. Tarman: Overall, tracking is considered one of the more—you know, your two out of ten, your statement that 10 percent is good would lead one to believe that tracking is a difficult skill?

Officer Ocker: Because of the elements and the scene being contaminated. That's what makes it—the percentage of doing it successfully drops because of the elements, and a lot of times, until a canine unit is called, the scene is contaminated. However, on the training field, when everything is laid out and the track sits for a half hour, an hour, or four hours, and we can control that and it's done when there is no adverse weather conditions, then it is a relatively easy task once you become certified with your dog and continually work with that exercise.

Mr. Tarman: There are some breeds that are specialized in just one skill; is that right?

Officer Ocker: Some breeds are used to just one skill, yes.

Mr. Tarman: In particular, the bloodhound, I believe, has a reputation as being a dog that's the most skilled in scenting, which would include tracking?

Officer Ocker: They are used a lot for tracking, yes.

Mr. Tarman: In the case of a bloodhound, they're used almost exclusively for that, as opposed to apprehension and attack and things like that, right?

Officer Ocker: Yes.

Mr. Tarman: Now in this case, your resume for the dog indicates that ten tracks were made—two have led to the discovery of evidence or the apprehension of the suspect. How many of the ten led to the apprehension of the suspect?

Officer Ocker: Just one.

Mr. Tarman: Just one?

Officer Ocker: Yes.

Mr. Tarman: So it's one out of ten, as far as finding a suspect on a track?

Officer Ocker: Yes.

Mr. Tarman: You started your track at the rear of this residence at 1:18 a.m., is that right? I'm taking that right from your report, but go ahead and refer to it.

Officer Ocker: Yes.

Mr. Tarman: And I think there's just a minor correction here—that, actually, was over two and a half hours after the incident. We have reports that the 911 phone call was made at 10:35 p.m. and the person would have fled right about that time, and you didn't arrive there until 1:18 a.m. So we're a little bit over two and a half hours, aren't we?

Officer Ocker: Like I said, I wasn't aware of when it happened. I got my initial call at one minute after midnight.

Mr. Tarman: But given those figures I just gave you, we can agree it's over two and a half hours, am I right?

Officer Ocker: Yes.

After Mr. Tarman tried to suggest that other persons might have walked over the same area that Ajax covered on his tracking, he moved on to question Officer Ocker about media vehicles at the scene of the crime when he and Ajax arrived. Officer Ocker reported only the forensic unit and two other patrol vehicles parked outside.

Mr. Tarman: Were you given any surveillance of this route as to who may have worked up and down the route in question, which is on your chart, during that two and a half hours?

Officer Ocker: The officers at the scene advised me that there was no one that attempted to locate evidence or follow the path they believed the suspect would have gone. In fact, they advised me they did not know which direction he went. That's why they called the patrol dog out.

That was not the response Mr. Tarman wanted from Officer Ocker. He continued to question him about policemen searching the backyard and officers driving to the suspect's house. Officer Ocker testified to having no knowledge of such activity. Knowing that Officer Brubaker had already testified to being at the suspect's residence for some time prior to the tracking, Mr. Tarman seemed frustrated that he could not get Officer Ocker to testify to the movement of patrol cars to that area.

Mr. Tarman: Were you aware of the fact that before that, there may have been one, if not several, police cars outside of that area?

Officer Ocker: I'm not aware of that, no.

Mr. Tarman: You haven't been made aware of that until just now, until I just asked this question?

Mr. Tarman's frustration was evident by the tone of his question, but it did not seem to affect Officer Ocker, who said, "I was not aware if there was anyone in the area. There was no one in the area when I performed the track."

Debbie enjoyed seeing Mr. Tarman fail at demonstrating bias on the part of Officer Ocker. The officer maintained his untainted treatment of the tracking from her house to Paul Ferguson's house. She had been so worried that the police might not have done a perfect job with the evidence in her case, but so far, Officer Ocker and Ajax were her heroes. She was amazed that not one policeman at the scene said anything to Officer Ocker that could have been used by Tarman to suggest that the police knew their suspect and did not follow other possible leads elsewhere.

Having failed to get the responses he wanted from Officer Ocker on the subject of patrol car contamination, Mr. Tarman moved on to the diagram of the tracking that Officer Ocker had created. After Mr. Tarman had Officer Ocker point out the location of the dead rabbit, he continued his cross-examination.

Mr. Tarman: So your dog had already just about passed the Ferguson residence. When I say passed, I mean he would be going in a westerly direction. He had already passed the Ferguson residence. He was just getting by it when he encountered this dead animal, is that right?

Officer Ocker: Actually, it was a little bit before. This is not to scale. After I had done the track, I drew this in my notepad and then transferred it over. So this is not to scale, but it was in the middle of the block, or a little bit toward Second Street.

Mr. Tarman: Then he goes on—he goes out into the street, but never goes across the street. I think your chart certainly reflects that. He never went across Bergner Street, did he?

Officer Ocker: No.

Having established that Ajax did not cross from the middle of Bergner Street to the other side of the street to Paul's house should have been enough to satisfy Mr. Tarman. However, it wasn't, because he began to suggest that the dog tracked to Front Street.

Officer Ocker maintained that the track did not go past the Ferguson residence, but Mr. Tarman was determined to have it do so.

Mr. Tarman: At any time, did you attempt to take your dog across Front Street to see if he could pick up the scent?

Officer Ocker: No. He did not indicate to me by body posture that there was any interest to go across Front Street.

Mr. Tarman: Well, given the high speed of the cars on Front Street, is it not possible that, that could have really disturbed the scent there and allowed somebody to cross Front Street, and because of the speed of those cars and the volume of those cars, could have really disrupted the scent to the point the dog just would not be able to pick up a scent and go across Front Street?

Officer Ocker: In my opinion, if someone were to cross Front Street, even with the traffic and everything, he would have indicated an odor in this area downwind from where that person crossed Front Street.

Officer Ocker pointed to an area downwind on the tracking diagram.

Mr. Tarman was not satisfied. He suggested a suspect could have crossed Front Street to the riverbank. Officer Ocker assured him that the scent would have been held within the banks of the river. When

Mr. Tarman asked Officer Ocker why he did not go across Front Street to see if Ajax could pick up a scent on the other side, Officer Ocker explained, "The dog didn't lead me to Front Street. He's pulling me. I'm not leading him."

When Mr. Tarman suggested that he should have taken Ajax across Bergner to see if he would have tracked to the Ferguson residence, Officer Ocker again responded, "He did not lead me to that direction, so no, I would never take him—he's basically pulling me. I'm not pulling him."

Despite Mr. Tarman's attempts to make the track go in directions it had not gone, Officer Ocker concluded that the trail of the suspect ended right in front of Paul Ferguson's house. Mr. Tarman concluded his cross-examination of Officer Ocker.

Mr. Matangos' redirect examination began by reemphasizing Ajax's abilities.

Mr. Matangos: Officer Ocker, you were asked if tracking is the most difficult thing for a dog to do, and you indicated in your answer, 'It depends on the dog.' How did Ajax take to tracking?

Officer Ocker: Like I said before, I have to put a lead on him to slow him down a little bit. He's a highly motivated dog. Some dogs require a lot of praise and attention for them to perform a task. I'm fortunate enough that he wants to do well to please me and to get a reward at the end of the track, so he's good at tracking. He's better at air tracks than ground disturbances, because oftentimes, instead of staying on the ground disturbances, he'll air-scent and cut corners. If the person made an abrupt left turn, he's going to cut that corner short if he picks up air scent rather than keeping his nose on the ground, as we would rather a Schutzund dog do.

Mr. Matangos: Does Derry Township Police Department have a bloodhound?

Officer Ocker: No.

Mr. Matangos: Why not?

Officer Ocker: Because bloodhounds are used for one thing, and that's tracking. There's a lot of opinions on which breed is better at performing tracking. We use our dogs for all purposes in law enforcement, and through our history, German shepherds have proved to be the more versatile breed of any other.

Mr. Matangos: Approaching with two photographs marked as Commonwealth's Exhibit 24. Do you recognize these depictions?

Officer Ocker: I believe this is the house on Bergner.

Mr. Matangos: And in the center of the photograph leading to the front driveway of the Ferguson residence, what's indicated?

Officer Ocker: Sidewalk.

Mr. Matangos: And the photo with the vehicles on it, what are the cars parked on?

Officer Ocker: Concrete driveway.

Mr. Matangos: A concrete driveway that leads out to Bergner Street; is that correct?

Officer Ocker: Yes.

Mr. Matangos: If the individual that you were tracking ran down Bergner Street and on to that driveway, which is also a hard surface, would you have been able to get Ajax tracked from the position he was air-scenting there at the corner of Second and Bergner?

Officer Ocker: Only if the air scent was concentrated enough that would lead him up there. With a two-hour delay and a breeze from north to south, my opinion is I don't know if he would have been able to go to that direction with that hard surface.

Mr. Matangos: Mr. Tarman mentioned your report and that you could refer to it. I don't see any mention of Front Street in your report.

Officer Ocker: No.

Mr. Matangos: I see lots of mentions of Second and Bergner. Your diagram that you've indicated—and you've indicated it's not to scale—what were you really trying to do? This indication that you have with the circling in front of the house on Bergner, what are you trying to do with that?

Officer Ocker: Indicate that Ajax lost—he discontinued following the track in the area of the circling and that he was concentrated on trying to pick up the odor which, again, is being carried by the wind going north to south.

Mr. Matangos: After you found out where the defendant's house was, did that play a part in your diagram?

Officer Ocker: No. This is the location the tracking ended. There could have been five houses here, and the circling lines would have stayed the same.

Matangos had completed his redirect examination of Officer Ocker, and Mr. Tarman had one more opportunity to question Officer Ocker in his recross-examination. He obviously did not like Mr. Matangos's reference to Officer Ocker's report not mentioning Front Street. He returned to his fixation on the tracking leading to Front Street even though Officer Ocker had clearly established in prior testimony that it had not.

By the time Mr. Tarman had nearly finished his interrogation of the witness, even Judge Kleinfelter had grown weary as indicated by his question to Mr. Tarman: "Haven't we beaten this to death?"

Even Mr. Tarman had to agree as he answered, "Probably so."

Chapter XXXI

The Doctor is Back

After Mr. Tarman beat to death his attempt to discredit Officer Ocker, it was obvious that Judge Kleinfelter needed a brief recess. Debbie had no idea who was to testify next for the prosecution, until Dr. Albracht entered the courtroom. She hadn't seen him since her hospital treatment, which was nearly eight months ago, but she recognized him immediately. Before she could approach him to thank him for agreeing to testify, he found her.

As she extended her hand to greet him, he immediately took it in both his hands and began a caring inspection of its condition. She responded by extending her left hand as well in a proud presentation of fully functioning, flexing fingers. He admired her progress as she thanked him profoundly for playing such a huge role in the success of her recovery. By the time she was thanking him for agreeing to testify, he was humbly shrugging off her compliments as no big deal. He was a big deal for her. He advised her thoroughly enough in the hospital for her to know her hands weren't right at her first follow-up doctor's appointment with Dr. Brown.

Dr. Albracht's professional care and concern inspired her to seek a second opinion with Dr. Mauer, and to endure the hours and pain of hand therapy with Donine. She did not have the words or the time to express her gratitude as Judge Kleinfelter returned to the courtroom. The jury and the prosecution were ready for the next witness.

While Mr. Matangos was swearing in Dr. Albracht, Debbie reflected upon her discussion with George about the need for a physician's testimony to establish serious bodily injury and the intent to kill. While she was not sure how Dr. Albracht could testify to either since he spent his time repairing her hands, she knew she did not want Dr. Brown to testify. All he did was the surgery and aftercare plan, which he botched up. She was actually angry with him for not allowing Dr. Mauer to assist in her surgery and for not recommending hand therapy upon her discharge from the hospital. She had no respect for him as an orthopedic surgeon, and she did not want him testifying at her trial.

George did not know about Dr. Albracht until Debbie described him. From studying her records, he saw Dr. Brown had performed her tendon surgery and seemed to George to be the doctor he should try to contact to testify. At Debbie's urging, George was able to reach Dr. Albracht and was able to obtain his commitment to testify.

Debbie recalled George's positive reaction to Dr. Albracht after he had a chance to meet him. She had not been included in that meeting, so she had not seen or talked with Dr. Albracht since her hospital stay. Dr. Albracht had not been present in the courtroom for any of the prior testimony due to the sequestration ruling, and Debbie was wondering how his medical expertise would impact upon her case. She was amused when she heard that his first name was Brandon. Brandon was such a young name, she thought, as she reflected upon how she and her friends had found him so attractive in the hospital. His name suggested that he was young enough to be her son.

When Dr. Albracht began to describe her injuries on the night of the attack, her amusement quickly ended.

Mr. Matangos briefly reviewed Dr. Albracht's education, training, and experiences to establish his expertise as an orthopedic resident in training. His training included assisting and performing surgery as well as being on call to assess patients that enter the emergency room with orthopedic injuries. Mr. Matangos decided this portion of Dr. Albracht's testimony was a perfect time to transition to the night of the attack.

As Dr. Albracht described Debbie's injuries for the jury, his account sounded much like Debbie's testimony, only in medical terms. The cuts to her right middle and ring fingers were referred to as lacerations with U-shaped openings at the top called "distal," meaning "away from the body." Dr. Albracht used medical terminology, but clarified his terms so that the jury members could understand.

As Dr. Albracht detailed his assessment of her injuries, Debbie recalled vividly being in the trauma bay hearing his concerns about nerve, blood vessel, and tendon damage that could "compromise the function of her hands." She remembered all too well his description of how tendons function and his assessment that corrective surgery and hand therapy would be necessary for full recovery of both her hands. As Debbie grew nauseous again on hearing the graphic nature of her injuries, Mr. Matangos asked Dr. Albracht if in order to assess or evaluate her injuries, he had asked Mrs. Bird what had caused her injuries.

Dr. Albracht: Yes, that's something we do as we're assessing a patient. We are going over the nature of their injuries and what had happened.

Mr. Matangos: What did she tell you had happened to her right hand?

Dr. Albracht: Well, she had mentioned that she was attacked, and when—I was there for quite a long time, and we had an ample opportunity to discuss exactly what happened. But over that course of time, she had reflected that she was attacked by a known assailant or somebody that came into her home that she knew, and she reflected to me it was a friend of her son's and that she was in her bedroom at the time when she heard some noises, that she apparently called out to her daughter—

Debbie sat stunned in the courtroom as tears began to stream down her face. She wasn't sure what was most upsetting to her at that point. Was it hearing the attack played back to her and feeling as though it was happening to her again? Or was it the fact that Dr. Albracht remembered her story well enough to include details like "she was attacked by a known assailant" and "it was a friend of her son's"? After over eight months, Dr. Albracht could describe the attack she experienced nearly as accurately as she had related it to the jury during her testimony.

She knew, as she wiped the tears from her cheeks, that Dr. Albracht was moved enough that night by the trauma she had experienced to recall it in detail all these months later. She wanted to remind the jury members that she hadn't spoken to Dr. Albracht since she was in the hospital. She wanted to remind them that he was not present in the courtroom for her testimony. Did they realize the significance of how closely his account of her attack matched hers?

Mr. Tarman: Your Honor, I really don't think it's relevant to this witness's testimony to get into the facts of something that he's been told in the hospital. I just don't know the relevance.

Judge Kleinfelter: Well, the objection is overruled. You may continue.

The judge's response to Mr. Tarman obviously demonstrated to all those in the courtroom that he saw the relevance.

Dr. Albracht: She had mentioned that she was—had called out to her daughter and that she was scared because nobody had replied, and if I recall, she said that she went to go see what was going on and realized—she looked down the hall and saw her daughter's door, and I can recall she had mentioned something about the door being in a position it's not normally in, and so that brought concern.

Debbie had to work hard to suppress her sobs as she heard more details that she thought only she could recall as Dr. Albracht continued.

Dr. Albracht: She went to go check it out, and at that time, somebody attacked her. She felt that she was—initially felt like she was being punched. She didn't realize what was going on.

Mr. Matangos: Where did she indicate that was taking place?

Dr. Albracht: That I don't recall.

Mr. Matangos: Where on her body.

Dr. Albracht: Oh, on her body? She mentioned that whoever was attacking her appeared to be punching her in the head, all over her head. She wasn't really sure what was going on.

Mr. Matangos: Did you see wounds that correlated to that?

Dr. Albracht: Yes, I did.

Mr. Matangos: And you've indicated that others were assessing those at that point?

Dr. Albracht: Yes.

Mr. Matangos: What next?

Dr. Albracht: With respect to her story, she had mentioned that she attempted to defend herself as one naturally would, and in doing that, apparently had realized that she saw blood and at that point, figured out that she wasn't being hit with a fist, that she must have been hit by an object or a knife or something sharp. So she then attempted to grab the object, and she had mentioned at that point she grabbed the knife and grabbed on to it tight, and he pulled the knife out of her hands, which would have given her the injuries that she did sustain.

Mr. Matangos: You've indicated those two on the middle fingers of the right hand. "What did you notice about her left hand?

Dr. Albracht: The one injury was a similar injury to the small finger of the left hand which had a U-shaped laceration, once again in the same orientation in addition to one on the palm of her hand, a somewhat large U-shaped laceration. And the final injury, the most significant, was a laceration to the side of her thumb, and that laceration had actually gone deep enough to not only involve one of the tendons that lifts the thumb like this.

He demonstrated for the jury the thumb action made possible by the damaged tendon.

Dr. Albracht: But also, it entered the joint space in between this part of the thumb—what we call the metacarpal phalange joint.

Mr. Matangos: And that's the joint that actually allows you to traverse?

Dr. Albracht: One of the joints that allows you to, what we call, oppose your thumb. The thumb is one of the most important digits of the hand because it's the only digit that allows you to do what we call opposition. It allows you to grab things. Without a thumb, the only way to grab is to close the adjacent fingers together. That's one of the joints that allow you to do that.

Mr. Matangos: You observed the other individuals working on Mrs. Bird's head wounds, is that correct?

Dr. Albracht: Yes, I did.

Mr. Matangos: What did you see after the assessment was done when they were beginning to work on those wounds?

Dr. Albracht: Well, although the wounds to the hands proba-bly—being in orthopedics, I felt those were the more severe injuries, I'd say, than the injuries to her head. Those to the head appeared more gruesome than the injuries to the hands, and what I mean by that is that she had a significant laceration to the scalp that had actu-ally gone down to the skull. Upon evaluating those injuries, one of the things we do is irrigate everything out that may have entered that wound, and you have to do that effectively to try and prevent the incidence of infection, and that's when I saw what he was doing. And at that point, he had the area open, and because of the nature of the laceration, it created somewhat of a flap of her scalp that could be reflected back. Those are the injuries that he was dealing with, the other physician.

Mr. Matangos: Did you see what they eventually did with the smaller wounds on her head? Did you watch what they did with them?

Dr. Albracht: Well, I was working at the same time on her other injuries, and I had seen the final result after the lacerations had been sutured.

Mr. Matangos: Doctor, I'm approaching you with Commonwealth Exhibit 4 and Commonwealth Exhibit 3. Do you recognize those photographs?

Dr. Albracht: Yes, I do.

Mr. Matangos: First, Commonwealth Exhibit 3. What is that a picture of?

Dr. Albracht: This is a picture of at least two of the lacerations, which were probably some of the more significant lacerations on her scalp.

Mr. Matangos: When would have that photograph been taken? Is that prior to treatment or after treatment?

Dr. Albracht: This is after treatment.

Mr. Matangos: And that's the way you would have seen it? You indicated you saw it after they were done?

Dr. Albracht: I saw it before they were suturing, during, and after.

Mr. Matangos: And that's the condition after the suturing?

Dr. Albracht: Yes.

Mr. Matangos: And Commonwealth's Exhibit 4. Do you recognize that as well?

Dr. Albracht: Yes.

Mr. Matangos: What is that?

Dr. Albracht: This is another view of the laceration, another view from a different perspective.

Mr. Matangos: And you recognize that as being post-treatment as well?

Dr. Albracht: Yes.

After establishing that Dr. Albracht had seen enough of Debbie's head injuries to testify to their seriousness later, Mr. Matangos directed Dr. Albracht to describe in detail the treatment of her hand injuries. With the medical terms of a doctor and the sensitivity to his layman audience, Dr. Albracht articulated his thorough assessment and treatment of Debbie's hand injuries. From the significance of irrigating and scrubbing the wounds to prevent infection to his evaluation of her finger disabilities due to the lacerations of the tendons, Dr. Albracht didn't miss one gruesome detail on either hand. As if his words weren't graphic enough, Mr. Matangos reintroduced the pictures Mr. Tarman had objected to so adamantly during Mrs. Bird's testimony of her injuries.

Debbie watched the faces of the jury members as they viewed the pictures of her injuries. She had been too nervous to pay attention to the reactions of the jury members during her testimony. For the first time, she noticed the foreman of the jury wiping tears. George would tell her later that the Susquehanna Township teacher was frequently moved to tears throughout the trial, suggesting to him that she was sympathetic to the prosecution.

George showed the jury Commonwealth's Exhibit 13 as Dr. Albracht described his treatment of the "violated capsule of the joint" of Debbie's left thumb.

Dr. Albracht: I'm sewing up the capsule, which has been violated at the joint. You can see a suture coming from that area. The capsule was split open, and you could see the inside of the joint because of that violation.

Debbie wondered if any of the members of the jury really wanted or needed to see this much detail.

Mr. Matangos: What's the danger—is there any danger when that's an evident injury as it was in this case?

Dr. Albracht: Well, anytime a joint is violated, it raises concern for fear of infection. The goal is to try and clean out anything that possibly may have invaded the joint. Once the joint is closed up, the organisms or bacteria you hear about that may have gotten inside are difficult for the body to fight because they are contained within the joint. So they may develop joint infections, which could lead to subsequent problems.

Commonwealth Exhibit 12 was an equally graphic and gory picture of the palm of Debbie's left hand. As Dr. Albracht described the U-shaped laceration to the small finger and the large U-shaped laceration of the palm of the hand, Mr. Matangos made sure each jury member could view the blown-up, close-up picture. When explaining the flap of skin that was "filleted back," Dr. Albracht actually referred to Debbie as being very fortunate to have not suffered tendon and nerve damage to her left hand from that injury.

Debbie did not recall hearing that concern from Dr. Albracht while in the hospital, but she did remember all his concerns about losing the large flap of skin. She knew it was compromised by the location of the laceration and the lack of blood supply. She knew she was fortunate, but it wasn't because she hadn't lost the portion of skin or that she hadn't sustained permanent nerve damage to her hand. She was lucky to have had such a caring, professional orthopedic surgeon. As Dr. Albracht continued to outline the potential post-surgical problems and the delicate balance between allowing movement of the tendons without tearing the sutures, Debbie took a moment to reflect upon all her blessings as she sat with her children and family while George Matangos carried them through the trial.

Judge Kleinfelter eventually grew tired of the treatment details and prompted Mr. Matangos into his next task to be accomplished through the physician's testimony.

Judge Kleinfelter: We're interested in the severity of these injuries, what the likelihood may have been that there could have been permanent impairment of bodily function, or at least a protracted loss of the use of a bodily member, and we're interested in whether any of these injuries were life-threatening. What the likelihood may have been for death or serious bodily injury. So the entire treatment procedure and aftercare procedure, again, while interesting, are not part of your case.

When Mr. Matangos was not able to transition quickly enough into the "serious bodily injury" phase of his questioning, Judge Kleinfelter was more adamant.

Judge Kleinfelter: Why don't you ask him, with this kind of injury, what is the likelihood from this kind of injury that someone might suffer a permanent loss of the use of the fingers, or at least a protracted loss? We know what happened in this case. I believe Mrs. Bird said, by and large, she's recovered. But what's the likelihood that she may not have been so successful?

Mr. Matangos: Doctor, just to put closure on the hand injuries, if you could state from your own knowledge, what is the likelihood of potential permanent loss of function of the hands or permanent damage to the joints or anything like that in this case?

Dr. Albracht: I don't think I'd be able to give you an incidence of what the possibility would be of developing contracture or limitations disability, but I would be just able to tell you that's one of the possibilities; developing contractures to the point she wouldn't be able to open her hand or open her fingers.

Mr. Matangos: Can you tell us if that injury to her neck, either by itself or in combination with the other injuries, could have been life-threatening?

Judge Kleinfelter: I haven't even heard him talk about the laceration to the neck. I heard her talk about it, but I haven't heard the doctor describe what he saw. I heard all about the scalp and face, back of the head. I didn't hear him describe injuries to the neck.

Judge Kleinfelter was absolutely correct. Mr. Matangos had not asked Dr. Albracht any questions about Mrs. Bird's neck injury.

Mr. Matangos: Could you, Doctor, please describe what you witnessed?

Dr. Albracht: I witnessed a small laceration over the thyroid cartilage in this region of the neck, in addition to abrasions to the ones I mentioned.

Mr. Matangos: When you were evaluating that neck wound, did Mrs. Bird tell you how that occurred?

Dr. Albracht: No, she didn't.

Mr. Matangos: Did she tell the other doctors in your presence how that happened?

Dr. Albracht: She may have before I got there but not during the time I was there.

Mr. Matangos: From the injuries you saw then, including the hand injuries, the neck injuries, the injuries to the scalp and side of the head, just from your knowledge, were any of those injuries, either by themselves or in combination, a threat to Mrs. Bird—a threat to her life?

Dr. Albracht: The injuries that she had across her neck were not. The injuries to her hands were not. The injuries to her scalp, theoretically, if she had lain there unconscious for whatever reason and had not gotten medical attention, she could have bled to death from them because of the fact that the scalp bleeds profusely when it's injured.

Mr. Matangos: Had the laceration across her neck where the bruising was, if this had been a continuous cut, was there a danger of striking anything vital with that injury?

Dr. Albracht: Yes. The carotid artery goes along the side of the neck just adjacent to the esophagus and the trachea. The trachea, which is the tube that leads to your lungs, just adjacent to that, as I mentioned, is the carotid artery, which supplies blood to your brain.

Mr. Matangos: Had that been penetrated and had those been cut open, what would have occurred?

Dr. Albracht: Once again, depends on how much of it is injured and the time she's seen, but most often it ends up being a fatal injury.

The chills ran up Debbie's spine each time Dr. Albracht used the words *fatal*, *life threatening*, and *death*.

With the help of Commonwealth's Exhibit 32, Mr. Matangos moved from serious bodily injury to intent to kill. It was subtle, and even Debbie didn't notice the transition until George presented the knife used in the attack to Dr. Albracht.

Mr. Matangos: What would have happened if this knife was drawn against both carotid arteries?

Dr. Albracht: She certainly would have bled profusely and probably died.

Debbie remembered lying on her back after Paul had done precisely what George had described. She could hear that voice inside her telling her, "You're going to die on your bedroom floor if you don't fight for your life?" Perhaps she had learned to listen to the voice inside her instead of needing Elizabeth Hoffman in her pocket after all! As Debbie reflected upon her blessings, George continued to nail down the last goal of Dr. Albracht's testimony, to establish Paul's intent to kill her and Jaredd on the night of the attack.

Mr. Matangos had Dr. Albracht describe the two veins similar to the carotid arteries that bring the blood back to the heart from the brain. When he asked Dr. Albracht what Debbie's fate would have been if the knife had cut one side of the neck and penetrated the large vein and artery, his answer was similar. "She would have, once again, bled profusely, and the potential is there for death."

Mr. Matangos surprised Debbie by asking permission to have her approach the witness stand in order for Dr. Albracht to point out and specifically discuss her injuries. As Dr. Albracht showed the jury members the scars on Debbie's hands, she realized that he was demonstrating permanent scarring.

Mr. Matangos: Are those scars readily visible to you?

Dr. Albracht: Yes.

Mr. Matangos had Dr. Albracht point out and describe the scars on Debbie's left hand, neck, and temple. He once again characterized the scars as "readily visible." Dr. Albracht attested to the permanent scarring to Debbie's head that would be visible if not covered by her hair.

Although Dr. Albracht had not seen Jaredd during treatment for the laceration to his face, Dr. Albracht did recall Jaredd coming in to see his mother while he was treating her hand injuries. Since Mr. Matangos did not have a picture of Jaredd's facial injury and Jaredd had left the courtroom earlier to attend his basketball practice, Mr. Matangos had no model. Debbie was concerned that Jaredd's absence would foul things up for George. Had she and Jaredd known that George was going to need him for his line of questioning to Dr. Albracht, he would have stayed and gone late to his practice.

George proceeded as if he hadn't even planned to involve Jaredd in his next questions. Since Dr. Albracht had previously testified to seeing Jaredd's facial laceration in the trauma bay, Mr. Matangos refreshed his memory by describing for him Jaredd's forty-eight-suture laceration.

Mr. Matangos: In the area that he was cut, what was the potential damage that this knife could have caused, and if you could just direct the jury's attention to your own face as to what could have happened.

In his medical terms, Dr. Albracht expounded upon the branches of the trigeminal and facial nerves. He informed the jury that if Jaredd's attacker had cut one or more of the branches of his facial nerve, Jaredd would have experienced paralysis of the side of his face, resulting in a "drooping of the face." Debbie felt the blood drain from her face. She was still struggling with accepting the scar on her son's face; and imagining him with a *drooping* face was just too much for her to handle.

Mr. Matangos: Had the knife wound been, instead of on the jaw line and on the bone—had it been the same depth but an inch or two lower, but below that jaw line, what could have occurred?

Dr. Albracht: I don't know what the depth of his wound was to his jaw, but once again, just being close to that area with that length, it's hard to say what the depth was, so I don't know.

Mr. Matangos: If I told you Jaredd already testified he could see his jawbone and could see all the fat pockets and other things because the wound kind of separated as he went into the bathroom—if I told you he could see his jawbone and the knife had actually penetrated to the bone, what would have been the potential had it been an inch or two lower and underneath?

Dr. Albracht: It's hard to give a percentage, but the percentage is high. If it had truly gone down to the bone, it certainly would have been deep enough to violate that area.

Mr. Matangos: It's possible or it's certain that death is inevitable?

Dr. Albracht: That's certain.

Mr. Matangos: In fact, would it turn to a probability if no medical treatment was available, that probably death would occur in a relatively short amount of time if those blood vessels were broken or interrupted?

Dr. Albracht: If he had not received medical attention, and if it had violated those structures, then the chances are much greater that he would have died rather than survived. And once again, even receiving medical attention for violation of those vessels certainly is no guarantee that he would have pulled through.

A dismal point to end the testimony of Dr. Albracht, but more than likely, Mr. Matangos had planned it that way. When Mr. Tarman had no questions for Dr. Albracht, Debbie recalled that Mr. Tarman had conceded the injuries by maintaining that someone other than his client did them.

As Dr. Albracht was leaving the courtroom, Debbie wondered if she would ever see him again. She was grateful for his professional and personal contributions to her case and wanted to tell him so. He had helped her through the physical ordeal of the attack and was available to help her through the legal battle. She hoped he knew how much she appreciated all his special care.

Chapter XXXII

A Call for Help

When Detective Nelson was called to the stand, he testified to being called to work on the night of April 18 for a "multiple stab wound incident." He arrived at the Bird residence at approximately 11:45 p.m. and received his orders to report to the police station to complete paperwork and interview Mrs. Ferguson. Detective Nelson reported that he interviewed Mrs. Ferguson at the station and talked briefly to Paul's father, Mr. Ferguson, who had arrived later.

Mr. Matangos confirmed through his questions that Detective Nelson interviewed all three victims the following day. Detective Nelson testified to interviewing Alisha Bird at eight o'clock on the morning of the nineteenth.

Mr. Matangos: When you spoke to Alisha, was she able to identify the attacker?

Detective Nelson: Yes, she was.

Mr. Matangos: Who did she identify?

Detective Nelson: Paul Ferguson.

Mr. Matangos: Did you interview Jaredd Bird?

Detective Nelson: Yes, I did.

Mr. Matangos: Do you recall what time you interviewed Jaredd?

Detective Nelson: Ten fifteen in the morning of April 19.

Mr. Matangos: And was Jaredd able to identify the attacker?

Detective Nelson: Yes. He identified Paul Ferguson as being his attacker by recognizing his voice.

Mr. Matangos: Did you then have an opportunity to interview Mrs. Bird?

Detective Nelson: Yes, I did. That happened at about one o'clock in the afternoon on the nineteenth. I interviewed her at Polyclinic Medical Center.

Mr. Matangos: And was she able to identify the attacker?

Detective Nelson: Yes.

Mr. Matangos: Who did she identify?

Detective Nelson: Paul Ferguson.

It was soon clear that Mr. Matangos was not seeking details of the interviews from Detective Nelson as his line of questioning went on to the 911 tape. Detective Nelson testified that he applied for a court order to get the 911 tape and got the court order signed by Judge Hoover of the Dauphin County Court of Common Pleas. Detective Nelson further indicated that he took the signed court order to the Dauphin County Emergency Management Agency, where he was able to listen to the actual 911 tape and make a copy of it. He stated that he had logged the tape into evidence.

Mr. Matangos requested that the audiotape be marked as Exhibit 51 for identification. Detective Nelson identified Commonwealth Exhibit 51 as "the tape of the 911 call that Debra Bird made that evening, at approximately 10:35 p.m. on April 18, 1996." Mr. Matangos moved for the admission of Commonwealth Exhibit 51, with no objection from Mr. Tarman.

After Mr. Matangos requested for the tape to be played in open court, he asked for an opportunity to approach Judge Kleinfelter with Mr. Tarman. What they discussed in sidebar that was not information for the jury was two parts of the tape that Mr. Tarman had objected to prior to the trial.

At one point in the tape, John McGreevy had told the dispatcher that Paul has "been in trouble before," and Mr. Tarman objected to that "because it alluded to his prior record." The part where Mrs. Bird stated that Paul "needs to be locked up," Mr. Tarman did not care about. The three agreed that Mr. Matangos would stop the tape prior to Mr. McGreevy's part of the call.

As the recording of Debra Bird's call for help echoed throughout the courtroom, Debbie silently wept, and the jury sat spellbound:

County dispatcher: Nine-one-one.

Debra Bird: I need an ambulance.

County dispatcher: Okay. Where at?

Debra Bird: 3323 North Third Street, Harrisburg, Susquehanna Township.

County dispatcher: What's the problem?

Debra Bird: We've been attacked by a neighbor- hood boy, named Paul Ferguson. He had a knife. He stabbed me repeatedly. My son woke up and helped. We need help.

County dispatcher: Where were you stabbed, ma'am?

Debra Bird: We need an ambulance. I don't know how bad I am, hurry.

County dispatcher: What's your name, ma'am?

Debra Bird: Debra Bird.

County dispatcher: What's your phone number?

Debra Bird: 233-2244.

County dispatcher: How old are you, ma'am?

Debra Bird: Forty-three.

County dispatcher: Are both you and your son injured?

Debra Bird: Yes, we both are injured. We're both cut.

County dispatcher: Okay. Where are you cut, ma'am?

Debra Bird: All over. He stabbed me in the head, the temple, the fingers. I don't know if I even have all of my fingers. I think my shoulder's dislocated. He was fighting with me. I kept yelling for Jaredd to wake up.

County dispatcher: Just stay on the phone. 'Cause
I want to stay on the phone until someone
arrives there. All right? Do you understand?

Debra Bird: Yes.

City police: Mrs. Bird. This is the police on the
line too. How many people were injured?
You and your husband and who else?

Debra Bird: No, I am alone. I am a single parent. I have three children. My son has been
stabbed too.

County dispatcher: How old is your son?

Debra Bird: My son is fifteen. It was Paul
Ferguson, John. (*The neighbor, John
McGreevy just entered the bedroom.*)

County dispatcher: So you know who it was?

Debra Bird: Yes. He's a neighborhood boy. He's
fifteen. He needs to be locked up. He had a
knife.

At the conclusion of the 911 recording, Mr. Matangos looked
at Judge Kleinfelter and declared, "Your Honor, at this point, the
Commonwealth rests."

Judge Kleinfelter looked at the jury members and announced,
"All right, ladies and gentlemen, that means you have heard the
Commonwealth's case."

Mr. Tarman was waiting for the prosecution to rest so he could
request to approach the judge. In another private meeting with Judge
Kleinfelter and Mr. Matangos, Mr. Tarman began his motions.

Mr. Tarman: Your Honor, I, at this time, make a motion for
a directed verdict on the count of aggravated assault against Alisha.
I don't believe that the Commonwealth has proved that there was
any attempt or infliction of serious bodily injury upon her. All we've
heard is she had a pillow over her face and she felt something on the
pillow, but nothing more than that. As we've heard, she was not hurt
in any way, and I would say that the Commonwealth simply hasn't
met their burden on the count.

Judge Kleinfelter: All right. Anything else?

Mr. Matangos: Your Honor, the Commonwealth's argument on the charge naming Alisha Bird as the victim is that, in fact, Mr. Ferguson began this entire incident within her room. He was found there by the mother who walked across the hallway. He's already got the knife in his hand. The circumstances and events surrounding the occurrence—the entire occurrence to be taken at face value and to be viewed as a whole indicate there was at least enough to meet the prima facie burden at this level, in that after leaving Mrs. Bird bleeding on the floor, the evidence, whether circumstantial or not, however viewed by the court, is that he then returned to Alisha's bedroom. She did feel the pressure on the pillow and she could not see that the knife was being wielded or could have been, but I believe the criminal intent can be inferred at this level knowing immediately thereafter that he went and slashed Jaredd, following Alisha to that room as well.

Judge Kleinfelter: I agree. An attempt is the taking of a substantial step. He entered the premises. He had a knife and went into her room. He certainly cut other people. He went back into the room. I think when he went back, although she didn't know what he was doing, she felt pressure on the pillow. He certainly had the knife in his hand at the time. I think you met the prima facie requirement to get over the demurrer. We're ready for your case.

Chapter XXXIII

The Defense Begins

Halfway through day 3 of the trial, Debbie was not sure she was ready for the defense to begin. She had been so confident with the testimonies of all the witnesses that George had introduced, but she was not looking forward to the lies she was sure to hear from Mrs. Ferguson. As she tried to comfort herself and prepare for the next phase of the battle, she noticed a discussion between Mr. Tarman and Judge Kleinfelter. It was one of those asides during the trial that was not for the jury or audience to hear, but George would explain to her later that Tarman wanted a "brief recess" to "assemble" several exhibits. According to George, he wanted to prepare Mrs. Ferguson for her testimony. Perhaps Judge Kleinfelter had the same concern and wasn't convinced that recess time to assemble several exhibits was necessary. He denied Tarman's request and directed him to continue.

Mr. Tarman's first witness was not Mrs. Ferguson. He called Nancy McGann, a contract administrator for the Primary Care Medical Department in Dauphin County Prison. She was subpoenaed to testify on the health assessment of Paul Ferguson that was performed on April 20, 1996, just one day after his admission to prison. Ms. McGann testified that Paul's height and weight on the day after his admission to Dauphin County Prison was five feet six, 233 pounds. Mr. Tarman then asked his witness to read Paul's most recent weight as recorded on the health assessment. She reported

Paul's weight as 191 pounds on October 15, 1996—a difference that Mr. Tarman reemphasized as a weight loss from 233 to 191 pounds. Before Debbie could determine the significance of the witness's testimony, Mr. Tarman had no further questions of Ms. McGann.

On cross-examination of the witness, Mr. Matangos had three questions for Miss McGann.

Mr. Matangos: Ms. McGann, on that assessment form, does it indicate that Mr. Ferguson told whoever was doing the assessment that he had been kicked above the eye and had an injury to the left side of his face that required some treatment?

Miss McGann: He stated no health problems at this time.

Mr. Matangos: Does it say anything in there about Mr. Ferguson requiring treatment for injuries received from a football game played the day before?

Miss McGann: No.

Mr. Matangos: Does it say anything about scratches, bruises, or any abrasions that Mr. Ferguson told the nurse about or that there was a record made of?

Miss McGann: No, sir.

With just three questions of Mr. Tarman's first defense witness, Mr. Matangos clearly established that Paul did not tell prison personnel any of the alibis that Mrs. Ferguson had created to explain the scratches Paul received during his attack on Debbie and her family. Reflecting upon Ms. McGann's testimony, Debbie could still not see the value of her testimony for the defense, but could clearly see how George was laying the groundwork for the testimonies to follow. He was a master, and Debbie was proud to have him on her team.

When Mrs. Ferguson was called to the stand as Mr. Tarman's second witness, Debbie could feel the anger swelling inside her. She felt a perverse satisfaction in knowing that Mrs. Ferguson had been waiting outside the courtroom for all of the previous testimony. She would not be able to modify her testimony to mirror the details of what the jury had already heard, and she could thank her attorney for his preliminary motion for sequestration. Debbie was grateful to Judge Kleinfelter for denying Mr. Tarman's later request for a brief recess.

In the midst of trying to see the positive in the worst of moments, Debbie wished Mrs. Ferguson could have heard the gory details of her son's crime and the painful details of the recovery process for her and her children. Debbie was drifting back into her fantasy world, where people actually told the truth and accepted responsibility for their actions—a world far removed from that of Paul's or his mother's.

When Mrs. Ferguson's testimony began, Debbie was quickly jolted back to reality and to Mrs. Ferguson's web of lies.

Mrs. Ferguson answered the preliminary questions regarding her family members, which included her son, Paul (sixteen), her daughter, Natasha (fourteen), and twin sons Tyler and Travis who were two years old. Mrs. Ferguson testified that Mr. Ferguson also resided with them, but that they had divorced two and a half years ago.

When Mr. Tarman pushed her to clarify why Mr. Ferguson resided with them given they were divorced, Mrs. Ferguson explained, "We had our problems, but we reconciled, and we're trying to get things together."

That was not Debbie's understanding of the situation. When she had nightmares about Mr. Ferguson immediately after the attack, she recalled George explaining that Mr. Ferguson had moved back into the Ferguson residence. He had heard it had something to do with Paul and Natasha being the owners of the house rather than Mr. or Mrs. Ferguson. Debbie further clarified that situation from what she had heard back when she first met Paul. Dorsey told Jaredd that after Paul's grandparents passed away, Paul's parents moved in with Paul and Natasha. Paul's grandparents had left the house to their grandchildren, Paul and Natasha, to ensure that the children would reside in Susquehanna Township and attend the Susquehanna Township School District. Up until then, Paul and Natasha lived in the city with their parents and were dropped off at the grandparents' house to ride to and from school, a violation of the residency requirements of the school district that apparently went undetected or ignored.

Having that additional background information, it all made sense to George that Mr. Ferguson had moved out of the house at the time of the divorce, but had subsequently moved back, asserting that he had as much right to live in the house with his children, Paul and Natasha, as Mrs. Ferguson had. George had no knowledge of a reconciliation and believed Mrs. Ferguson was presenting information in such a way that she believed would be viewed more positively by the jury—in other words, lying.

Regardless of the reasons, two adults, two teenagers, and two toddlers lived at 110 Bergner Street, and Mr. Tarman's Defense Exhibit No. 5 was about to shed more light upon the living arrangements in the Ferguson house. Exhibit 5 was a floor plan that illustrated two bedrooms and a bathroom on the second floor. The bedroom that Mrs. Ferguson referred to as Natasha's room was also the room that she and the twins slept in.

That sounded crowded and odd to Debbie that an adult, a fourteen-year–old, and twin two-year-olds all slept in the same bedroom, but Mr. Tarman took the whole image another step further when he asked, "And was that all in the same bed, or did you have two different beds there?"

When Mrs. Ferguson answered, "Same bed," Debbie was shocked as much by the answer as she was by Mr. Tarman's line of questions. What was he thinking? She wondered why he would go there with such detail when he stated, "So it was you and the twin boys and Natasha in that room?"

Mrs. Ferguson's testimony indicated that they all slept in the same bed, and that was more information than anyone needed to know. Debbie's confusion over the significance of many details of the defense's line of questioning would continue throughout Mrs. Ferguson's testimony.

Mr. Tarman moved on to establish with the use of Exhibit No. 5 that Paul occupied the second bedroom of the upstairs portion of the Ferguson residence. He pointed out the TV in Natasha's room and the location of the linen closet next to Paul's room, the significance of which would later become clear in Mrs. Ferguson's alibi for Paul.

When Mr. Tarman began to establish the location and position of Paul's bed, Debbie knew that he would be using his chart in the same way that George used the floor plan of her home to reenact the

defense. Unfortunately for Mr. Tarman, Mrs. Ferguson again provided more details than needed. She clarified that Paul's bed was "two
mattresses on the floor because of—okay—what had happened: Paul
had some of his friends over. It used to be two beds here, and he
used to have all his friends. When they come over, Paul would play
with his Nintendo, and they have the disc player for the Genesis. He
had a little party, and they broke the beds. So his bed is now the two
mattresses on the floor."

Debbie looked at Mr. Tarman, trying desperately to understand
why he would want Mrs. Ferguson to tell the jury that Paul and
his friends broke his bed in order to establish for the jury the position of Paul's bed on the night of the attack. She was sure he didn't
want Mrs. Ferguson to continue along those lines when his questions
abruptly moved on to the night of the attack.

Tarman: Now, Ivonne, I want to direct your attention to April
18, 1996, which was the night in question. Can you recall what night
of the week that was?

Mrs. Ferguson: It was a Thursday night.

Tarman: And can you recall whether or not that was a school
night?

Mrs. Ferguson: Yes, it was.

Tarman: And you've already said that Natasha was thirteen
then. Where was she attending school?

Mrs. Ferguson: Susquehanna High.

Debbie immediately stiffened at the inaccuracy of her testimony. Natasha and Alisha were in the eighth grade at the middle
school at the time of the attack. Mr. Tarman didn't attempt to correct
Mrs. Ferguson.

Tarman: And what grade was she in?

Mrs. Ferguson: Ninth grade

Tarman: And what about Paul? Where was he attending school?

Mrs. Ferguson: Excuse me?

This was a phrase Mrs. Ferguson would use frequently throughout her testimony to give herself time to sort out the question or to
calculate her answer.

Debbie recalled George's reassurance to her that testifying would not be difficult for her and her children because they were telling the truth. It would be much more difficult for the witness who was lying. Debbie could tell that it was going to be a tough time on the stand for Mrs. Ferguson if she was unclear about the grade and school Natasha was attending the previous year. George's words echoed through Debbie's mind, the words he had spoken to her on the phone after he had first listened to the tape of her 911 call: "Mrs. Ferguson is claiming you were confused on the night of the attack and misidentified her son as your attacker. This is not a tape of a confused woman."

Debbie felt a bit of smug resentment as she focused upon Mrs. Ferguson's confusion under the pressure of her own attorney's questions.

Mrs. Ferguson: She was in the middle school. Excuse me.

Tarman: She was in the middle school in what grade?

Mrs. Ferguson: Ninth grade. I'm sorry.

And wrong again, Debbie thought as she wondered if the jury was picking up Mrs. Ferguson's inconsistencies. She was in ninth grade; she was in high school.

Tarman: What about Paul?

Mrs. Ferguson: Paul was in high school, also tenth grade.

Tarman: Now, on Thursday evening, April 18, can you recall what time you returned home from work?

Mrs. Ferguson: A little bit after four thirty. About quarter to five.

Tarman: Is that the normal hour for you to return from work?

Mrs. Ferguson: Yes, it is.

Tarman: And can you tell me who was home when you arrived and what was going on there?

Mrs. Ferguson: Okay, I got home. One of the twins was sick. He had a virus. He was doing a lot of vomiting. I came in and laid him down on the couch. Now, I have a couch-bed in the living room as well as another couch. I laid him down. And Paul's father was there, and I asked him, you know, where were the rest of the kids? He said Paul was upstairs cleaning his room, and Natasha was in her room doing her homework. Now, Paul had gone to a trip the night before to see the 76ers in Philadelphia, and he wanted to go to a party that Friday coming, and his room was really—a real, real mess. Typical teenager with clothes all over the place. You couldn't even walk in his room. He also had to do the shutters outside, and I said I'm going to go upstairs and tell Tasha to take care of Tyler, and Paul will go outside with me and do the shutters because the shutters are looking pretty bad.

Debbie tried to imagine coming home from work with twin two-year-olds, one of which was sick and vomiting, and being concerned about getting outside to scrape shutters. She obviously got to the shutters a bit too quickly for Mr. Tarman as well, because he had her back up to the sick child.

Mrs. Ferguson testified that Tyler was ill when she picked him and Travis up from the day care. "He had the flu. Vomiting, did not want to eat. All he wanted to do was just sleep."

When Mr. Tarman asked her what time Mr. Ferguson left the house to go to work that evening, she replied, "I was outside. Paul and I were outside working on the shutters. I couldn't be specific to the exact time he left." She guessed, "Around 6:00 p.m."

To which Mr. Tarman prompted her back to the shutters alibi.

Debbie knew from George's trial preparations that Mrs. Ferguson would alibi the scratches on Paul's arms and legs by claiming that he got the scratches while he was scraping the paint off the shutters. In order to provide the alibi for her son, Mrs. Ferguson actually testified to witnessing his injuries.

Mrs. Ferguson: I would go out there and help him, and when we were doing the shutters—I have bushes around the shutters and trees, and I was basically trying to pull some of the trees down for Paul to get in there and work on the shutters. I was getting cut on my fingers, and he was getting cut on his arms. We went around the house, and I was grabbing on to the bushes and grabbing on to the trees which he was going in there.

Debbie looked at the jury members in an effort to determine if Mrs. Ferguson's story sounded as implausible to them as it did to her. Each member of the jury watched intently as Mrs. Ferguson testified, and one gentleman in the front row seemed to be nodding in affirmation. It occurred to Debbie in her later discussion with George that she had been unable to really focus upon the jury throughout her own testimony in any way other than to convey her information. George reassured her that the jury member of concern nodded throughout all of the prosecution's testimony as well, and not to worry. It didn't help; she still worried.

Mrs. Ferguson continued ad nauseam about the "hour or so" difficult task of helping Paul scrape the shutters and the cuts they both sustained. All the while making no mention of her sick two-year-old or the plans for dinner that was always Debbie's first order of business when she returned home from work or from transporting one or more of her children to afterschool sports or dance activities.

Tarman: How was Paul dressed when you were doing this?

Mrs. Ferguson: He had sweat pants and sweat top.

Sweatshirts are usually long sleeved, Debbie thought, *and should have protected Paul from scratches from the bushes.* Debbie imagined Mr. Tarman wishing he had not asked that question or had prepped his client to indicate that the shirt Paul wore was short-sleeved, thus allowing him to sustain scratches on his arms.

Tarman: Prior to this time, had you noticed—had Paul mentioned anything to you about any cuts or bruises that he received that day?

Mrs. Ferguson: Yes, he did. When I came home and I told him we had to go out and do the shutters, he said earlier that day he was playing football and he did fall on his knee, and he told me his knee was hurting him. I put ointment on his knee. I told him, "You'll be all right. You still got to do your chores."

She put ointment on her fifteen-year-old son's knee. *You must be kidding*, Debbie thought as she searched the faces of the jury in a desperate attempt to see any expression that would suggest they were getting as sick of Mrs. Ferguson's lies as she was. Debbie was literally feeling sick to her stomach as she visualized anyone believing that a mother of a sick two-year-old returned home from a full day of work to put ointment on her fifteen-year-old son's scraped knee before helping him scrape shutters, a knee she knew he actually injured in his knife attack on another mother of three. Debbie felt anger as she relived the force Paul hit her with as he knocked her to the floor of her bedroom. He bruised his knees as he fell onto the hardwood floor of her bedroom and remained straddled over her on his knees while he stabbed her temple and slit her throat.

Debbie despised this woman who never put ointment on her son's knee or helped him scrape shutters on the evening of April 18, 1996. Her son viciously and without cause attacked a family in her neighborhood, and she knew it. This testimony was all made up to hide the sin of her son and her own shame and failure as a mother. Debbie wanted to scream out at her lies, but turned instead to the jury in silent prayers that they would be able to separate the lies from the truth.

The ointment became the repeated theme throughout Mrs. Ferguson's description of Paul's injuries.

Tarman: The scratches that he got from working with the shutters, you observed that?

Mrs. Ferguson: Yes, I did.

Tarman: And in what part of his body were they located?

Mrs. Ferguson: His arms.

Tarman: What part of his arms?

Mrs. Ferguson: The upper part of his arms.

Tarman: You're pointing actually, Ivonne, to your forearm between your elbow and your wrist?

Mrs. Ferguson: Right.

Tarman: Was it just one scratch or more than one?

Mrs. Ferguson: It was more than one. It was welts, as well. I was the main one that was getting cut on my hand. I have the one gash from the bushes.

Tarman: Ivonne, can you remember—you're saying that you put some ointment on him. What parts of his body did you put ointment on at that time?

Mrs. Ferguson: His forearms.

Tarman: And you mentioned—

Mrs. Ferguson: And his knee.

Tarman: All right. Now, what kind of ointment did you use?

Mrs. Ferguson: I used A&D ointment.

Judge Kleinfelter: Why does that have to be marked?

Tarman: There was testimony of beads of sweat on his face, and she put it on his face.

Judge Kleinfelter: What?

Tarman: There was testimony about beads of sweat on his face. She applied the same ointment later on in the day, as the testimony develops, to his head and his nose area.

Judge Kleinfelter: Okay. But why do we actually need the ointment?

Tarman: Well, she has it here. It's the same stuff she applied, and I think it adds more credibility to her testimony.

The tube of A&D ointment was marked as Defense Exhibit No. 6, despite how ridiculous it appeared to Judge Kleinfelter and, hopefully, to the jury members that a tube of ointment was a defense exhibit.

Tarman: Ivonne, placing in front of you Defense Exhibit No. 6. Can you identify that?

Mrs. Ferguson: Yes, I can. The vitamin A&D ointment I put on Paul.

Tarman: You said you applied that to his knees and also to his arms, is that right?

Mrs. Ferguson: Yes.

Tarman: Can you give me a description of the injuries that you observed to his legs at that time?

Mrs. Ferguson: On his knees, he had scraped—he had scrapes to his knees.

After the hour or so of "working on the shutters," Mrs. Ferguson testified that she "warmed up the food" for dinner. After dinner, she was in the kitchen doing the dishes while Paul and Travis were wrestling in the living room. She testified that she "heard Paul scream 'Ouch.' I ran in to the living room, and I said, 'What happened?' Paul is holding his face. He said, 'Travis just kicked me in the face.'" Mrs. Ferguson told the jury that she took Paul to the bathroom, cleaned out his cut, and put some ointment on it.

So that's how Paul got ointment on his forehead—the ointment that the police later mistook for beads of sweat. The police testified that they got Paul out of his bed on April 18 after he claimed to be sleeping soundly. They thought the beads of sweat on his forehead were consistent with the perspiration that would be present on a 233-pound perpetrator of a crime who had just sprinted two and a half blocks from the scene of the crime. But those beads of moisture were actually A&D ointment that his mother had applied to the scratches he sustained while wrestling with his two-year-old brother. Paul had a rough day playing football, scraping shutters, and wrestling with his little brother. No wonder he was so beat when he went to bed on April 18, and why he was snoring so profusely as his mother would soon testify. Debbie was feeling more nauseous as Mrs. Ferguson's lies continued. Just in case the jury needed more evidence to support her fabricated alibi, Mr. Tarman presented Defense Exhibit No. 7 and Defense Exhibit No. 7-A.

Tarman: Ivonne, placing in front of you now Defense Exhibit No. 7 and Defense Exhibit No. 7-A. Would you describe those to the ladies and gentlemen of the jury, please?

Mrs. Ferguson: These are Travis's shoes. He wears special shoes because when he was born, I'm not that big, so I'm carrying twins, and when he was born, he was born with a clubfoot. So he wears a special shoe to try to correct his foot.

Tarman: This is the twin, Travis, that was not sick that day, is that right?

Mrs. Ferguson: Right.

Tarman: Is this the same—did these shoes belong to the same little boy that was playing with Paul that you just mentioned?

Mrs. Ferguson: Yes, yes.

Tarman: And back in April of 1996, he, of course, was wearing these shoes. Is that what you're saying?

Mrs. Ferguson: Yes, yes.

Tarman: And now when he was playing with Paul and you heard Paul yell, were you able to determine what the cause of the injury was to Paul?

Mrs. Ferguson: Well, when I ran in there right away, he was holding his face, and he said, "Travis just kicked me." Travis has a problem with kicking. He has kicked me. I've had bruises, cuts.

Natasha has too. My side door, the second door, he practically kicked the door. You know, he has a problem with his feet.

Tarman: And, of course, this is a small white shoe?

Mrs. Ferguson: Yes.

Tarman: It has the brace on, and I notice it also has a piece at the bottom, which is a little bit—

Mrs. Ferguson: Right. That's what caught on to Paul's face. When he kicked him and he went up, he gave him the cut.

Tarman: You've already pointed to your face, Ivonne. Could you point to it again? What part of Paul's face received the cut from the shoe brace from Travis? If you could point to your face and just indicate what part of Paul's face was cut?

Mrs. Ferguson: I was looking at him. I was looking at his right side. I realize his cut was on the left side because when I'm looking at you and I'm thinking your left is my right, and my right is your left, so it's really on the left side.

Tarman: Point to the facial area and show me where the cut was.

Mrs. Ferguson: The cut was here, and when his feet went up, it kept on going up.

Debbie felt outraged as Mrs. Ferguson tried to attribute the two scratches on Paul's face to the brace on the foot of a two-year-old. Debbie could visualize those two cuts from her index finger and her little finger—the only two fingers on her right hand that could flex. And they were on the left side of Paul's face because she had to use her right hand because her left arm was dislocated and couldn't be lifted as defense from her attacker.

Mrs. Ferguson said the brace made the scratch on the left side of Paul's nose then went up his forehead. One motion of a brace could not make those two cuts, but one motion of her hand with two fingers flexed into Paul's face could. Debbie wanted an expert to testify that the scratch on Paul's forehead was made by a downward rather than an upward motion. She wanted to stop Mrs. Ferguson's lies.

Meanwhile Mr. Tarman had established for the jury through Mrs. Ferguson's testimony a defense for the scratches and beads of "ointment" on Paul's face and was moving on to the details of the evening.

With guidance and help from Mr. Tarman, Mrs. Ferguson outlined the evening of April 18 through a timetable of the television shows she and her family watched. According to her testimony, Mrs. Ferguson, Paul, Natasha, and Travis watched Martin from 8:00 p.m. to 8:30 p.m. Mrs. Ferguson took Travis to bed at 8:30 p.m. after changing the sheets that Tyler had thrown up on. She returned to watch *Living Single* with Paul and Natasha, but had to change the bottom sheet again during the program.

When *Living Single* ended at 9:00 p.m., the three began watching *New York Undercover*. Halfway through the hour-long show, Mrs. Ferguson sent Paul and Natasha upstairs to shower and go to bed. After all, Paul had been "falling asleep" because he was so tired from getting home late from the 76ers game the night before.

Paul took his shower first. Mrs. Ferguson got him a Tylenol for his headache and applied A&D ointment on his cuts one more time while Natasha took her shower. Mr. Tarman made sure that Mrs. Ferguson repeated specifically that she applied ointment to Paul's face, arms, and knees. She mentioned that Paul always wore sweatpants and sweat tops to bed, and that night was no exception. He wore purple sweatpants and a beige sweatshirt to bed.

According to Mrs. Ferguson, Natasha negotiated permission to finish watching *New York Undercover* in her room on her TV as long as she kept the volume low, but when *New York Undercover* ended at 10:00 p.m., Mrs. Ferguson insisted that she turn off the TV. Natasha was not permitted to watch *Comicview*, and Mrs. Ferguson returned to the show she had been waiting to watch. The documentary *48 Hours* was about the Oklahoma bombings, and she planned to watch the show by herself downstairs in the living room.

Unfortunately for Mrs. Ferguson, the show she was so interested in watching was interrupted repeatedly. She had to go upstairs two times between 10:00 p.m. and 10:15 p.m. to reprimand Natasha for watching *Comicview* despite her instructions to go to sleep. Mrs. Ferguson made a point to remind the jury that she saw Paul sleeping and heard him snoring each time she went upstairs.

At approximately 10:20 p.m., Mrs. Ferguson heard noises in Paul's room while she was watching *48 Hours*. When she went upstairs, now for a third time in the first twenty minutes of her TV show, she caught Natasha coming out of Paul's room with one of Paul's shirts on a hanger. Mrs. Ferguson took the shirt from her, went into Paul's room, and returned the shirt to his closet. She saw Paul sleeping and heard him snoring, stating, "Paul is knocked out. He is beat tired from the night before."

The discussion Mrs. Ferguson had with Natasha about taking Paul's shirt resulted in Tyler waking and Mrs. Ferguson noticing that he had thrown up again, requiring her to change his bottom sheet again. While she was at the linen closet getting another sheet, she stated that, "Of course Paul is there with his snoring."

Mr. Tarman made a point to ask if the bedroom doors were open or closed. According to Mrs. Ferguson, the doors were always open, and the bathroom light was always on, providing enough light for her to see Paul sleeping each time she came upstairs.

The perfect alibi, Debbie thought sarcastically and with a rage that she could barely contain. From the 10:20 p.m. phone call that woke her to 10:30 p.m. when she heard the floorboards creaking, Mrs. Ferguson was in her son's bedroom and outside his room seeing him sleeping and hearing him snoring. And the worst part of all the lies she was hearing was remembering George's plan for cross-examination of Mrs. Ferguson. He was not going to have her repeat her lies. He was merely going to have her state that she'd do anything for her son, including lie for him and allow the jury to figure it out. Debbie was beginning to be angry with George at the thought of letting Mrs. Ferguson tell her lies and go unchallenged.

Mrs. Ferguson testified that she returned to her TV program at, coincidentally, 10:30 p.m., which was halfway through the show and precisely the time Debbie heard her floorboards creak. Mrs. Ferguson went up the stairs two more times before *48 Hours* was over. In fact, she never saw the end of her program because the second trip up the stairs was at Natasha's request so she could see the police officers outside their home.

Mrs. Ferguson testified that she went to the windows of her home and could see policemen all around the outside, searching in her bushes, and said to Natasha, "Go to your room. I don't know what's going on. Are you okay? Are the boys okay? Paul's okay? The bathroom okay?"

"The bathroom okay" question jumped out at Debbie as she imagined the hundreds of times she wondered what had happened to the plaid shirt Paul was wearing during the attack that surely had her bloody handprints on the front of it. Since she and George had concluded that Paul was naked under that big, long plaid shirt because he had taken his pants off in the kitchen and was prepared to rape Alisha, they had also concluded that Paul had to have worn that bloody shirt home; otherwise, he would have been running through the neighborhood totally naked. Having worn that bloody shirt into his house, it was likely to have ended up in the bathroom or his bedroom. George's theory was that Mrs. Ferguson did not come outside immediately when she saw the police outside her home because she was busy collecting the shirt and hiding it in her van until she could dispose of it on her way to the police station. Debbie was sure Mrs. Ferguson was wondering if the bathroom was "okay" before she went into the garage and opened the garage door to the police outside.

Mrs. Ferguson continued to testify that she was thinking there might be a fire. Debbie immediately tried to imagine looking outside her home and seeing police and worrying about a fire. Fire trucks or sirens might evoke such fears, but not police cars without sirens and police officers searching through her bushes. And how long would she spend inside looking outside the windows before she would open the door and ask the officers what was going on?

Mrs. Ferguson had a reason for not opening her front door and asking the police what was happening. All her house doors were double-locked, and she could not find her keys. According to Mrs. Ferguson, Natasha provided the explanation that Travis had been playing with the house keys.

Now that explained the delay in Mrs. Ferguson's appearance to the police. She wasn't grilling Paul about where he had been and what he had done. She wasn't collecting the bloody shirt and hiding it in her van in the garage or under the twin's mattress. She actually was unable to open any of her house doors because Travis had hidden her house keys. After searching the house for her missing keys while the police searched the perimeter of her home, she finally went through the garage and met them outside her garage door.

Mrs. Ferguson said that the police wanted to know if her son was home and wanted to see him immediately. She assured them that he was in bed sleeping and led them to his room. Mrs. Ferguson testified that the police asked, "Is this Paul's room?" She replied, "Yes, it is" and further stated, "There's a sign that says 'Paul's Room,' and he [the police officer] opened the door and Paul was still sleeping and snoring."

Her statement, "He opened the door" again echoed in Debbie's mind. The officer opened the bedroom door that had been open all evening so that Mrs. Ferguson could see Paul sleeping and hear him snoring? George, did you hear that? Jury members, did you catch just one more discrepancy in her pack of lies? It was difficult for Debbie to hear Mrs. Ferguson's lies go unchallenged.

The police would not tell Mrs. Ferguson why they needed to get Paul out of his bedroom, into handcuffs and into the back of their police car, but Mrs. Ferguson testified that she kept hearing through their Walkie Talkies the repetitious "Debra Bird stabbing."

At this point in the court proceedings, Judge Kleinfelter announced the end of day 3 of the trial. It was 4:57 p.m. on Wednesday, December 11, and time for the jury members to go home. It was also time for Debbie to talk with George. He needed to speak with her too, and what he had to say put most of her concerns to rest. He asked Debbie if she remembered his plans to be brief in his cross-examination of Mrs. Ferguson so as not to have her repeat lies that could become more believable by the jury through the repetition. Debbie not only remembered his plan, she had grown angrier at his plan with each lie that Mrs. Ferguson told, and she told him so. He told her not to worry because his plan had changed. He said Mrs. Ferguson had told too many lies, and she wasn't good at it, so he was going after her.

Chapter XXXIV

The Trial: Day 4

The fourth day of the trial began at 9:00 a.m., with Mrs. Ferguson back on the stand and Mr. Tarman continuing his examination. He made sure that Mrs. Ferguson did not hear anyone come in or out of her house during her ten o'clock TV program. He also established through her testimony that Paul did not have a key to their house because, according to Mrs. Ferguson, he always lost his keys. Mr. Ferguson, Mrs. Ferguson, and Natasha each had a key, and Paul gained access to the house each day after school with Natasha and her key.

Defense Exhibit 8 was a Voluntary Consent Form for Search and Seizure that Mrs. Ferguson signed at the police station at 12:23 a.m. during her meeting with Detective Nelson. It was clear that Mr. Tarman presented the form to establish for the jury that Mrs. Ferguson had nothing to hide in her home on the night and early-morning hours of the attack.

Mr. Tarman introduced Defense Exhibit 42, which Mrs. Ferguson described as a diagram of her neighborhood. Mr. Tarman used the diagram to illustrate again for the jury how close Mrs. Ferguson's house was to Front Street and the route Mr. Tarman wanted the jury to believe the real perpetrator of the attack traveled as he fled the scene of the crime.

Defense Exhibit 9 A, B, and C were pictures of Paul's cuts. Exhibit 9-B was a close-up of the cuts on Paul's face, which Mrs. Ferguson testified were caused by Travis's brace, and 9-A showed the abrasions on Paul's knees—cuts that Mrs. Ferguson swore she saw and applied ointment to prior to Paul going to bed at approximately 9:30 p.m. on April 18. Defense Exhibit 9-C was a picture of Paul's arms with the scratches he got while scraping the shutters.

Defense Exhibit 9 was the knife used in the attack. Mrs. Ferguson never saw the knife; no such knife had ever been in her home, and Paul never had such a knife. Paul never owned a pair of black sneakers like the ones labeled as Defense Exhibit 35. They were the sneakers left at the scene of the crime by the perpetrator of the crime. Despite the fact that Paul wore size 13 sneakers, he would never have worn such sneakers because he only wore Reebok, Nike, or Fila name-brand sneakers, according to his mother. When Mr. Tarman presented Commonwealth Exhibit 26 and 26-A, Mrs. Ferguson identified the white size 13 sneakers as Paul's, emphasizing that they were Reeboks and the same sneakers that Paul put on when the police picked him up on the night of the attack.

With Mr. Tarman's help, Mrs. Ferguson testified to never seeing a flashlight or tips of gloves in her home like those presented as evidence by the prosecution. When Mr. Tarman told Mrs. Ferguson that there had been testimony in the trial that "the assailant of the Bird family wore a flannel, short-sleeved shirt, blue or black in color. Have you ever observed your son, Paul Ferguson, wearing a flannel short-sleeve shirt of that kind?" she said "no."

Debbie wished she could be seated with George at the prosecution table, because she needed to make sure he caught the comments such as bathroom okay, Paul's bedroom door closed, and now the flannel shirt. *Where did the flannel shirt come from? It was never a flannel shirt.*

Mr. Tarman: Does your son, Paul Ferguson, own flannel shirts?

Mrs. Ferguson: Yes, he does.

Mr. Tarman: And have you, since the charge has been brought, gone through his clothing to try to see if you could find a shirt like that?

Mrs. Ferguson: Yes.

Mr. Tarman: And even before April 18, 1996, you're saying you never saw him or knew him to have a short-sleeved flannel shirt?

Mrs. Ferguson: Not short-sleeved. All his flannel shirts are long-sleeved. The short ones have little flowers or designs on them, but not a short-sleeved flannel shirt.

Mr. Tarman: Thank you, Ivonne. Your witness.

It didn't take long in George's cross-examination of Mrs. Ferguson for Debbie to know that George picked up on the flannel shirt discrepancy.

Mr. Matangos: Mrs. Ferguson, in your answer you're relying on Mr. Tarman to tell you it's a flannel shirt, right?

Mrs. Ferguson: He asked me the question. Did I ever see a flannel shirt? Did Paul own a flannel shirt?

Mr. Matangos: So you're relying on Mr. Tarman indicating that it's flannel?

Mrs. Ferguson: Excuse me?

Mr. Matangos: You're relying on Mr. Tarman indicating to you that it's flannel?

Mrs. Ferguson: No, I was answering his question.

Mr. Matangos: How else would you come up with the terminology *flannel*, unless Mr. Tarman told you flannel?

Mr. Tarman: "Your Honor, I would—I think that's an unfair question.

Judge Kleinfelter: I don't know. You used the term—somebody used the term *flannel*. First time I've heard *flannel* in this trial.

Mrs. Ferguson: I took it as flannel shirt, Your Honor.

Mr. Tarman: Well, Your Honor, Ivonne has been present at the preliminary hearing.

Judge Kleinfelter: Well, just a moment. Do you have an objection?

Mr. Tarman: Yeah.

Judge Kleinfelter: State your objection.

Mr. Tarman: I think it's an unfair question.

Judge Kleinfelter: The objection is overruled.

Mr. Matangos: Would you answer the question I asked?

Mrs. Ferguson: When he was talking about the shirt, I assumed he was talking about the flannel shirt.

Mr. Matangos: Because that's what you looked for at your house?

Mrs. Ferguson: Right, because I heard—

Mr. Matangos: I don't want to hear what you heard. That's what you looked for at your house?

Mrs. Ferguson: Right.

Mr. Matangos: And you didn't find any flannel shirt?

Mrs. Ferguson: Not with that description.

Mr. Matangos: What description?

Mrs. Ferguson: Excuse me?

Mr. Matangos: What description?

Mrs. Ferguson: When the police came in, in the paper it had said something about a short-sleeved flannel shirt. They gave me papers when I was in the police station.

Mr. Matangos: And it said flannel shirt? Is that your recollection?

Mr. Ferguson: Yes.

Mr. Matangos: And that's why you looked for flannel?

Mrs. Ferguson: Right. Well, first, in one paper, it said they were looking for a black nylon shirt.

Mr. Matangos: I'm not asking about the black nylon shirt. I was asking why you came up with this flannel shirt?

Mrs. Ferguson: Okay.

Mr. Matangos: Because what the shirt was that was described was a plaid shirt—a cotton plaid shirt. That's all that was described, and it was described as being blue-and–white, or black-and-white. Did you know that?

Mrs. Ferguson gave no response, and Mr. Matangos continued.

Mr. Matangos: Did you know that?

Mrs. Ferguson: In one of the papers, it said black nylon shirt.

Mr. Matangos: I'm not—once again, you're going back to something I didn't ask you. It was described—Paul was described as wearing a blue-and-white or black-and-white plaid shirt—

Mrs. Ferguson: Right.

Mr. Matangos: At the time of the assault with a dark collar—dark blue or black. Does Paul own a plaid shirt like that?

Mrs. Ferguson: Blue or black and—

Mr. Matangos: Blue or black-and-white plaid shirt with a dark collar?

Mrs. Ferguson: No.

Mr. Matangos: He doesn't own a shirt like that?

Mrs. Ferguson: I would have to see what you're talking about, Sir.

Mr. Matangos: You just said you went through all his clothing.

Mrs. Ferguson: You said blue, black, or white?

Mr. Matangos: Plaid. You know what plaid means?

Mrs. Ferguson: Boxes and lines across.

Mr. Matangos: So you do know what I'm talking about?

Mrs. Ferguson: Yes.

Mr. Matangos: Does he own a shirt like that?

Mrs. Ferguson: Yes, he does.

Mr. Matangos: Thank you.

Well, George was right, Debbie thought. He was going after her, and Debbie loved it. Every time Mrs. Ferguson hesitated, repeated herself, or said "Excuse me" to give herself time to think up the right answer or hope that the question would go away, Debbie hoped that the members of the jury, the judge, and everyone in the courtroom was taking notice. She enjoyed watching Mrs. Ferguson struggle with her lies, and she felt all the anger and frustration that Mr. Matangos was feeling as he put the pressure on her with his quick questions and his determination to uncover the truth for the jury even if it wouldn't come from her answers.

And he was brilliant with the questions of Mrs. Ferguson regarding the shirt. She couldn't say Paul never had a plaid shirt because she knew Mr. Matangos saw the picture of Paul in the yearbook in the plaid shirt. George knew that without a colored picture of Paul, Mrs. Ferguson could change the dark color to any dark color other than blue or black, and there was no way of proving otherwise. Since the yearbook picture did not include the shoulders or arms, she could also change that plaid shirt to long-sleeved, which she had already indicated in her responses to Tarman's questions. Debbie settled back in her seat and looked forward to the grilling to continue.

Mr. Matangos: These pants [he held up Paul's purple sweat pants] do you recognize these as being the ones Paul had on that night?

Mrs. Ferguson: Yes.

Mr. Matangos: And that he had on when he went to the police station and took all those photographs?

Mrs. Ferguson: Yes.

Mr. Matangos: Your Honor, if I may have this marked for identification purposes?

The pants were marked as Commonwealth Exhibit 52, and the beige sweatshirt was presented for identification.

Mr. Matangos: Do you recognize this? It's inside out, but do you recognize that?

Mrs. Ferguson: Yes. The shirt Paul had on that night.

Mr. Matangos: How do you describe that?

Mrs. Ferguson: A sweatshirt, Nike.

Mr. Matangos: And what color is that?

Mrs. Ferguson: Like a gray—beige-gray.

Mr. Matangos: Is there any question that's the sweatshirt he had on when the police officers came to the house?

Mrs. Ferguson: No.

Mr. Matangos: Is there any question this is the shirt he was wearing that night?

Mrs. Ferguson: I don't think this was the shirt. His shirt was more beige.

Mr. Matangos: Could I have that photograph, Mr. Tarman? I'm showing you Exhibit 3. See the photograph?

Mrs. Ferguson: Yeah.

Mr. Matangos: What is the photograph of?

Mrs. Ferguson: This shirt.

Mr. Matangos: So it is the same shirt?

Mrs. Ferguson: Yes.

Mr. Matangos: What size was that sweatshirt?

Mrs. Ferguson: XL-1, I believe.

Mr. Matangos: Can you see what I'm holding up, ma'am?

Mrs. Ferguson: Yes.

Mr. Matangos: What are these?

Mrs. Ferguson: They're pants.

Mr. Matangos: They're pants that are marked as Commonwealth Exhibit 34. Do you know where these pants were found?

Mrs. Ferguson: In the Bird's residence, I guess. I don't know.

Mr. Matangos: Well, I'm only asking if you know. Do you know?

Mrs. Ferguson: I'm not sure.

Mr. Matangos: If I told you these were the ones found in the kitchen that were left there on the floor with the black sneakers Mr. Tarman showed you earlier, he didn't show you these though?

Mrs. Ferguson: No.

Mr. Matangos: Only showed you the sneakers?

Mrs. Ferguson: Yes.

Mr. Matangos: Paul owns a pair of pants just like these, doesn't he?

Mrs. Ferguson: Yes, he does.

Debbie was shocked. She was sure Mrs. Ferguson was going to deny that Paul had any items like those that had been left in her house. Hadn't George told her that Mrs. Ferguson was going to provide a denial that Paul ever owned items like the sneakers, knife, flashlight, and pants that were left behind? Or did George just notice that Mr. Tarman failed to present the pants for Mrs. Ferguson to alibi? Debbie wondered why Mrs. Ferguson was not lying that Paul had black nylon pants like she did for the other items as Mr. Matangos's questions continued.

Mr. Matangos: You can tell by looking at it that it is something Paul would have worn before, isn't it?

Mrs. Ferguson: Can I look at the inside of the pants? I believe Paul's say 'Nike' inside.

Mr. Matangos: Well, that's your testimony—that everything he wears is Nike or Reebok or Fila. Right?

Mrs. Ferguson: Right.

Mr. Matangos: What do these pants have inside?

Mrs. Ferguson: A hundred percent nylon.

Mr. Matangos: There's nothing in here that indicates a make or model, is there?

Mrs. Ferguson: No.

Mr. Matangos: There's no brand name, right?

Mrs. Ferguson: No.

Mr. Matangos: What size are these? Did you notice when you looked at that tag that these are double-XL, XXL?

Mrs. Ferguson: Right.

Mr. Matangos: And Paul weighed 233 pounds back in April of 1996, didn't he?

Mrs. Ferguson: Right.

Mr. Matangos: That would have been the size of the other pants he wore, isn't it?

Mrs. Ferguson: His are 3-XL. The pants he wears are bigger.

Mr. Matangos: He doesn't own 2-XL pants?

Mrs. Ferguson: No.

Mr. Matangos: That's your testimony now. You never bought one pair of 2-XL pants?

Mrs. Ferguson: Of those pants, I know he bought 3-XL when I went to the store with him.

Mr. Matangos: What was his waist size?

Mrs. Ferguson: Excuse me?

Once more, Mrs. Ferguson was too deep into that tangled web of deceit she was weaving for her to turn back now. She was stalling, and George was standing over her like a hawk over a field mouse. He was playing with her because she had no place to go to get away or hide, and he was in no hurry. In fact, it seemed as though Mrs. Ferguson was spinning so many traps for herself that he didn't know which one to go after first.

And Debbie was having a field day watching the performance. Let's see, Paul owned black nylon pants like the ones left in her kitchen by her attacker, but Paul's pants were size 3-XL rather than 2-XL. And Mrs. Ferguson knew that because she was with him when he bought them, and she remembered their size. Debbie couldn't remember the size of the dress she was wearing at that moment or day, let alone the size of any of the clothing her children had on that day in the courtroom. Of course, she couldn't remember the last time she applied ointment or a band-aid to Ashley, let alone Jaredd.

Mr. Matangos: If you went to the store to buy clothing, you know his waist size.

Mrs. Ferguson: I usually go to the store and he tries the clothes on.

Mr. Matangos: You know it was 3-XL each time. What was his waist size?

Mrs. Ferguson: When he picked it up, he picked 3-XL. He's somebody whose pants are 38, some are 36. Depends on the style of the pants. Sometimes he wears 40.

Mr. Matangos: Tell me when you're done.

Mrs. Ferguson: Paul's weight fluctuates and I've seen him have 38 on or 40 on.

Mr. Matangos: We're talking about April of 1996.

Mrs. Ferguson: Right.

Mr. Matangos: Okay. And you're telling me he wore 36 and 38 when he was buying 3-XL pants?

Mrs. Ferguson: Depends on the style of those pants. Those pants are worn big.

Mr. Matangos: So he could have worn 2-XL?

Mrs. Ferguson had no response. She knew the correct answer was yes, but that answer could make those black nylon pants Paul's, and she was desperately trying to avoid admitting that to the jury. Instead of saying "Excuse me" to buy herself more time, she was trying the no-response answer—like that was going to work with Mr. Matangos.

Mr. Matangos: A 2-XL would have been big on somebody wearing a 38 or 36.

Mrs. Ferguson: Right.

Mr. Matangos: A 2-XL is around a 52 waist. As a matter of fact, I fit into a 2-XL.

Mr. Tarman: Your Honor, we're offering facts not in evidence now. The district attorney is getting into other—his own pants size— and I don't think that's a proper form of question.

Mr. Matangos: Strictly for comparison opinion from the witness.

Mr. Tarman: That is very, very confusing to a witness to be asking a question in that form.

Judge Kleinfelter: We'll allow it.

Mr. Matangos: Is there other clothing in this courtroom that he wore that day?

Mrs. Ferguson: Excuse me?

Mr. Matangos: Is there other clothing in this courtroom that Paul wore on April 18?

Mrs. Ferguson: That I'm looking at right now?

Mr. Matangos: No. Is there other clothing besides what we've seen?

Mrs. Ferguson: I don't understand the question.

Mr. Matangos: Did you give Mr. Tarman some clothes to bring to court?

Mrs. Ferguson: I gave Mr. Tarman all of Paul's shirts; flannels, prints, whatever was in the home.

Mr. Matangos: Did you give him the one you described earlier that you finally admitted he owned? Did you give him that one?

Mrs. Ferguson: You said if he owns a blue-and-beige or white. I said, "Yes, he owns blue and beige and white," but what I said to you as far as flannel has to be long-sleeved. That's all he owns as far as flannel.

Mr. Matangos: Do you see the clothing I'm holding up now?

Mrs. Ferguson: Um-hmm.

Mr. Matangos: Do you see that?

Mrs. Ferguson: Yes.

Mr. Matangos: Can I have this marked, please, as Commonwealth Exhibit 53?

(A sweatshirt was marked as 53 and sweatpants as 54).

Mr. Matangos: Mrs. Ferguson, this is Commonwealth's Exhibit 53. What is that?

Mrs. Ferguson: A sweatshirt.

Mr. Matangos: Whose sweatshirt is it?

Mrs. Ferguson: This is Paul's sweatshirt.

Mr. Matangos: That's a Hanes sweatshirt, isn't it?

Mrs. Ferguson: Yes.

Mr. Matangos: Like the kind you pick up at a department store?

Mrs. Ferguson: I usually buy these since he likes to sleep in sweatshirts. I usually buy Hanes or something. I usually go to a department store.

Mr. Matangos: And there's no question in your mind this is Paul's sweatshirt? You brought this to court, didn't you?

Mrs. Ferguson: Excuse me?

Was she stalling because she was beginning to realize that all her testimony about Paul only owning name-brand clothing was going down the tubes?

Mr. Matangos: You brought this to court to give to Mr. Tarman?

Mrs. Ferguson: Right.

Mr. Matangos: Showing you Commonwealth Exhibit 54 for identification. Then George went back to asking Mrs. Ferguson, What is that?

Mrs. Ferguson: Sweatpants.

Mr. Matangos: Whose sweatpants are those?

Mrs. Ferguson: These are Paul's.

Mr. Matangos: How do you know they're Paul's?

Mrs. Ferguson: Looking at it. I gave it to Mr. Tarman.

Mr. Matangos: So there's no question in your mind these are Paul's clothing?

Mrs. Ferguson: Right.

Mr. Matangos: These are larges; is that right?

Mrs. Ferguson: Right.

Mr. Matangos: That's a large size?

Mrs. Ferguson: Right.

Mr. Matangos: Not double-XL or triple-XL; just a regular large?

Mrs. Ferguson: Right.

Mr. Matangos was done proving Mrs. Ferguson was lying about brand-name clothing and sizes. He moved right to the times and events Mrs. Ferguson had described for Mr. Tarman the day before in her testimony.

Mr. Matangos: You had a very good recollection yesterday of all those events, didn't you?

Mrs. Ferguson: Right.

Mr. Matangos: Is that because that night you made sure to remember what happened, right? Because you knew how important that would be?

Mrs. Ferguson: No. To me it was more like a nightmare. I'll remember that night the rest of my life. It was a nightmare to me.

Mr. Matangos: You recall it because it was important?

Mrs. Ferguson: Yeah. It was a nightmare.

Mr. Matangos: Whether it was a nightmare or not, it was very important what happened. Now, I'm going to put some times on this diagram. I'll start at the top with 5:00 p.m., then 6:00 p.m. Do you see me doing this—7:00 p.m., 8:00 p.m., 9:00 p.m., 10:00 p.m., 11:00 p.m., and finally, midnight, or 12:00 a.m.?

Mr. Matangos proceeded to list the events of Mrs. Ferguson's testimony to Mr. Tarman regarding the events of April 18. He described each detail as Mrs. Ferguson had outlined, challenging her to affirm each event and specific time as he charted it. Debbie was amazed at how well George remembered so many details of Mrs. Ferguson's testimony that even Mrs. Ferguson seemed to have trouble recalling. Other than Mrs. Ferguson appearing nervous about each time and event that Mr. Matangos seemed to be making her commit to, the events seemed to become repetitious of the previous day.

For abandoning his previous theory about repeating lies, George seemed to be doing just that. He was allowing Mrs. Ferguson to repeat her alibis without challenge, until he got to the ointment. At that point, you could see how the devil was in the details, and there were some details that Mrs. Ferguson had not thought out ahead of time. When Mr. Matangos got to the ointment, he had already established that Paul had taken his shower and was dressed for bed in his sweatpants and sweatshirt.

Mr. Matangos: And who rolled up the sleeves? Did Paul pull them up or you pulled them up? Who did that?

Mrs. Ferguson: He always does that. Like the hives—he has the hives or whatever—it bothers him in the arms, and he cuts the cuffs off so he can have flexibility, so forth, on them.

Mr. Matangos: You'd agree with me the cuffs and the sleeve here are not cut?

Mrs. Ferguson: No.

Mr. Matangos: Were these rolled up to get to his arms? Did you roll them up to get to his arms?

Mrs. Ferguson: No, he pulled it up.

Mr. Matangos: After he pulled them up like that so you could reach the cuts and everything—the scratches that you say were there from scraping the shutters and the bushes—he slid them down himself, or you pulled it back down?

Mrs. Ferguson: He pulled it down himself.

Mrs. Ferguson: He just pulled it back down his arm?

Mrs. Ferguson: Right.

Mr. Matangos: Same thing with the pants? Just rolled them up, slipped them up over his leg like that?

Paul had scratches on his upper arms and knees, and George had the jury visualizing sliding sweatpants and sweatshirt sleeves with cuffs up over the cuts to apply ointment and sliding them back down over the cuts.

As George continued, Debbie wondered how he went from his initial plan for cross-examination that involved only a few key questions for Mrs. Ferguson to such a detailed interrogation on her every word. If she remembered the details she chose to share with Mr. Tarman, perhaps she should be able to recall if she pulled Paul's pant legs and sleeves up or if Paul did that himself. Perhaps she should be able to remember how long Paul took in the shower the night of April 18 and how long Natasha took. When Mrs. Ferguson estimated three minutes for Natasha's shower and four minutes for Paul's, Mr. Matangos did have some obvious disbelief in his tone.

Mr. Matangos: Maybe four minutes in the shower?

Mrs. Ferguson: You're asking me to time the shower. You know, I went downstairs, got the ointment, and came back upstairs.

Mr. Matangos: That's done a lot throughout these trials. I hope you understand. Lots of witnesses on the stand have been asked about times, so we understand you're estimating.

Mr. Matangos's efforts to kindly reassure Mrs. Ferguson that everyone understood he was only looking for her best estimate of the times and events that occurred nearly eight months ago were no indication that he intended to let up. He continued outlining the times of every aspect of her testimony, including the interruptions to her *48 Hours* television program, the arrival of the police, and her trip to the police station.

By midmorning, Judge Kleinfelter interrupted Mr. Matangos for a timing question of his own. "Mr. Matangos, will you be some time yet?"

When Mr. Matangos answered, "I'm afraid so, Your Honor," the judge announced a fifteen-minute recess.

Chapter XXXV

Moments that Last Forever

When the recess ended, Mr. Matangos launched immediately into questioning Mrs. Ferguson about many aspects of her previous testimony. She was unable to describe what Paul did with his friends at the Birds' residence prior to the "relationship change" in February of 1994, while insisting that the restriction of her son from the swimming and basketball at the Birds' house had made him angry. When she offered that she was angrier than Paul, Mr. Matangos jumped on her comment and challenged her as to what efforts she had made to learn the nature of the problem. She hadn't called or tried to talk with Mrs. Bird regarding the restriction, and claimed that even Paul had not told her what had happened.

Only Debbie and her family knew about Paul's theft from their home, and Debbie worried that George was getting dangerously close to aspects of the trial that were not to be shared with the jury. As Debbie reflected upon the real reason Mrs. Ferguson made no effort to talk with her; the fact that she was angry that the police had questioned her and her son about the day Paul hooked school and hung out and stole things from the Birds' house, Debbie noticed George thumbing through Jaredd's yearbook, and she knew where he was going next.

Mr. Matangos: We talked about a plaid shirt, Mrs. Ferguson. What is that?

Mrs. Ferguson: Yearbook.

Mr. Matangos: Where is that yearbook from?

Mrs. Ferguson: Susquehanna Township High School.

Mr. Matangos: Your son attends Susquehanna Township High School, doesn't he?

Mrs. Ferguson: Yes.

Mr. Matangos: Did he receive a yearbook?

Mrs. Ferguson: No. You could purchase it and I didn't.

Mr. Matangos: Did you receive any photographs that were taken of Paul during the school year last year?

Mrs. Ferguson: No.

Mr. Matangos: Do you see a person that you recognize on the page you have open, which is page 45?

Mrs. Ferguson: Yes, my son.

Mr. Matangos: Your son's pictured in that yearbook?

Mrs. Ferguson: Right.

Mr. Matangos: Do you recognize the clothing he's wearing?

Mrs. Ferguson: Yes.

Mr. Matangos: He owns a shirt just like that, doesn't he?

Mrs. Ferguson: Yes.

Mr. Matangos: It is a plaid shirt?

Mrs. Ferguson: Right.

Mr. Matangos: It's a dark plaid shirt?

Mrs. Ferguson: Green and beige that particular shirt.

Mr. Matangos: Green and beige?

Mrs. Ferguson: Right. Green around the collar and the dark color is green and then it's got that light beige—

Mr. Matangos: What color is the collar?

Mrs. Ferguson: Green.

Mr. Matangos: That's not a color photograph, is it?

Mrs. Ferguson: No, but I know that shirt.

Mr. Matangos: Do you have that shirt with you here today?

Mrs. Ferguson: No.

Mr. Matangos: Didn't you tell me you went through all the clothing and you gave clothing to Mr. Tarman?

Mrs. Ferguson: Right.

Mr. Matangos: You don't have that shirt here?

Mrs. Ferguson: I would have to look and see. I don't know. I know I take somebody's clothing when they don't wear it anymore and I bring it to Goodwill.

Mr. Matangos: So it's possible you don't even own that shirt anymore.

Mrs. Ferguson: Could be.

Mr. Matangos: Mrs. Ferguson, had you seen that photo before today?

Mrs. Ferguson: Excuse me?

Mr. Matangos: Had you seen that photo of your son before today?

Mrs. Ferguson: I don't remember. It's so many pictures from school. I really don't remember.

Mr. Matangos: Did your attorney tell you I had that photograph?

Mrs. Ferguson: No, he didn't.

Mr. Matangos: Paul's attorney didn't tell you I had shown him this photograph?

Mrs. Ferguson: Which photograph? Another photograph you have?

Mr. Matangos: Mr. Tarman didn't tell you that I showed him this yearbook and this photograph?

Mrs. Ferguson: Oh, he said there was a book with a photograph that he wants—that you could see one of Paul's plaid shirts. I'm saying plaid shirt. I'm looking at this. I'm nervous. You're interrogating me. I'm a little bit nervous. I'm sorry.

Mr. Matangos: You do admit Mr. Tarman told you about this yearbook and this photograph?

Mrs. Ferguson: I don't know if it was that photograph or not. He just said Jaredd has a photograph, something about a shirt, a beige shirt or blue shirt. I don't remember.

Mr. Matangos: He told you that Jaredd said that?

Mrs. Ferguson: Excuse me?

Mr. Matangos: Who told you Jaredd said that?

Mrs. Ferguson: You ask me questions. I really don't remember. I only remember it was Foreman that asked me for a shirt. That was my previous lawyer. I don't remember that.

Mr. Matangos: You were shown some glove tips?

Mrs. Ferguson: Yes.

Mr. Matangos: Do you remember being shown glove tips?

Mrs. Ferguson: Yes.

Mr. Matangos: Those are just ordinary gloves you wear to wash dishes, right?

Mrs. Ferguson: I wear disposable gloves. I have boxes and boxes of disposable gloves.

Mr. Matangos: Was that my question?

Mrs. Ferguson: Excuse me?

Mr. Matangos: Was that my question?

Mrs. Ferguson: Repeat your question.

Mr. Matangos: My question is those tips are from ordinary gloves you use to scrub like a pot?

Mrs. Ferguson: Right.

Mr. Matangos: I didn't ask you if you owned them.

Mrs. Ferguson: Okay. I was just having a conversation.

Mr. Matangos: You've talked plenty about what you're going to say on the stand here today, haven't you?

Mrs. Ferguson: Excuse me?

Mr. Matangos: You've talked plenty about—

Mr. Tarman objected, Your Honor, that's an improper question, "talked plenty."

Judge Kleinfelter: Overruled.

Mr. Matangos: Talk about your alibi you're giving today? You've talked to Mr. Tarman?

Mrs. Ferguson: Yes.

Mr. Matangos: Spoke to Natasha?

Mrs. Ferguson: Yes.

Mr. Matangos: Spoken to your husband?

Mrs. Ferguson: Oh, yes.

Mr. Matangos: Spoken to Paul?

Mrs. Ferguson: What do you mean, spoken to Paul?

Mr. Matangos: I'm just going down a list. You're stopping when I say Paul. You talked to Paul about what you're going to testify to as far as the alibi. Right?

Mrs. Ferguson: I don't understand what you mean. For me to talk to Paul and say I'm going to say this and say that? Is that what you're saying?

Mr. Matangos: Yes.

Mrs. Ferguson: No.

Mr. Matangos: You never talked to Paul about what you're going to testify here today?

Mrs. Ferguson: I talked to Paul not to worry about it. All I could do is talk to him about Jesus and don't worry about it.

Mr. Matangos: When you sat down with Natasha and talked about what you were going to say today—

Mrs. Ferguson: When I sat down with Natasha?

Mr. Matangos: Yes. When you sat down and talked about it, how many times would you say you've talked about it?

Mrs. Ferguson: I have no idea. You know, I have talked to her, yes, I have. You know we talked about the TV shows, yes.

Mr. Matangos: Ma'am, your son is here charged with attempted homicide, aggravated assault—

Mrs. Ferguson: Right.

Mr. Matangos: --and burglary.

Mrs. Ferguson: Right.

Mr. Matangos: Now, I'm asking you how many times have you talked with Natasha specifically about this testimony about where he was, where you were, the entire circumstances about that evening?

Mrs. Ferguson: When I got home and she woke up that morning, we talked about it, and I said, 'We did this and we did that.' But as far—what are you trying to say to me?

Mr. Matangos: I think you know what I'm trying to say. I'm trying to say you and your daughter have talked.

Mrs. Ferguson: I talked several times, of course. This is a nightmare. This is all we live. It's a nightmare.

Mr. Matangos: It's also a nightmare for the Bird family.

And the tears welled up in Debbie's eyes instantly as she felt the tone and significance of George's words. She felt the nightmare of the attack all over again, but she was overwhelmed by the passion of her attorney. He didn't forget for a second that it was a nightmare for her and her family. He was fighting the battle for them, and he had lived the nightmare with them personally enough to never forget what Paul had done to them, even though Mrs. Ferguson never felt their pain. When he reminded Mrs. Ferguson that this wasn't about her and her nightmare, it was about the Bird's nightmare, he proceeded to help her feel their pain.

Mrs. Ferguson: Yes, it is. It sure is.

Mr. Matangos: Did you ever call the Birds?

Mrs. Ferguson: No, I haven't. I wanted to, but I was afraid to.

Mr. Matangos: Did you ever try to go see them that night?

Mrs. Ferguson: I wanted to, but I was afraid to.

When Mr. Matangos realized he had made his point, that the nightmare the Bird family experienced was never felt by Mrs. Ferguson, he moved on to the finale of his performance—the way he planned to end his cross-examination of Mrs. Ferguson.

Mr. Matangos: So you started talking to Natasha that very next morning about what you recalled about the night's events. And since that morning when you started talking about it, April 19, you've had seven and a half months to discuss what your testimony would be today, haven't you?

Mrs. Ferguson: We talked about it, yes.

Mr. Matangos: Since Paul was arrested, there have been two prior hearings?

Mrs. Ferguson: Right.

Mr. Matangos: You attended both of those?

Mrs. Ferguson: Right.

Mr. Matangos: There was a preliminary hearing May 1st?

Mrs. Ferguson: Right.

Mr. Matangos: You didn't testify, did you?

Mrs. Ferguson: No, I didn't.

Mr. Matangos: At that time you didn't tell anybody this testimony that you're providing today, did you?

Mrs. Ferguson: Just my lawyer.

Mr. Matangos: You were before Justice Shugars at that time; is that right?

Mrs. Ferguson: Right.

Mr. Matangos: You heard all the testimony that the Birds gave at that hearing. Right?

Mrs. Ferguson: Right.

Mr. Matangos: So you knew the entire sequence of events?

Mrs. Ferguson: Right.

Mr. Matangos: You knew the times?

Mrs. Ferguson: I don't recall a lot out of it. I mean, there were policemen all around me. There were camera people asking me questions.

Mr. Matangos: During the hearing, ma'am?

Mrs. Ferguson: Mm-hmm.

Mr. Matangos: In a matter of such great importance in your life, you didn't pay attention to the testimony that was given?

Mrs. Ferguson: I did pay attention.

Mr. Matangos: That's what I asked you the first time. So you heard them testify and you heard them give the times, and you heard them give the location and injuries. You heard them give the defense that Mrs. Bird said she made, striking out at the assailant. You heard all that, didn't you?

Mrs. Ferguson: Right.

Mr. Matangos: You heard the testimony of Alisha who said she saw Paul over Mrs. Bird?

Mrs. Ferguson: Right.

Mr. Matangos: And you heard what he did from Alisha's own mouth and the circumstances and events that took place that night?

Mrs. Ferguson: Yes, I heard.

Mr. Matangos: You know where he went in the house. You know what time he was there, isn't that right? You knew this occurred at 10:30 p.m. You heard the testimony that it was about 10:30 p.m.?

Mrs. Ferguson: Yes.

Mr. Matangos: You knew the testimony that the 911 call took place about 10:35 p.m. because Mrs. Bird testified to that on the stand, didn't she, right in front of you?

Mrs. Ferguson: I don't recall the time of the 911 call.

Mr. Matangos: Since that time you have reviewed all the police reports with Mr. Tarman that were taken that night, haven't you?

Mrs. Ferguson: I—yes, I read some of them, of the—what they had said, the family members.

Mr. Matangos: And from those you also know the times, the places, when he was supposed to have been there and when he was supposed to have left, don't you?

Mrs. Ferguson: Yes.

Mr. Matangos: And you know because you didn't have to hear the testimony. It's written down and you could see it?

Mrs. Ferguson: Yes.

Mr. Matangos: You knew the time, specifically, was 10:30 p.m.?

Mrs. Ferguson: Right.

Mr. Matangos: Somewhere about 10:30 p.m. It was after 10:23 p.m. You knew that from the report?

Mrs. Ferguson: Every time I read it, it couldn't be, because I knew where my child was.

Mr. Matangos: That's right. Because you knew the times then, didn't you?

Mrs. Ferguson: Right.

Mr. Matangos: Mrs. Ferguson, you were here in this courtroom before Judge Kleinfelter previously, weren't you?

Mrs. Ferguson: Right.

Mr. Matangos: And you testified?

Mrs. Ferguson: Right.

Mr. Matangos: And at that time you didn't testify to anything about what you're testifying to today, did you?

Mrs. Ferguson: No.

Mr. Matangos: You didn't make a mention of where Paul was, how you saw him so many times that night?

Mr. Tarman: Your Honor, I would object to this. The nature of that hearing was not—

Judge Kleinfelter: Sustained.

Mr. Tarman: As to the guilt or the innocence of Paul Ferguson, and she would have no right to even say those things.

Judge Kleinfelter: Sustained.

Mr. Matangos: Before today's date and coming into this courtroom, you knew all the times that this incident involved, isn't that correct?

Mrs. Ferguson: Right.

Mr. Matangos: Your Honor, at this time, I don't have any further questions.

Debbie understood the significance of the chart of times and events when George ended his cross-examination of Mrs. Ferguson. He wanted to underscore for the jury that her alibi was built around her knowledge of the timeframe she had to have Paul at home and the events that would account for his injuries and the beads of *ointment* on Paul's forehead. George was a master, and Debbie was so proud of him.

Mr. Tarman had just a few points to clarify in his redirect examination. He made sure Mrs. Ferguson acknowledged that she understood that flannel and plaid were considered to be the same in their discussions, and that the *green and beige* shirt that Paul was wearing in the yearbook picture was long-sleeved. He apparently noticed that she failed to mention that as she described the shirt as different from the shirt the Birds had described on their attacker. Mr. Tarman made sure to have Mrs. Ferguson state that she had not found any such short-sleeved, plaid shirt in Paul's clothing.

When Mr. Tarman introduced Defense Exhibits 1-D and 1-E in his redirect examination, Mrs. Ferguson identified them as photographs of the shutters, bushes, and trees around her home—the shutters she and Paul scraped on April 18. After Mr. Tarman led Mrs. Ferguson to confirm that Paul would not have worn the Hanes sweatpants to school, he too was finished questioning his primary defense witness.

Mr. Matangos jumped on Mrs. Ferguson's acknowledgment that Paul wore Hanes sweatpants in his recross-examination.

Mr. Matangos: When he was around the house, he didn't wear—he didn't have to wear Nike, Fila, or Reeboks, did he?

Mrs. Ferguson: No.

Her answer seemed to clear the record for Paul to be wearing the generic black nylon pants and the black sneakers left on the kitchen floor of the Birds' home. With that out of the way, Mr. Matangos focused upon the photos of the shutters.

Mr. Matangos: And the photographs that were taken of those shutters that Mr. Tarman showed you as Defense Exhibits 1 and 2, when were those photographs taken?

Mrs. Ferguson: That photograph was taken about three months ago.

Mr. Matangos: September?

Mrs. Ferguson: I think so, yes.

Mr. Matangos: After full-growing season from the spring, right?

Mrs. Ferguson: Right.

Mr. Matangos: Right. And this would not have been the condition of that area on April 18, would it?

Mrs. Ferguson: I haven't touched it since, so you could see how some of them were just growing and need to be cut.

Mr. Matangos: That's right. They've grown. That's not the condition they were in on April 18th.

Mrs. Ferguson: Right.

Mr. Matangos: And those shutters are in the same condition they were on April 18?

Mrs. Ferguson: Right. We didn't get to paint it.

Mr. Matangos: And that's one that you've already scraped?

Mrs. Ferguson: Excuse me?

Mr. Matangos: That's one that you've already scraped?

Mrs. Ferguson: I didn't scrape it. Paul scraped it.

Mr. Matangos: It was already scraped and prepared to be painted. It just never got painted?

Mrs. Ferguson: Right.

Mr. Matangos: That photograph in the yearbook, that would have been taken—this is the 1996 yearbook, right? And these are given out in the spring/summer of '96 at graduation. So these photographs they take in the fall of '95?

Mrs. Ferguson: Right.

Mr. Matangos: Specifically, do you know that this photograph was taken in September of 1995?

Mrs. Ferguson: No. But yes, I agree with you. I don't know.

Mr. Matangos: You mentioned before that Paul has a habit of pulling up his sleeves, doesn't he?

Mrs. Ferguson: To go to bed.

Mr. Matangos: Just to go to bed?

Mrs. Ferguson: Yes.

Mr. Matangos: If he pulled those sleeves up, could that have looked like a short-sleeve shirt?

Mrs. Ferguson: Couldn't go all the way up. It has the hand things.

Mr. Matangos: Would have shown the forearms, wouldn't it?

Mrs. Ferguson: Yes.

Mr. Matangos: You don't have this shirt, though, do you?

Mrs. Ferguson: I don't know.

Mr. Matangos: You said you looked through everything. You said you spoke about—

Mrs. Ferguson: I picked up all the plaid shirts. I don't know if I had it. I don't know. I take things to Goodwill.

Mr. Matangos: You said that plaid and flannel is the same thing to you, right? That means the same thing to you?

Mrs. Ferguson: Right.

Mr. Matangos: So if someone had said flannel, you would have known they meant plaid, so you would have looked for a plaid shirt?

Mrs. Ferguson: Right.

Mr. Matangos: You didn't find this shirt?

Mrs. Ferguson: No.

Mr. Matangos: Thank you. Nothing further.

Lee Ann Grayson was Mr. Tarman's next witness for the defense. She was a state police forensics specialist who analyzed the evidence the police had sent to the lab. Because she was an expert on hair sample analysis and Mr. Matangos knew what she was going to testify to for the defense, he quickly interrupted Mr. Tarman to stipulate that Ms. Grayson was a hair and fiber expert and he could dispense with the line of questions to establish such.

Ms. Grayson's testimony amounted to the determination that two hair fibers found in the pocket of the black nylon pants left on the Birds' kitchen floor by the perpetrator of the crime were not Negroid hair. While her analysis was inconclusive as to Caucasian or animal, she could rule out that they were not hair from a black individual, and Mr. Tarman saw her testimony as favorable to the defense.

Mr. Matangos's cross-examination of Lee Ann Grayson focused upon a few questions.

Mr. Matangos: If the detectives, Fox, Nelson, Heilig; officers that were at the scene, reached into those pants as one has indicated on the stand, is it possible those hairs that you found there were parts of their hair fragments from their hand or palm or rear of their hand?

Ms. Grayson: Could have been.

Mr. Matangos: You don't really know how those hairs could have come to be in those pockets, do you?

Ms. Grayson: No, sir.

Mr. Matangos: If I told you that the Bird family owns a cat and the cat has free reign of the house and this item was found in the kitchen floor, it may even be the cat's hair?

Miss Grayson: That's correct.

When Mr. Matangos concluded his cross-examination of Ms. Grayson, Mr. Tarman called his last witness for the defense. Natasha Ferguson, Paul's sister, took the stand, and her testimony sounded a lot like her mother's. She recalled the events as they coincided with the television like they had been rehearsed with her mother. Mr. Tarman's questions continued to the lunch break and after the lunch break; and when Mr. Tarman had no more questions for his witness, he seemed pleased with the job Natasha had done on the stand.

Debbie recalled that George had assured her that Mr. Tarman would not be too harsh with her children because of the chance of alienating the jury, so she expected that George would do the same with Natasha in his cross-examination. It did not take long for

Debbie to realize that George had changed his plans for Natasha as he had done for Mrs. Ferguson.

Mr. Matangos: Who was your brother playing football with in school that day?

Natasha: I don't know.

Mr. Matangos: You don't know?

Natasha: No.

Mr. Matangos: You rode the bus home with Paul, didn't you?

Natasha: Yes.

Mr. Matangos: And it is interesting because you rode the bus to school with him, right?

Natasha: Yes.

Mr. Matangos: You do every day?

Natasha: Yes.

Mr. Matangos: And yet you thought you were going to wear the shirt you stole out of his room to school?

Natasha: Yes.

Mr. Matangos: When he saw that, what did you think he was going to do to you?

Natasha: Get upset with me and argue.

Mr. Matangos: You thought that was a good idea?

Natasha: Yes.

Mr. Matangos: The whole idea of sneaking into the room was so he couldn't find out.

Natasha: Excuse me?

Like mother like daughter, Natasha used the same phrase her mother used when she needed to stall to plan her answer. Their well-planned alibi that enabled them both to "see Paul sleeping and hear him snoring" suddenly did not make a lot of sense.

Mr. Matangos: The whole idea of sneaking into his room was so he couldn't find out you had his shirt?

Natasha: Yes.

Mr. Matangos: He was going to see it when you got to the bus stop, wasn't he?

Natasha: No.

Mr. Matangos: He wasn't going to see the shirt?

Natasha: No, because I would have worn a shirt over it.

Mr. Matangos: He wasn't going to see the shirt as you prepared to go to school either?

Natasha: No.

Mr. Matangos: Your rooms are right across from each other. Mr. Tarman showed you the photographs where you can see into his room and right back into your room from the doorways, isn't that right?

Natasha: Yes.

Mr. Matangos: You can see right in there. He can see you and you can see him?

Natasha: Yes.

Mr. Matangos: You can certainly hear each other, right?

Natasha: Yes.

Mr. Matangos: You could hear him snoring from your bedroom, couldn't you?

Natasha: No.

Mr. Matangos: You couldn't hear him in your bedroom snoring?

Natasha: No.

Mr. Matangos: Your mom could hear him downstairs.

Mr. Tarman: Your Honor, that's an unfair question to be asking; what their mom can hear. She's telling Mr. Matangos what she can hear. What her mom can hear is another question.

Judge Kleinfelter: The objection is overruled.

Mr. Matangos: When Paul came home from school that day and you guys got off the bus, what did you do?

Natasha: I opened the door.

Mr. Matangos: You opened the door?

Natasha: Yes.

Mr. Matangos: That's because your mom said Paul has trouble keeping hold of keys?

Natasha: Pardon me?

Mr. Matangos: He has trouble with keys?

Natasha: Yes.

Mr. Matangos: So he doesn't have keys?

Natasha: No.

Mr. Matangos: But you have keys?

Natasha: Yes, I do.

Mr. Matangos: So you had to let Paul into the house?

Natasha: Yes.

Mr. Matangos: And after you let him in the house, what did you do?

Mr. Matangos questioned Natasha through the entire time frame, from getting home from school until the police came. He asked her for details throughout her statements that made her come up with answers to questions she hadn't prepared to answer:

Mr. Matangos: Where was Paul at 5:00 p.m.?

Natasha: He was in his room until my mom told him to go help with the shutters.

Mr. Matangos: What was he doing in his room?

Natasha: Cleaning his room.

Mr. Matangos: What do you mean by that?

Natasha: He was cleaning his room.

Mr. Matangos: What was he doing?

Natasha: He was cleaning his room. You know.

Mr. Matangos: Was he vacuuming? Picking up? Folding? Putting away papers? What was he doing?

Natasha: Dusting.

Mr. Matangos: What else?

Natasha: Picking up his clothes.

Mr. Matangos: What else?

Natasha: Picking up his clothes and dusting.

Mr. Matangos: And you saw him doing this because your room is right across the hall?

Natasha: No.

Mr. Matangos: How did you know what he was doing up there?

Natasha: Because I saw his room, and I know he did it.

Mr. Matangos: So you didn't actually see him pick up his clothes?

Natasha: No.

Mr. Matangos: You didn't actually see him dusting?

Natasha: No.

Mr. Matangos: But you know he did because afterwards you saw the room?

Natasha: Yes.

Mr. Matangos: And it was dusted?

Natasha: Yes.

As it turned out, Natasha did not actually witness Travis kick Paul in the face, but she knew it happened. Perhaps she would have said she witnessed it if Mr. Matangos had presented his questions differently:

Mr. Matangos: So we're up to 7:30 p.m., and Travis kicked Paul?

Natasha: Yes.

Mr. Matangos: You don't know where he kicked him?

Natasha: What do you mean by where he kicked him?

Mr. Matangos: You didn't see it, did you?

Natasha: Nope, I didn't see it.

Mr. Matangos: But you said he did it with his shoe.

Natasha: I know he did it with his shoe.

Mr. Matangos: You know that how?

Natasha: (*No response.*)

Mr. Matangos: Did someone else show you?

Natasha: No. That's the only reason—the only way he could have got cut.

Mr. Matangos: Could he have been cut with a fingernail?

Natasha: No.

Mr. Matangos: No?

Natasha: No.

George was able to interject details so quickly into his questions of Natasha that Debbie hoped the jury was paying close enough attention to pick up the inconsistencies.

Mr. Matangos: Was there anything else that happened between 7:00 p.m. and 8:00 p.m.?

Natasha: No, except for my mom bringing up Tyler. That was like—that was after dinner and before he got cut.

Mr. Matangos: You say "bringing up." You mean taking up, because you stayed downstairs. Right?

Natasha: Yes.

According to Natasha, her mother didn't get a chance to sit and watch *Martin*, *Living Single*, or *New York Undercover*. At nine thirty, just as her mother indicated in her testimony, Natasha and Paul went upstairs for showers at their mother's request. But Natasha never saw her mother put ointment on Paul.

Mr. Matangos: What time was it when you got out of the shower?

Natasha: I would guess around 9:40 p.m.

Mr. Matangos: And what did you do?

Natasha: I got dressed and watched the rest of *New York Undercover*.

Mr. Matangos: Paul was already in bed sleeping by then, right?

Natasha: Yes.

Mr. Matangos: You sure?

Natasha: Yes.

Mr. Matangos: You only took a three-minute shower, though, right?

Natasha: No, I took a four- or five-minute shower.

Mr. Matangos: Three, four, five—whatever it was, it was quick so you could get back to see *New York Undercover*, right?

Natasha: Yes.

Mr. Matangos: And you didn't see Mom putting the ointment on your brother before you got in the shower?

Natasha: No.

Mr. Matangos: Was he dressed when you got in the shower?

Natasha: Yes.

Mr. Matangos: So Paul had time to get out of the shower, dry, go in his room and get his clothes on before you went into the shower?

Natasha: Yes.

Mr. Matangos: And before you asked him about borrowing his shirt?

Natasha: Yes.

Mr. Matangos: Your mom was never up there?

Natasha: She could have been. I don't know.

Mr. Matangos: It's a small upstairs. You say you can see everything. You can see in from this room to this room, doors are always open. Was she or wasn't she upstairs when you were there?

Mr. Tarman: Asked and answered, Your Honor. She said she could have been, but she doesn't know. The question has been asked and answered.

Judge Kleinfelter: The objection is overruled.

Mr. Matangos: That means you have to answer.

Natasha: While I was taking a shower, she could have been upstairs.

Mr. Matangos: But not before?

Natasha: I didn't see her before, no.

Mr. Matangos: All you know is when you got out of the shower, Paul was already under the covers and asleep?

Natasha: He was under the covers, yes. And his lights were turned off.

Mr. Matangos: And his door was open so you could see in there?

Natasha: Yes.

Mr. Matangos: And you could see in because of the light coming through the windows?

Natasha: Yes.

Debbie remembered how George told her that Mrs. Ferguson would be using the description of floorboards creaking and the light coming in from the bedroom windows just like Debbie had during her preliminary hearing. She would say the floorboards creaked to alert her that Natasha was in Paul's room. She would also use the light coming in the windows to see Paul in a dark bedroom. George was mocking Mrs. Ferguson's testimony with Natasha, and she was agreeing with him.

Mr. Matangos: He's already asleep in his bed?

Natasha: I don't know if he was asleep. I think he was asleep. His eyes were closed.

Mr. Matangos: I thought you told me you heard snoring?

Natasha: No. That's when I—

Mr. Matangos: Snuck in to steal the shirt?

Natasha: Yeah.

Mr. Matangos: So from where you were in the hallway, from that little light in the bathroom, you could see his eyes closed?

Natasha: Yes.

George was not easy with Natasha as he had suggested he would be since it was risky to be tough on kids with a jury. But it was obvious throughout the cross-examination that George was not going to tolerate Natasha telling her mother's lies for her and that Natasha took her alibi directions from her mother. When George got to the morning of Mrs. Ferguson's return home, he caught her several times in misstatements.

Mr. Matangos: Let's talk about that next morning. Mom comes home. You immediately start talking about the testimony you're presenting today, isn't that right?

Natasha: Can I explain to you what happened?

Mr. Matangos: I'm just asking a question. You can say yes or no.

Natasha: That she came home and we started talking about it?

Mr. Matangos: Mm-hmm.

Natasha: It didn't happen like that.

Mr. Matangos: You didn't start talking about the previous night's incidents when she got home?

Natasha: She was home for a while, and I came downstairs, and I asked her what happened, and then she told me what happened. And I said that Paul couldn't have done it because he was home in his room asleep.

Mr. Matangos: You didn't have to tell your mom that, right?

Natasha: Of course, I didn't have to tell her that.

Mr. Matangos: Because Mom saw him there?

Natasha: Yes, she did.

At that point, Mr. Matangos launched his repetitious line of questions that he posed to Mrs. Ferguson about the number of times Natasha and Mrs. Ferguson discussed what they were going to testify to in defense of Paul. Denying that they talked did not work any better for Natasha.

Natasha: We talked about it. Only thing we talked about, she told me her story, and I told her my story.

Mr. Matangos: You told it once to each other?

Natasha: No, more than once.

Mr. Matangos: Dozens of times?

Natasha: No.

Mr. Matangos: No?

Natasha: No.

Mr. Matangos: Twice?

Natasha: I don't know. I don't know how many times.

Mr. Matangos: Well, you told it to Mr. Tarman too, didn't you?

Natasha: Yes.

Mr. Matangos: And didn't you talk about it with your mom before you went down to talk about it with Mr. Tarman?

Natasha: Yes.

After offering Natasha a series of times she would have had to discuss the details of the night of the attack and had to answer yes, Mr. Matangos asked Natasha if she discussed the times her mother learned at the preliminary hearing.

Mr. Matangos: And you talked about what time Paul was supposed to have been at the Bird residence?

Natasha: No, we didn't talk about that stuff.

Mr. Matangos: How did you know Paul was home? How about if they said it happened at two o'clock in the afternoon when he was still in school?

Natasha: I would have known it wasn't true.

Mr. Matangos: But you had to talk about it to know exactly where Paul was for you to say, "I know it can't be Paul." So you did talk about it, didn't you?

Natasha: She didn't tell me that much about the preliminary hearing.

Mr. Matangos: No, but you talked about the series of events. You talked about what things happened, what time they happened, where they say Paul was supposed to have been. You talked about that?

Natasha: No, we didn't.

It appeared through much of Natasha's testimony that Mr. Matangos posed questions to her that logically would be answered in such a way that denial made her look like she was lying. After Mr.

Matangos's lengthy grilling of Natasha, Mr. Tarman had no redirect questions for Natasha. It appeared as though Mr. Tarman was anxious to get Natasha off the stand and to rest his case.

With the prosecution and defense phases of the trial complete, Debbie thought the trial was finally over, until Judge Kleinfelter asked Mr. Matangos, "Do you have any rebuttal testimony?"

Mr. Matangos called Detective Nelson to the stand.

Detective Nelson was asked to describe in detail the statement he took from Mrs. Ferguson at the police station on the night of the attack. He testified that he had taken notes during the interview, and he referred to those notes to answer Mr. Matangos's questions. Detective Nelson indicated that Mrs. Ferguson told him that Paul was upstairs "cleaning his room" from 7:00 p.m. to 8:30 p.m. The whole family watched *Martin* on TV from 8:30 p.m. to 9:00 p.m., but prior to watching TV, she had put ointment on Paul's face where the baby kicked him. At nine thirty, Natasha and Paul went upstairs for bed, and Paul took a shower. After she told Paul to go to bed, she did not see him until the police arrived. When Natasha told her mother that the police were outside, Mrs. Ferguson told Detective Nelson that she asked Natasha if Paul was in his room, and Natasha indicated that he was.

Mr. Matangos: Does that report mention anything about scraping shutters?

Detective Nelson: No, sir.

Mr. Matangos: Does that report mention anything about cuts that he would have received while he was scraping shutters?

Detective Nelson: No, sir.

Mr. Matangos: Does it mention anything at all about the time frame after nine thirty when she saw Paul Ferguson?

Detective Nelson: No, sir.

Mr. Matangos: Does it say anything in that report about her going upstairs and interrupting Natasha in his room while taking a shirt out of Paul's room at about ten fifteen?

Detective Nelson: No, sir, it does not.

George had saved the best for last, Debbie thought as she learned how different Mrs. Ferguson's initial statements were from the testimony she offered after she had time to prepare her alibis, after she had heard the details of her son's attack on the Bird family from the hearings she attended and the documents she studied. Debbie wondered what Paul had told her during those minutes that the police surrounded their home to prepare Mrs. Ferguson to hide the bloody shirt and to alibi the cuts to his face. Debbie wondered just how much Mrs. Ferguson knew before she got to the police station for her to put up such a defense so quickly. As Detective Nelson continued, Debbie grew more curious.

Detective Nelson reviewed his notes and testified that Mrs. Ferguson told him, "What the officers saw on Paul's face was not sweat, it was ointment."

Mr. Matangos: How did that information come up?

Detective Nelson: She told me.

Mr. Matangos: Did you ask her about the sweat?

Detective Nelson: No, I was pretty much letting her tell her story.

Mr. Matangos: She's the one who told you about the sweat being ointment?

Detective Nelson: Yes.

Mrs. Ferguson also told him that Paul could not have gotten out of the house without her seeing him, and that she came through the garage because she could not find her house keys. She blamed Mrs. Bird for the trouble her son was in, stating, "Mrs. Bird doesn't like him."

Detective Nelson indicated that he took notes throughout Mrs. Ferguson's statements and was prepared to tape-record her when she declined. Instead, he read back the notes he had written and asked her if they accurately reflected her account of the evening. She agreed, and Detective Nelson had her sign his account of her statements.

Just when Debbie thought Mr. Matangos was about to end Detective Nelson's portion of the rebuttal, he asked Detective Nelson if he saw Mrs. Ferguson again that early morning after his interview with her. The detective said he had seen her speaking to Paul after he had taken Paul down to Dauphin County night court for his preliminary arraignment. He said he overheard her telling Paul, "Don't forget to tell the officers you got those scratches playing football today."

What seemed to be a bombshell was ignored by Mr. Tarman in his cross-examination of Detective Nelson. Mr. Tarman had Detective Nelson repeat that Mrs. Ferguson stated that one of her twins kicked Paul and she put ointment on Paul's face. He also focused on Mrs. Ferguson's statement that Paul could not have gotten out of the house without her seeing him. When he had Detective Nelson admit that he did not conduct follow-up interviews with the Fergusons to see if the shoe brace was relevant to the case, or to talk with Natasha, Debbie could see how Mr. Tarman was implying that the police did not do enough to investigate the possibility that Paul had not committed the crime. That seemed to be a good place for the defense to end with Detective Nelson.

Mr. Matangos put more witnesses on the stand in the rebuttal phase of the trial, but none could top the impact Detective Nelson had on Debbie's feelings of confidence. She listened to Detective Heilig, who shared an office with Detective Nelson and was present during Detective Nelson's interview with Mrs. Ferguson, echo Detective Nelson's testimony. Lieutenant Fleisher was called to the stand to testify that he had seen Paul Ferguson wearing pants identical to the nylon pants left at the scene of the crime. Debbie would learn later that the lengthy sidebar that was held prior to the officer taking the stand was to ensure that the testimony of Lieutenant Fleisher did not include that the Lieutenant knew the pants were identical because they had been searched the day Paul was picked up for a previous crime.

Jaredd was called to the stand to testify that he had seen Paul wearing black nylon pants and black sneakers like the ones left behind by the attacker on numerous occasions prior to the attack, even though Mrs. Ferguson had claimed that Paul did not own such sneakers or generic nylon pants. Debbie returned to the stand to clarify how she discovered Paul's picture in the plaid shirt in the yearbook, and then Mr. Matangos was finished with his rebuttal witnesses.

Mr. Tarman brought Mrs. Ferguson back to the stand to allow her to clarify what she meant by her statement during her interview with Detective Nelson. She really didn't mean that she didn't see Paul again after 9:30 p.m. until the police arrived. What she meant was that she didn't speak to Paul from that time on. Mr. Matangos was quick to emphasize that when Detective Nelson read her statements back to her at the completion of her interview, she had an opportunity to make corrections and did not do so.

When Judge Kleinfelter asked Mr. Tarman if he was finished, Mr. Tarman responded, "Finally, Your Honor, that's it."

Mr. Matangos acknowledged that he too was finished, and the fourth day of the trial ended at 4:00 p.m. Judge Kleinfelter prepared the jury for the next day, which would include an overview of the case, closing arguments from both lawyers, and jury deliberations. Cautioning the jury as he had at the end of each day all week long, he stated, "Don't discuss the case with anyone or permit anyone to discuss it with you. Do not read any news accounts, and have a pleasant evening."

Debbie would have felt better if she had followed the judge's advice and not tuned in to the six o'clock news. The reporter for WHTM, Debra Pinkerton, appeared on the screen and described the defense for Paul Ferguson. She reported that the defense attorney, Robert Tarman, called two witnesses to the stand—Paul Ferguson's mother, Ivonne, and his sister, Natasha. As Ms. Pinkerton described Ivonne's and Natasha's testimony that Paul was with them on the night of the stabbings, Debbie worried that the reporter was supportive of Paul's defense. As Ms. Pinkerton presented details about Natasha sneaking into Paul's room at 10:17 pm and seeing Paul sleeping and snoring, Debbie resented that the lies of Paul's mother and sister were getting air time and that Mrs. Ferguson's claim that Mrs. Bird is blaming the stabbing on her son because she doesn't like him was discrediting her and her children's testimony. The news coverage made Debbie feel victimized again. How could the reporter inside the courtroom that day prepare such a one-sided slant on the trial?

Chapter XXXVI

Friday the Thirteenth

Debbie had to work at pushing Friday the Thirteenth out of her mind as she prepared for the fifth day of the trial. The day her case would surely go into jury deliberations could not be an unlucky day for her and her family. They had been through enough. Although the date would nag at her, she would not discuss it with her family. They had enough to worry about.

When Judge Kleinfelter addressed the jury, he prepared them for Mr. Tarman's and Mr. Matangos's closing remarks. As it turned out, nothing could have prepared Debbie for Mr. Tarman's presentation. Mr. Tarman began in a relaxed manner suggesting that he was just like each of the members of the jury. He promised to be brief, but nearly an hour later, he had filled the jury and the audience in the courtroom with so many examples of reasonable doubt that Debbie could picture O. J. Simpson's face in the courtroom the moment his jury declared him not guilty despite the abundance of evidence against him. He got away with murder, and Paul, according to Mr. Tarman, should be found not guilty as well.

At the conclusion of Mr. Tarman's closing remarks, Judge Kleinfelter called for a ten-minute recess. Mr. Matangos must have sensed Debbie's fears and apprehensions because he immediately turned around after the jury was dismissed and told her and her family, "Don't worry, I'll take care of you." Debbie had to believe in

George. He was their only hope. The testimonies were over, and the defense was finished articulating examples of reasonable doubt for the jury members.

As Debbie tried to trust George and push her insecurities behind her, George began to assemble his props for his closing remarks. He placed his time chart before the jury box and all the Commonwealth Exhibits he planned to use on the table before him. When he placed the size 13 white Reebok sneakers that Paul wore to the police station next to the size 13 black sneakers found in the Birds' kitchen, Paul said something to Mr. Matangos that prompted him to turn on his heels and approach Paul at the defense table. George made a comment back to Paul that caused Paul to attempt to get up. Restrained by Mr. Tarman's grasp and his stern command, Paul sat down, and George returned to his preparations.

For the rest of the ten-minute recess, Paul sat with an arm over the back of his chair and a look of smug confidence on his face. After Mr. Tarman's performance, Paul was totally confident that he was going to win the case. Debbie wanted the judge and the jury members to see Paul as he flaunted his cocky, arrogant self that he had hidden from the jury during the trial behind a quiet, serious persona and the large cross over his tie.

When George had all his materials ready for his presentations, he returned to Debbie for some final words of reassurance. Debbie asked him what had happened between him and Paul. He explained with some obvious rage that Paul had asked him, "When am I getting my Reeboks back after my acquittal?" George told Debbie that he leaned over his table and responded, "You ain't getting your Reeboks back 'cause you ain't going home." George was angrier than Debbie had ever seen him.

Although Debbie was furious that Paul was so confident after his defense attorney's closing remarks, she was scared too. If they didn't win this trial, Paul would get his Reeboks back and return to her neighborhood and terrorize her and her family by his mere presence.

Mr. Matangos was not scared. He was angry, and he was determined to see to it that Paul never got his Reeboks back. When the jury was seated in the courtroom and Paul was back to his proper courtroom façade, George began to recreate the attack with rubber gloves on his hands and the knife raised over his head. His reenactment of the stabbing made Debbie cry and her family cringe. As he systematically and methodically walked the jury through every piece of evidence that pointed to Paul's guilt, there was no reasonable doubt left in the courtroom. For an hour and thirteen minutes, Mr. Matangos had the jury members and Debbie's family on the edge of their seats and focused on his every word.

Mr. Matangos showed the jury every gruesome picture of Debbie's injuries over again, refreshing their memories about the pain and suffering and the horror she endured with each one. When he presented the pictures of Paul Ferguson, he explained with each photo what really caused each scratch and bruise as he recounted Paul's attack on the Bird family on the night of April 18. Aspects of the trial that seemed unimportant at the time came alive as he wove them into his detailed account of the crime. When he reminded the jury that the Birds' backyard was loaded with rosebushes and Paul's trail out of the backyard went close enough to those bushes to cause the scratches on his arms and legs, Debbie was amazed at how George had not missed a thing.

Mr. Matangos startled everyone in the courtroom when he displayed a picture of Paul's bloody toe that had not been explained by Mrs. Ferguson. He mocked the alibis of Mrs. Ferguson for each of Paul's other injuries, but Mr. Tarman had failed to have her create a lie to explain how Paul got a bloody toe. Mr. Matangos seized the opportunity to explain the injury. A bloody toe would have been exactly what would have occurred when Paul ran barefooted from the Birds' house to his home.

Mr. Matangos's hour-and-thirteen-minute closing remarks felt like minutes to Debbie; and just when she thought George could not impress her any more, he looked at the jury members, then back to Debbie and her children, who sat next to each other for the closing remarks. He asked the jury, "Think about why the Bird family, seated together before you, are here today. Are they here to have you find a person guilty who did not commit this horrendous crime against them, so that the real perpetrator of the crime can be free to do this to them again? Think about why they are here as you listen to these final words." He pushed the Play button on the tape recorder, and the jury heard Debbie's pleading words:

"I need an ambulance at 3323 North Third Street, Harrisburg, Susquehanna Township. We've been attacked by a neighborhood boy, named Paul Ferguson. He had a knife. He stabbed me repeatedly. My son woke up and helped. We need your help."

What had been Debbie's plea for help to the 911 operator on April 18 was now her final words to the jury members who held her family's fate in their hands. "We need your help."

Judge Kleinfelter called another ten-minute recess, followed by a detailed explanation to the jury of their responsibilities during deliberations and the definitions of the charges. He reminded them that while he was responsible for deciding all questions of law, they were the sole judges of facts. He directed them to consider the evidence, to find the facts and apply the law to the facts to determine if the defendant was guilty or not guilty of the charges.

After reminding the twelve members of the jury that their decision must be unanimous, Judge Kleinfelter excused the two alternate jury members and thanked them for performing their civic duties.

The jury was out less than two hours, which included their lunch, before the announcement was made that the verdict was in. At 2:20 p.m., the jury assembled, and Judge Kleinfelter asked for their verdict.

Debbie, her children, her family, and her friends joined hands in the courtroom and prayed for the guilty verdict:

The Clerk: Will you please rise? In the case of the *Commonwealth of Pennsylvania versus Paul A. Ferguson*, No.1353 C.D. 1996, on the charge of criminal attempt homicide against Debra Bird, how do you find?

The Foreperson: Guilty.

The Clerk: In the case of criminal attempt homicide against Jaredd Bird, how do you find?

The Foreperson: Guilty.

The Clerk: In the case of the *Commonwealth versus Paul A. Ferguson*, 1354 CD 1996, Count 1, a charge of aggravated assault against Alisha Bird, how do you find?

The Foreman: Guilty.

The Clerk: In the case of the *Commonwealth versus Paul A. Ferguson*, No. 1355 CD 1996, Count 1, aggravated assault against Debra Bird, how do you find?

The Foreman: Guilty.

The Clerk: Count 2, aggravated assault against Jaredd Bird, how do you find?

The Foreman: Guilty.

The Clerk: And Count 3, burglary, how do you find?

The Foreman: Guilty.

Chapter XXXVII

Sentencing

The three months following the trial should have been marked with celebration for the Bird family, but sentencing still loomed over their heads. Debbie was emphatic that Jaredd and Alisha speak at sentencing, although they let her know that they would be perfectly content to let her do the talking.

In a counseling session with Deb Salem, Deb convinced Jaredd and Alisha that they should not pass up the opportunity that the victim rights advocates made possible for them, the opportunity to speak at Paul Ferguson's sentencing. She reassured them that they should tell the judge just how they felt about what Paul did to them and their family and what they wanted the judge to do to punish him.

As Debbie, Jaredd, Alisha, and Ashley entered Judge Kleinfelter's courtroom on the afternoon of March 14, 1997, they knew this was the last big battle they needed to fight against Paul Ferguson, and they were ready. Paul was sitting with Mr. Tarman at the defense table, and his mother was seated on his side of the courtroom.

Mr. Matangos took care of some preliminary legal details, then informed Judge Kleinfelter, "The victims in this case—Debra Bird, Jaredd Bird, and Alisha Bird—would like to make a statement to the courts." After calling Jaredd to the stand, Mr. Matangos encouraged

Jaredd to "tell the judge anything you would like to tell him about what you would like to see happen to Paul."

And Jaredd did just that: "Let me start off at the beginning. On the night of April 18, I woke up to a seven-inch gash on my face, a blood-soaked mother, and two very distressed sisters. Later that night, I was taken to Polyclinic Hospital, where my mother and I were sutured.

"I did not know of the extent of my mother's injuries, which made me very afraid for her life. I found out later that she would be okay and undergoing surgery the following week.

"After the weeks following what happened that night, I felt very angry and very frustrated. I felt that this was probably my fault because I didn't wake up to put a stop to what was happening in my house. But it wasn't my fault. It was his fault. It was Paul Ferguson's fault that this happened to my family, and I ask you to please hand down the maximum sentence possible.

"I know that you can't hand down a sentence of death, which would be ideal. Since you can't do that, I would request that you hand out the maximum sentence possible. Thank you."

Matangos: Your Honor, at this time, Alisha Bird would like to speak to the court on this as well.

Alisha: "I woke up April 18 to my mom screaming and someone, who I had trusted a number of years ago, attacking her. Because of this, I lost a lot of trust in the people that I should be able to trust. I have trouble meeting new people because I am afraid that they will turn on me. I have just a lot of distrust for people.

"I walk in my own house, and I don't feel safe any longer. I am afraid to turn the corners and open doors in my house because I am afraid someone, once again, is going to be behind them trying to injure my family or me.

"I feel that Paul Ferguson had no right to do this. I think he should be in jail for the rest of his life, because for the rest of my life, I will be afraid, and I will never be able to feel safe again to the extent that I did before. He came in and intruded on my life and my family's lives."

When Alisha returned to her seat next to her mother, Debbie was overwhelmed with sadness at hearing her children's pain and fears, and, at the same time, pride for her children's courage while going through such an ordeal. She was proud of Jaredd and Alisha for their powerful statements, and Ashley for her strength and support of her mother, brother, and sister through it all. Beyond her strong feelings for her children, Debbie was determined to see that Paul got what he deserved, and it was her turn.

As she stepped up to the table before Judge Kleinfelter, Debbie was prepared to send a clear message to the judge, Paul, and Paul's mother that she was angry about Paul's attack on her and her family and disgusted with Paul's mother for lying during the trial. Crime Victims Assistance encouraged her to provide a statement of the financial, physical, and psychological impact of Paul's crime against her family, and she was more than ready to do just that.

Debbie described in detail the hospital, doctors' and emergency care bills, which totaled $12,611, and home damages and clean-up bills of $10,785. The individual and family counseling costs were over $2,835 at the time of the sentencing hearing. The hand therapy and plastic surgery costs had not yet been determined. All in all, the financial impact of the crime exceeded $29,000, without accounting for the costs of police services, legal fees, and court costs.

Knowing that Judge Kleinfelter was very familiar with the physical impact of Paul's attack from the trial proceedings, Debbie chose to make sure that Paul and his mother were reminded of the physical pain and suffering she and Jaredd experienced. In fact, Debbie prepared her entire impact statement with Mrs. Ferguson in mind.

Debbie's account of the financial and physical impact, while significant, paled in comparison to the psychological trauma caused by Paul Ferguson's evil action. This was the part of her victim's impact statement that she was most anxious to present.

"The psychological impact of this crime is the most significant. What you didn't hear in the courtroom, Your Honor, and the jury couldn't hear was Paul's relationship to my family prior to this attack.

"Up until February of 1994, Paul was a friend of Jaredd's, and he was welcome in our home. And although his mother didn't know what he did at my home, and you didn't hear, they played normal boy things. They played basketball. They swam in the pool. They took bike rides, and they played Nintendo and Sega Genesis in our home.

"Paul went with us to do things. He borrowed a bike to ride to City Island, to ride to White Mountain Creamery, to do things with our family. He was always welcome in our home. He stayed over. He was at our house when he was locked out of his own house. He needed rides to the movies and activities, and he was included as a friend of Jaredd's in our home.

"On the morning of February of 1995, I left for work and passed Paul walking toward his home. I thought he missed the bus. I went on to work. When I came home that day, the fish tank in the kitchen was stirred up. Four fish were missing; two were dead. I asked the girls what happened to the fish tank. They didn't know but the fish tank in their bedroom was full of fish food. We went on with our evening activities.

"The next morning, I went to get money out of a drawer where I kept lunch money that the kids didn't know about. The one-dollar bills were missing. I stood in my bedroom wondering what happened in my house. Fish tanks messed up and money missing.

"I remembered Paul walking home the previous morning, so I asked Jaredd if Paul missed his bus. Jaredd said, 'No, he didn't miss his bus. He got his bus at his stop but got off two stops later so his mother would think he went to school.'

"I looked around. My jewelry box was stirred up. Pieces of jewelry were missing. I thought, Paul was in this house. I called the police. After several weeks passed, the police followed up with a report that they were unable to prove Paul was in my house. They indicated that they thought Paul was the one who was in my home, but his mother was uncooperative, and they were unable to prove it without fingerprints or other evidence. I accepted the police's inability to address Paul's intrusion, but I told Jaredd that Paul was not welcome back in our house again.

"Two years after that, we are attacked in our home. One month after Paul was in our home and Jaredd no longer invited him back,

Paul was in juvenile court for burglarizing cars at the JCC. Somehow, he involved Dorsey and Bradon, the other friends in the neighborhood. They ended up in the courtroom against him, and they no longer were friends with Paul. Paul lost his three main friends in our neighborhood by his own actions.

"Two years after that, on April 17, Paul was in juvenile court for burglarizing three homes. He was not with these boys anymore. They no longer were friends of his. He was with someone else doing more burglarizing, more vandalism. One day after that, he attacked my family."

Debbie described with passion the effects of the attack on her and her children. She shared their struggles in counseling to deal with their guilt, fears, and anger. And she spoke about the unanswered questions: the difficulty they all had with trying to understand why Paul targeted them. They got those answers from a prison inmate, and Debbie intended to make sure Mrs. Ferguson and Paul knew those answers.

"We read the statement, the words of Paul through a fellow prison inmate. We read that Paul was bragging in jail that no one left the door open; he had a key. The police didn't know how he got in because they didn't realize he took a key from Jaredd when they were friends. He had that key, and he said he could have been in our home anytime he pleased.

"These are Paul's words through an inmate. Paul planned to get me back because I had no right to not let him come back to my house because I couldn't prove he stole from my house. I didn't need to prove it. I knew it. That's why he wanted to get us back. Because I punished him for something he did, and he didn't like it. He wasn't used to being punished for his bad behavior.

"He tried to get us back. He put pool chemicals in my lawnmower, and he bragged about it to the inmate. He also said that it didn't work because nobody talked about it. Nobody talked about it because nobody knew. When I went out to my shed and I found my lawn mower covered with pool chemicals and pool chemicals in my gas canister, I called my neighbor, John McGreevy. He came over and noticed that the chemicals were not in the motor of the lawnmower.

We took the gas canister off the mower, dumped the chemicals, and added the gas, and I was able to mow the lawn.

"I didn't discuss the incident with my kids, and I didn't call the police. There was no point in responding to it in any way, and no one talked about it. That wasn't good enough for Paul. His act of vandalism did not satisfy him because no one talked about it. It was like it never happened. Interestingly, only two people and Paul knew about the incident—John McGreevy and me. And yet, the inmate knew about it. I wonder how he knew. Maybe he is lying in this document? I don't think so."

Debbie was getting angrier as she spoke. She picked up the copy of the informant's interview and held it out in front of her. She recalled how angry she felt when she first read it and knew that Paul's attorney had a copy of the document and was still defending him. She recalled reading the truth about what Paul did and wanting to have Mrs. Ferguson try to lie her way out of the facts according to the informant, only to learn that the interview could not be used in the trial.

When George told her she could say anything she wanted in her victim's statement, and that she could refer to the interview, she knew exactly the parts of the document she wanted to throw in the faces of Paul and his mother. The time had finally arrived when she could confront Paul and his mother with what he had said in jail and what he had done on the night of the attack. With document in hand, she continued.

"Paul got a knife, borrowed a knife. He planned this act. And the lawnmower wasn't enough. He thought about being in our house some night when we came home. Or maybe he would burn our house down. These are the ideas that came from Paul Ferguson, all because he couldn't come back to my house or swim in my pool. And he couldn't do that because he violated our boundaries and had a consequence for his actions for a change.

"Paul borrowed a knife and bragged that there weren't any prints on the knife because the kid who gave it to him, put it in his bag without Paul touching it. So the kid dropped the knife in Paul's bag leaving his own prints on it. Paul wore gloves when he attacked us and he left the knife in Jaredd's room after he slit Jaredd's face because his prints were not on the knife. He planned this horrible act and thought he would walk home that night, crawl into bed, and read about it the next day.

"Alisha read in this document that Paul planned to get her back by raping her, that he thought he could come into our home, rape her, cut her up, and get back at her and me. Alisha struggles with knowing, at her age, that someone had been thinking about raping her, planning it, and actually tried to carry it out.

"Well, I am very grateful for the floorboards in my home that creaked, because Paul never got a chance to touch her. But he did see her, and he bragged to the informant about what position she was lying in on her bed when he came into her bedroom with his plan.

"We have been in counseling for our anger, and we have been in counseling for our fear. We have a security system in our home because none of us can live without it. I wake up at night, and the first thing I do is look at the security system on my bedroom wall. And if the light is red, it means we are all secure. If it is green, it means the security system wasn't on. This is the first thing I do even if there is not a sound in my house. I look to see if we are safe and secure.

"We all have trouble being home alone. This fall, when Jaredd stayed after school for soccer and Alisha stayed after school for field hockey, Ashley came home from school by herself. Typically, she would be home waiting for me to get home from work to take her to dance. But this fall, Ashley was not there each day. I would come home and find a note from Ashley telling me which friend she was visiting and to pick her up there. When I finally told Ashley that I wanted her to be waiting at our house after school, I found her sitting on the curb in front of our house doing her homework. I asked her what she was doing sitting on the curb. Ashley said, 'I am afraid to be in the house, and I am a lot more comfortable outside where it is open and I know I can see what's coming.' Despite the security system, Ashley was afraid to be in her house alone five months after the attack.

"These are the kinds of concerns Paul Ferguson has created for my family. We can't be alone. We can't move in our house without announcing we are coming. We all have exaggerated startle reflexes. If one of us walks into a room unannounced, we jump. We can't enter our home without announcing our entrance. When the door opens, the security system beeps. I quickly learned that if I did not call out when I came home, Jaredd would be upstairs in a panic and ready to fight an intruder. We all talked about how we panic and can't deal with the fear, so we announce our presence when we enter the house.

"Alisha talked about strangers and how Paul robbed her of her sense of security, trust, and safety. When I approach strangers on the street, I experience a sense of panic as I watch them and worry what they might do until I am safely past them. This is the kind of psychological turmoil Paul's attack has had upon us. During our greatest moments of fear, I think about my children and reflect upon what we've gone through together. This violation of our sense of safety, security, and trust has been significant.

"What do I want, Your Honor? I want you to keep Paul Ferguson out of my life and my children's lives. I want you to keep him out of our lives for a lifetime. He has learned to live off people, to prey upon people, to take what he wants, and to take out his rage on women in the form of rape and violence.

"Paul believes he can have no consequences for his actions because you can't prove it. He lies, and his mother lies for him. Why she does that, I'll never understand because she has created a monster. There is no remorse in this young man, no regret. The only thing he regrets is that he didn't get to carry out his plan—actually to do a big crime and be famous, I think were the words I have heard people say who know Paul; that his big goal in life was to commit a big crime and be famous. That's the profile of an individual who is evil, cruel, and a menace to society.

"For all the victims of the car vandalism at the JCC, for all the victims of Paul's thefts in their homes, and his burglaries, thefts, and vandalism, for all the neighbors in my community who have been plagued by his predatory behaviors, for my children, my family, my relatives, and my friends who have suffered through this trauma, this horrible nightmare, and for all the future victims of Paul Ferguson, I request, Your Honor, that you ensure that we are not victimized by him again. Thank you."

When Debbie finished and returned to her seat, Mr. Matangos acknowledged to the judge that he had very little to add because, "Mrs. Bird said it best." Mr. Matangos reminded the court that the day before his attack on the Bird family, "Paul Ferguson was before the Honorable Judge Jeannine Turgeon in Courtroom No. 7 on the fifth floor of this courthouse and admitted to the acts as indicated in the presentence investigation, Your Honor, involving the burglaries and presented himself, to be placed on community-based treatment, as a good student. His mother presented him as a caring individual. All the while, Your Honor, during that false presentation to the court, it is clear that the defendant had in his mind and had already taken preparatory steps to commit this violent act the very next evening. The preparation, as indicated by the trial testimony—the gloves, having the knife wrapped in electrical tape, knowing how to get in, when to get in, probably being by the house at other nights to see what time bedtime was, arranging it so he could sneak out of his house. Your Honor, within Mr. Ferguson's mind, on the date he was in court, he had already had this planned. I ask the Court to take that into consideration.

"Your Honor, within the pre-sentence investigation, there is mention of the discussion that the probation and parole officer had with Mr. Ferguson in prison and Mr. Ferguson's comments of how proud he is of his accomplishments while he has been incarcerated, and how productive he has made the use of his time while incarcerated, and how there is no proof whatsoever in his mind that he committed this act—no fingerprints, no physical evidence, and his questioning why the jury would have believed the Birds' word over his.

"Within the entire discussion with that probation and parole officer, Your Honor, there is not one mention of remorse, not one mention of regret, not even a hint of any remorse for the suffering that the family went through, whether it be at his hand or not. Not even an offhanded comment that whoever did this did a terrible thing to the Birds—a family, as you have heard from Mrs. Bird, that treated him almost like one of their own for the years that he spent playing with Jaredd. If you recall the testimony at trial, playing on the same basketball team, having the same circle of friends—Paul made not one mention of the victims' suffering.

"Paul's only care throughout that entire discussion with the probation and parole officer was, as usual, himself, Paul Ferguson. His only comments, self-serving in nature, are concerned with his time, his activities, not those whose lives he put in danger that night, whose lives he intended to take, Your Honor, that evening.

"Mr. Ferguson intended to leave that household with Mrs. Bird dead. He intended to enter that house and leave Alisha Bird, fourteen years of age, raped and dead in her bed, Your Honor. His prior record is indicated on the guidelines, Your Honor, and also on the presentence investigation.

"Your Honor, on behalf of the Commonwealth, we respectfully request that you sentence the defendant to a maximum term of incarceration on each of the charges presented, each of the charges that the defendant has been convicted of: two counts of criminal attempt homicide, aggravated assault against Alisha Bird, and burglary. And as Your Honor is aware, the maximum period of incarceration for attempted homicide, effective as of May 8 of 1995 where serious bodily injury results, is twenty to forty years.

"Your Honor, it is the Commonwealth's request that at both counts of criminal attempt homicide, you sentence the defendant to consecutive terms of twenty to forty years. It is the Commonwealth's request that at the charge of aggravated assault on which the defendant was convicted for Alisha Bird, that you sentence him to a maximum period of incarceration, also consecutive to both of those first two sentences, and also a consecutive maximum term of incarceration on the burglary counts, Your Honor."

When George was finished, Debbie knew that the time had come for Judge Kleinfelter to announce the sentence for Paul. After presenting a lengthy description of the pre-sentencing deposition, Judge Kleinfelter spoke the words that would echo in Debbie's mind long after the sentencing proceedings had ended.

"Regardless of exactly what he had in mind when he entered the house—whether it was a sexual assault, whether it was to steal, whether it was to assault these family members—whatever it was, it was a horrible, horrible crime. And you know, had that knife moved just a few inches one way or the other with respect to either Mrs. Bird or her son, these would be homicides. They would be absolutely, first-degree murders, and he would be looking at, at least a life sentence, if not the death penalty.

"By the fast actions of the emergency medical technicians and the surgeons that attended, particularly to Mrs. Bird, that's not the case. But when somebody repeatedly rains blows on another human skull with a knife and then attempts to cut their throat, only one intent can be considered—and that is the intent to take life.

"This person who came into a home, a family that befriended him in many, many ways, as we heard both today and in the course of the trial, what kind of a fiend does this?

"Well, we may not have the answer to that question, but one thing is abundantly clear to this Court, and that is, that not only the Birds, but anyone else in this community, deserves absolutely to be protected from Paul Ferguson, and our sentence is designed to accomplish that fact."

With those strong words, Debbie knew that Judge Kleinfelter was going to, as Detective Nelson put it, "slam-dunk" Paul Ferguson. It was reassuring to hear the person, with the power to make the final determination of Paul's prison time, speak so emphatically against the attack of Paul Ferguson against her family.

Judge Kleinfelter continued, "Confession, contrition, remorse—these are some of the hallmarks, in my opinion, that indicate that a person is ready to take a first step towards rehabilitation. And Paul Ferguson had demonstrated none of these things—not at trial, not during the pre-sentence investigation, and certainly not here today. While we are concerned that a lengthy prison sentence will deprive this young man of his youth, we believe that no sentence other than the one we are about to impose would address the seriousness of these offenses.

"In the case of *Commonwealth of Pennsylvania versus Paul A. Ferguson*, at 1353 CD 1996, the first count of criminal attempt homicide against Debra Bird, it is the sentence of the Court that the defendant pay the costs of prosecution, make restitution as contained in the financial statement submitted by the victim, which we will also make a part of the record, and undergo imprisonment in the state correctional institution, the minimum of which shall be twelve and the maximum which shall be twenty-four years.

"On the second count, also being criminal attempt homicide involving Jaredd Bird, it is the sentence of the Court that the defendant pay the costs of prosecution and undergo imprisonment in the state correctional institution for a term, the minimum of which shall be twelve and the maximum of which shall be twenty-four years. This sentence shall be served consecutively with that imposed at the first count."

Consecutively, rather than concurrently, was the word Debbie needed to hear from Judge Kleinfelter, because *consecutively* meant that the years of incarceration assigned to each charge would be served back-to-back rather than all at one time. Paul was already, after two counts, serving a minimum of twenty-four years, and the judge was not finished with all the charges yet. She listened intently for his final words:

"At Docket 1354 CD 96, a charge of aggravated assault on Alisha Bird, it is the sentence of the Court that the defendant pay the costs of prosecution and undergo imprisonment in a state correctional institution for a term, the minimum of which shall be six and the maximum of which shall be twelve years. This sentence shall be served consecutively with the second count at 1353 CD 1996.

"At the third count, a charge of burglary, it is the sentence of the Court that the defendant pay the costs of prosecution and undergo imprisonment in a state correctional institution for a term, the minimum of which shall be six and the maximum of which shall be twelve years. The cumulative effect of our sentence is that the defendant is sentenced to a term of thirty-six to seventy-two years."

Debbie knew from her discussions with George that the minimum number of years assigned during sentencing meant the minimum number of years to be served without opportunity for parole. She did some quick math and determined that Paul would be fifty-one years old before he would come up for parole. By that time, she would be eighty years old. She vowed silently that if Paul did not confess after thirty-six years of incarceration, she would be attending his parole hearing to see to it that he didn't get out after serving his minimum sentence.

As the Bird family left the courtroom with Mr. Matangos, reporters surrounded them. Debbie expressed her gratitude for the outcome of the sentencing and for the help of the legal system, and they worked their way to the elevator. As Debbie turned around in the elevator and saw just one set of footprints following behind her and her children, she said a silent prayer of thanks. The elevator carried the Bird family to a renewed sense of security and courage to get on with the rest of their lives.

About the Author

Debra McDonald is a graduate of Lock Haven University, Shippensburg University, and the University of Pennsylvania. She is a retired educator, having dedicated thirty-six years as a high school health and physical education teacher and coach, a middle school assistant principal and an elementary principal all in the East Pennsboro Area School District from 1974 to 2010. She is happily married and enjoys her three adult children, two adult stepchildren, and eight grandchildren.